MIND over MARKETS

Power Trading with Market Generated Information

James F. Dalton, Eric T. Jones & Robert B. Dalton

IRWIN
Professional Publishing®
Chicago • London • Singapore

This publication is designed to provide accurate and authoritative information in regard to the subject matter covered. It is sold with the understanding that the publisher is not engaged in rendering legal, accounting, or other professional service.

ISBN 1-55738-489-4

Printed in the United States of America

BB

2 3 4 5 6 7 8 9 0

TABLE OF CONTENTS

PREFACE

Excellence in any endeavor, be it carpentry, medicine, athletics or futures trading, is only achieved through a careful balance between the analytical and intuitive powers of your mind.

A skilled carpenter blends his or her knowledge of angles, tools and building materials with the creativity of mind and body that comes only from years of experience in the craft. The expert surgeon is also keenly aware of the fusion of knowledge and intuition. Regardless of the number of diagnostic tests, once the incision is made knowledge takes a back seat to intuitive judgment, for every patient's physiology is different.

The key element that has long separated tremendously successful traders from all others is their intuitive understanding that time regulates all financial opportunities. In 1984, J. Peter Steidlmayer formally introduced the Market Profile as a way to graphically depict the acceptance or rejection of price over time. For the first time, what had once been the domain of the intuitive trader was now accessible to all traders.

The ability to record price information according to time has unleashed huge amounts of useful market information in a form never before available. In turn, this information explosion has triggered a new way of looking at markets and opened the doors for accelerated levels of market analysis.

Mind over Markets is a book about learning; learning the dynamics of markets through the organization of price, time and volume, and learning how to synthesize this information with your own intuition.

Our goal is to arrive at a healthy balance between the powers of objective observation and intuitive decision making—a rare talent possessed by only the best of traders.

Acknowledgements

Our thanks to the individuals and organizations named below extends far beyond the scope of the writing of this book. *Mind over Markets* is born out of years of teaching, research and trading. In one way or another, the following individuals and companies have made a significant contribution to this effort:

J. Peter Steidlmayer, who pioneered the theories upon which much of our work is based. When I[1] first met Pete in 1985, one of the first questions I asked was "If your theories are so good, why share them with anyone else?" Pete's response was not what one would expect from a successful commodity trader. He said, "The market has been good to me. Like Marshall Field's contribution to the city of Chicago was the Field Museum, my contribution to the financial world is a better way to trade."

Peter Steidlmayer has always encouraged his students to take the information he has provided and make it their own. In less than five years, we have witnessed the birth of new types of quotation software, databases, and all forms of expanded market research. Such is the natural process that follows any significant new discovery. Given the magnitude of the contribution that Peter Steidlmayer has made to the financial markets, this information expansion will likely continue for a long time.

Norman Hovda, who, as a broker in the Soybean Meal pit at the Chicago Board of Trade, observed Pete Steidlmayer as he came into the pit to trade. It was Norman who first introduced me to Pete, and that meeting has since changed the way we look at markets. One of the "equations" to which you will be introduced in this book is: *Market Understanding + (Self Understanding × Strategy) = Results*. Norman's specialty is Self Understanding. Although he remains a member of both the

---

[1] While this section reflects the thoughts of all three authors, for stylistic reasons, it is written from the perspective of James F. Dalton.

Chicago Board of Trade and the Chicago Board Options Exchange, his primary focus is consulting businesses, schools and families on 'tools' for Self-Help. Norman resides in Wilmette, Illinois.

Donald Jones, president of CISCO, a Chicago-based research and database firm, has helped us in countless ways over the years. CISCO was the first database to begin providing the Market Profile and Liquidity Data Bank to the public. In addition to providing the data for many of the illustrations presented in these pages, Don has also taken the time on numerous occassions to share his ideas and analytical research.

Elaine Dalton, for her unwavering support both as a partner in business and partner at home.

Barton J. Hanson, whose literary efforts and market research as Senior Editor of the Profile Report are indirectly woven into portions of this book.

Cletus Dobbs, for his vivid explanation of how the auction process works in the "real world"—at a livestock sale. Cletus is a rancher in Texas.

Commodity Quote Graphics (CQG), for their quality ongoing technical support over the years. CQG is also responsible for the majority of the charts and data presented in this book.

CBOT Market Profile®, Market Profile®, Liquidity Data Bank® and LDB® are registered trademarks of the Chicago Board of Trade (CBOT), which holds exclusive copyright to both the Market Profile® and Liquidity Data Bank® graphics. The graphics herein were reproduced with the permission of the Chicago Board of Trade. Nothing herein should be considered as a trading recommendation of the Chicago Board of Trade. The views expressed in this publication are exclusively those of Dalton Capital Management, Inc.

James F. Dalton
Eric T. Jones
Robert B. Dalton

CHAPTER 1
INTRODUCTION

Jim Kelvin was a retired cattle rancher from Texas. He had developed an interest in the futures market during the years when he would hedge his livestock at opportune prices. After he sold his ranching business, he began to experiment with a few small trades as a hobby.

Jim read everything he could find on futures trading. He studied all the technical models, read manual after manual on market analysis, attended seminars and kept point and figure charts. In time, he felt he had a firm grasp on all the factors that make the market tick and began to look at trading as a serious vocation. He wasn't making money, but he thought he was just "paying his dues" as he learned the intricacies of his trading system.

One morning Jim got up at 6:00, as he always did, and went to his study to turn on his quote monitors and prepare for the market's open. He picked up *The Wall Street Journal* to see what the bank traders and brokerage analysts were saying about the foreign exchange market. He had been watching the Japanese yen closely, because he felt the recent depth of coverage in the news would surely reveal some good trade opportunities. The U.S. dollar was expected to record new lows because of a slowing U.S. economy and consistently negative trade balances, forcing the yen and other currencies higher. All the foreign exchange related articles on his quote equipment news service were bullish for the yen.

A good friend and fellow trader called and commented on how the currencies should rally that day. Jim then checked the 24-day channel model and the 16–32-day moving average cross-over model, two longer term technical indicators on which he frequently based his trading—both had been generating buy signals for some time.

Jim glanced over his charts and volume numbers and chewed on the end of a pencil. At the end of every day, he conducted a personal analysis of the market's structure and wrote down possible trades for the following day. Last night he had written "weakening yen—look for opportunity to sell." The yen had been in an upward trend for some time, but in recent weeks volume was drying up. Price was moving higher, but activity was decreasing and there had been no substantial moves to the up side in over a week.

He knew from his ranching days that less volume was significant. When he would auction off his livestock, the price would continue up until the last buyer had bought. When the auction was nearing its end, the bulk of the buyers would have dropped out because they had fulfilled their inventory requirement or the price was too high. When no one was left to buy, the auction was over.

He read his analysis again. Common market sense told him that the up auction in the yen was over. There were no more buyers. But what about all the fundamental and technical indicators?

"All these professionals can't be wrong," Jim said to himself. "I can't sell the yen."

The market was going to open in less than five minutes. Jim stared at his blank monitor for a moment, thinking about what his friend had said. He put his hand on the phone, but did not pick it up.

The yen opened higher, rose a few ticks, and then stalled. The floor traders were acting on the recent bullish sentiment, but the buyers that had driven the yen up for the past month were nowhere to be found. He just sat and watched his terminal. *It's going to break . . . I should sell*, he thought. The flashing green price on his quote screen began to drop as he sank deeper into his chair and indecision tightened its grip.

What happened? Jim Kelvin's decision making process was jammed by the conflict between his own intuition and popular opinion. "How can the majority be wrong?"

The majority of people who trade futures don't make money. In fact, over 90 percent aren't successful enough to justify being in the market. If you trade with the majority, then you will fare only as well as the average, and the average market participant does not make money!

He was caught, like the goat that starves to death between two piles of hay, in the conflict of multiple sources of information indicating opposite conditions. Jim's common sense and firm understanding of the market's auction process told him the yen was weak and should have been sold, but he let himself become frozen by the power of the majority. All the fundamental and technical indicators agreed—everyone was predicting the bull trend to continue.

The difference is relatively simple. Jim was basing his opinion on current market information—he was "listening" to the evolving market—while all the other sources were based on information that was history and no longer relevant to what the market was doing *in the present tense.*

What if a baseball catcher waited to see how fast a man stealing second could run or pondered how often he was successful before he threw the ball? There is no way the throw would be in time. A good catcher operates solely in the present tense. He feels when the steal is on and reacts immediately, just as an experienced trader feels the direction of the market and reacts immediately.

Similarly, if a linebacker waited until he could see what the offense was doing or tried to read the play by watching the scoreboard, he would never make the key tackle. He reads the offense by recognizing patterns learned from experience and by trusting his intuition—sensing the play. To wait is to miss the opportunity. If you wait until a market has committed itself in a direction, you are too late.

In *Mind over Markets*, our goal is to teach you how to "read the plays." In more concrete terms, you will learn how to identify the information generated by the market, understand its implications, and act on your knowledge. However, this is not a book about a trading system that works or does not work. The Market Profile is not a black box that dogmatically tells you when to buy and sell commodities. This is a book on learning. This a book on observing and understanding the market.

Mind over Markets is organized around the five basic steps in the learning process, roughly corresponding to the five stages of skill acquisition discussed in the book *Mind over Machine*, by Hubert and Stewart Dreyfus.

To illustrate these stages, imagine a young man named David. He attends a concert at his college given by a well known contemporary pianist. While listening to Beethoven's haunting "Moonlight Sonata," he is moved by the pure emotion expressed in the piece and decides he must learn to play the piano. The next day he arranges for his first lesson.

In the first few weeks, David learns to "recognize objective facts and features relevant to the skill and acquires rules for determining actions based on those facts and features."[1] In other words, he reaches the first

---

[1] Hubert Dreyfus and Stewart Dreyfus, *Mind over Machine* (New York: The Free Press, 1986), pp. 21-36.

stage of learning: *the novice*. He learns that the black ellipse with a stem is a note, and that a note placed on the bottom line of the treble staff is an E. He is shown where the E is on the keyboard and can then press the corresponding key to sound the note.

David can look at a sheet of music, and by reducing it into individual parts, he can find the right keys and play the song. Of course, this is a slow, painstaking process that forces listeners to use their imagination when trying to make out any semblance of melody.

After a month of lessons and regular practice, David becomes an *advanced beginner*. By playing a song over and over, he goes beyond the note by note struggle and begins to achieve some continuity of melody. Experience improves his performance. He still sees the song as a series of notes on a page, but begins to feel the flow that allows a recognizable song to emerge. David can play "Amazing Grace" so it actually sounds like "Amazing Grace" and not some array of notes in random rhythm.

As the years go by, David reaches the third level and becomes a *competent* pianist. Most musicians never pass this stage to become proficient or expert. He sees each song as a whole, a certain expression to be performed with a definite goal in mind. He still plays by reading the notes, but he achieves some degree of emotion and purpose in his playing.

An important distinction must be made here. David plays with the emotion of the written expression in the piece (crescendos and fortes, etc.), not with individual interpretation. He performs much like a machine that very accurately converts the musical score into a sonata or concerto.

This level of competency can lead to excellent performances, for most written music is thoroughly marked to show the composer's emotion. These marks have literal meaning, such as quiet (pianissimo), or pronounced and sharp (staccato). David plays Bach's "Prelude in E Minor" flawlessly at a recital and receives a standing ovation for his technical excellence.

However, David is still a person playing an instrument, much like a computer running a complicated flow chart. To advance to the next level, *proficiency*, he must transcend the physical notes on paper (the rules) and become deeply involved in the music.

To reach the fourth level and become proficient, David must learn the actual notes of a piece so well that he no longer has to think of them. The written work becomes a part of his mind, a holistic image, allowing him to interpret the music. This comes from experience—in life as well as hours of practice at the keyboard. The pianist must rely on his intuitive ability to express emotion through the piano, leaving behind the fact that the piece is in E flat in 6/8 time. Therefore, if David is proficient, he will feel the emotion that Bach created and, drawing on his own emotions and experience, convey that emotion in his playing.

Music that surpasses the competent level goes beyond the auditorily aesthetic and involves the listeners. Hearing a proficient musician is often a deeply moving experience, for passionate music arises from the emotion of the performer and strikes similar chords in the listener. This cannot be explained in rational terms, for one cannot teach the expression of true emotion. Only through experience and involvement can proficiency be reached.

The final stage is labeled by Dreyfus and Dreyfus as *expertise*. David has studied piano for many years and knows the instrument inside and out. When he plays, the piano becomes an extension of his body. It is as if the music comes straight from his mind, which in an important way it does. He no longer thinks of individual notes or any rules when his hands are on the keyboard.

An expert musician feels the melody, and the song lives as an expression of his feeling. The mechanical aspects are fully ingrained, leaving the brain to its wonderful powers of creation. Listening to an expert musician is like peering into his thoughts and feeling the weight of his sadness or the exhilaration of his joy. It is a mode of expression that transcends all rules and calculative rationality to become pure expression. Few people reach the expert level, in any field.

This example was meant to introduce you to the basic levels of skill acquisition that we will attempt to take you through in learning to trade the futures market successfully. However, learning is a process that requires a great deal of time and effort, and learning to be an expert trader is no exception. The musician spends many hours of rote memorization and practice to develop experience and skill. Successful trading requires the same discipline and hard work.

Many perceive futures trading to be a glamorous, high-profit venture for those with the nerve to trade and that, through the purchase of mechanical systems and computer software, you can bypass the time and dedication it takes to succeed in other professions.

In reality, there are few glamorous professions. Some, like the music industry, reward the best quite impressively. It is easy for the naive music lover to glamorize performers like Bert Bacharach, Frank Sinatra and Billy Joel. However, if we dig deep behind the sell-out stadium concerts and multi-platinum albums, the music business is not much different than any other profession. For every Simon and Garfunkel there are literally millions of aspiring young musicians who spend endless hours of dedication and frustration learning and perfecting their profession. Even the established superstars spent uncounted days perfecting each song and their musical ability to achieve recognition.

Because of the difficulty of making it big, many musicians "burn-out." The process of becoming good enough to succeed brings with it the potential for failure, and the process of becoming an expert trader is just as difficult. The learning in this book goes beyond technical systems into areas of self-understanding that might reveal weakness in your abilities of self and market observation, discipline, and objectivity. Also, much of the information in this book differs from the accepted models of market analysis. Just as you will learn that the best trades fly in the face of the most recent market activity, the information in this book flies in the face of most current opinions and theories on trading and understanding the market.

Futures trading is not a glamorous or profitable experience for most of the people who attempt to trade. Futures trading is a profession, and it takes as much time and dedication to succeed as any other profession. You will start as a beginner, learning the objective basics about the profile, then proceed through the stages towards the ultimate goal of any professional in any trade—becoming an expert.

CHAPTER 2
NOVICE

Novice is the first stage in any process. No one starts out an expert, or even an advanced beginner. To learn any skill, you must begin by learning the necessary objective facts and features—the tools with which you will build your skill from the ground up. Just as a carpenter learns the function of a saw, hammer, and plane before attempting to make his first basic bird feeder, you must learn the mechanics of the Market Profile before you make your first basic market decisions.

The learning that occurs during the novice stage is largely rote memorization. The carpenter is taught the workings of his tools; the aspiring pianist is taught the definitions that form the base of all music theory. This learning comes from a derivative source, such as a book or a teacher, and does not involve the novice in any active way as he or she sits and listens or reads. Some degree of derivative learning is necessary, especially during the early stages, but in the words of the ancient Greek philosopher Heraclitus, "Much learning does not teach understanding." Only through experience and extensive practice and application will understanding and expertise arise.

Throughout this book (a derivative source) there are many definitions and patterns to memorize. It is important to remember, however, that the information is only part of a larger whole that will develop as you read and attempt to assimilate what you have learned with your personality, individual trading style, and experience. Keep an open mind and actively apply the new knowledge to your observations of the marketplace.

Perhaps some of your established beliefs have already been thrown into question. In the example at the beginning of the book, Jim the yen trader is torn between the different sources of information: fundamental, technical and market-generated. All the fundamental sources (newspapers, trade magazines, personal advice) and technical sources (channel models, moving averages, etc.) were predicting a rally in the foreign currencies. The market-generated information, which is the market's price activity recorded in relation to time in a statistical bell curve, was indicating a market that had reached the top of the up movement. This is not to say that all technical gurus, financial writers, and market analysts are useless—there is just no greater indication of what the market is doing than the market itself!

The Market Profile is a conduit for listening to the market. It is merely a graph that plots time on one axis and price on the other to give a visual impression of market activity. This representation takes the form of a statistical bell curve, just like your high school teacher used. Most students scored in the middle of the bell curve with C's, while fewer received A's and F's. Similarly, the majority of a day's transactional volume takes place in a common range of prices with less trading on the day's extremes (see Figure 2–1).

The Market Profile is simply a way of organizing market activity as it unfolds. It is not a system that predicts tops and bottoms or trend continuation any more than the teacher's grade chart is an indicator of overall student intelligence. The Market Profile is an evolving gauge that accurately reflects market activity in the present tense, a gauge being defined as a passive device that exists only to measure something. The key to the Market Profile lies in correctly reading this information.

Laying the Foundation

In this section, we will discuss the definitions and concepts that form the foundation for learning to understand the market through the Market Profile. As has been stated before, this is a challenging task. Everything you learn about the Market Profile is interrelated and integral to a complete understanding of the market. Each concept is like a piece in an intricate puzzle that should be studied to determine its place in the developing picture. If you file each piece away as a separately defined definition, you will be left with a jumble of seemingly unrelated facts. But, if you continually integrate each section of the book with what you have already learned, the picture will slowly emerge.

Figure 2–1　A statistical bell curve; the organization of price over time.

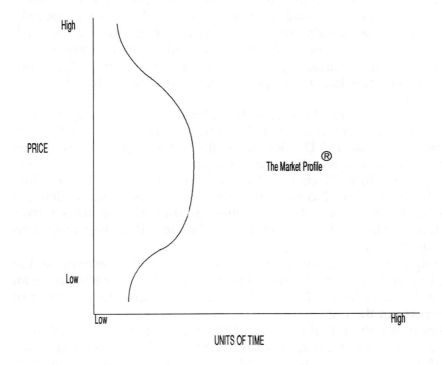

The Auction

Jim Kelvin intuitively knew that the bull trend in the yen was over because of his days in the ranching business. At first glance, the futures market seems to have very little to do with cattle ranching. However, they are both markets, and all markets share a common auction process through which trade is conducted.

As Jim Kelvin sat before his quote monitor on that morning, he recalled one of the last days he took his livestock to auction. Price for feeder cattle had been steadily climbing for several months, reaching a high of 86 cents, but the number of steers sold had fallen significantly during the previous week's auction. The meat processers had cut back their purchasing to the bare minimum at higher prices, buying just enough to keep their processing plants operating and to meet their contract obligations. Jim knew that price would have to auction lower to find renewed buying.

A steer was led into the auction barn. The sale barn manager at one end of the circular corral called out the starting price, "Do I hear 80 cents for this fine feeder steer?" The opening call was too high and did not get a "raise" from the men standing around the perimeter of the circle. "78? . . . 76? . . . do I hear 74 cents?" Finally, a buyer entered the auction, starting the bidding at 72 cents. After a small rally as buyers called out their offers, the steer was sold at 76 cents a pound. The up auction over the last few months in the cattle market had ended. Price had to auction lower to attract buyers.

During some auctions there would be an immediate response to the opening bid, and price would move up quickly. "Do I hear 82? I have an offer for 82 . . . Do I hear 84? . . . 85?" as the men around the perimeter of the ring cried out their offers.

Other times, the initial price would be too high, and the auctioneer would quickly lower the bid, "Do I hear 78? . . . 77? . . . 76 for this fine steer?" The price would back off until a buyer entered the auction, then price would begin to move upward, often auctioning beyond the opening price. Once the auction got started, competition and anxiety among buyers sometimes drove the market beyond the prices that were initially rejected as too high. Price would continue up until only one buyer remained. "Ninety two going once, twice, three times . . . sold," then the auction was over.

The futures market auctions in a similar manner. If the open is considered below value, price auctions higher in search of sellers. If the open is considered too high by the market's participants, price auctions lower, searching for buyers. Once a buyer enters the market, price begins to auction upward until the last buyer has bought. Similarly, the market auctions downward until the last seller has sold, constantly searching for information.

As you progress through this book, the importance of the market's auction process will become evident. And, with the aid of the Market Profile, you will soon see that the futures market's auction process is by no means a "random walk."

Organizing the Day

The basic building blocks of the Market Profile are called Time Price Opportunities, or TPO's. Each half hour of the trading day is designated by a letter. If a certain price is traded during a given half hour, the corresponding letter, or TPO, is marked next to the price. Figure 2–2 shows each half hour segment separately alongside the completed profile. On a side note, Treasury bonds trade in 32nds of $1,000, and one tick is worth $31.25 ($1,000 divided by 32). In the bond market on this day, the prices traded during the first thirty minutes (A period) ranged from $96^{29}/_{32}$ to $97^{10}/_{32}$. The next time period (B period) traded from $96^{31}/_{32}$ to $97^{4}/_{32}$, and so on. The resulting Profile is shown in Figure 2–2.

We will now proceed through the same day in the bonds step-by-step, explaining in detail how to read the basic information generated by the market through the Market Profile "gauge." The numbers in the following discussion refer to Figure 2–3.

1. The price range resulting from market activity during the first two time periods (the first hour) for most commodities is called the *initial balance* (slightly longer in the S&P). In the Treasury Bond example shown in Figure 2–3, the initial balance was established from $96^{29}/_{32}$ to $97^{10}/_{32}$ by the floor traders, or locals, during A and B periods. The initial balance represents the period of time in which the locals attempt to find a range where two-sided trade can take place—a range where both the buyer and seller agree to conduct trade. Locals trade mostly in the day timeframe and provide liquidity, not direction, in the market by acting as middlemen between the off-floor traders. Their purpose is not to make one or two big trades every day, but to make a few ticks on a large volume of trades. The local is typically responsible for over 50 percent of the day's trading volume.

    The local's role is like a car dealer—a middleman between the producer and consumer. The dealer's goal is to move his inventory quickly to make a small profit on each sale. He must

Figure 2–2 Segmented profile.

```
97-10    A  .  .  .  .  .  .  .  .  .  .  .        O
97-09    A  .  .  .  .  .  .  .  .  .  .  .        O
97-08    A  .  .  .  .  .  .  .  .  .  .  .        O
97-07    A  .  .  .  .  .  .  .  .  .  .  .        O
97-06    A  .  C  .  .  .  .  .  .  .  .  .        AC
97-05    A  .  C  .  .  .  .  .  .  .  .  .        AC
97-04    A  B  C  .  .  .  .  .  .  .  .  .        ABC
97-03    A  B  C  D  .  .  .  .  .  .  .  .        ABCD
97-02    A  B  C  D  .  .  G  .  .  .  .  L        ABCDGL
97-01    A  B  C  D  .  .  G  H  .  .  .  L        ABCDGHL
97-00    A  B  C  D  .  .  G  H  .  .  .  L        ABCDGHL
96-31    A  B  .  D  .  F  G  H  I  .  .  L        ABCDFGHL
96-30    A  .  .  D  .  F  G  H  I  J  .  L        ADFGHIJL
96-29    A  .  .  D  E  F  G  H  I  J  .  L        ADEFGHIJL
96-28    .  .  .  D  E  F  .  .  .  J  .  L        DEFJL
96-27    .  .  .  D  E  F  .  .  .  J  .  L        DEFJL
96-26    .  .  .  D  E  F  .  .  .  J  .  L        DEFJL
96-25    .  .  .  D  E  .  .  .  .  J  K  L        DEJKL
96-24    .  .  .  .  E  .  .  .  .  J  K  L        EJKL
96-23    .  .  .  .  .  .  .  .  .  .  K  L        KL
96-22    .  .  .  .  .  .  .  .  .  .  K  .        K
96-21    .  .  .  .  .  .  .  .  .  .  K  .        K
96-20    .  .  .  .  .  .  .  .  .  .  K  .        K
96-19    .  .  .  .  .  .  .  .  .  .  K  .        K
96-18    .  .  .  .  .  .  .  .  .  .  K  .        K
```

Figure 2–3 Elements of the Market Profile. "M" designates closing activity.

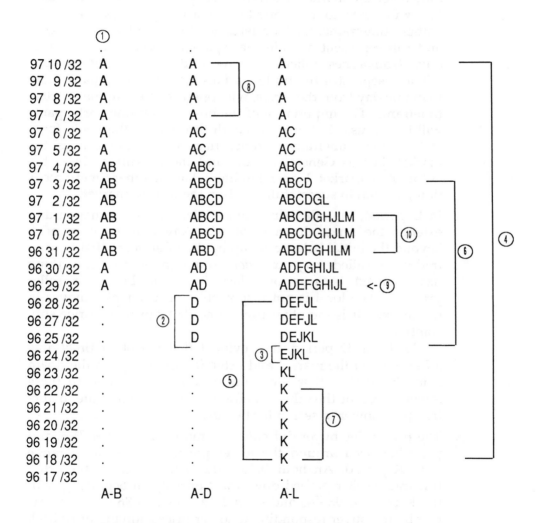

97 10 /32	A	A	A
97 9 /32	A	A	A
97 8 /32	A	A	A
97 7 /32	A	A	A
97 6 /32	A	AC	AC
97 5 /32	A	AC	AC
97 4 /32	AB	ABC	ABC
97 3 /32	AB	ABCD	ABCD
97 2 /32	AB	ABCD	ABCDGL
97 1 /32	AB	ABCD	ABCDGHJLM
97 0 /32	AB	ABCD	ABCDGHJLM
96 31 /32	AB	ABD	ABDFGHILM
96 30 /32	A	AD	ADFGHIJL
96 29 /32	A	AD	ADEFGHIJL
96 28 /32	.	D	DEFJL
96 27 /32	.	D	DEFJL
96 25 /32	.	D	DEJKL
96 24 /32	.	.	EJKL
96 23 /32	.	.	KL
96 22 /32	.	.	K
96 21 /32	.	.	K
96 20 /32	.	.	K
96 19 /32	.	.	K
96 18 /32	.	.	K
96 17 /32	.	.	.
	A-B	A-D	A-L

Important Note: The letters A,B,C, etc. vary between quote services and exchanges. The importance here is not in the letters themselves but the fact that they represent half-hour periods of time.

buy from the producer, like General Motors, at a price he finds fair, then turn around and sell to the consumer at a price that will attract buying while maintaining a degree of profit. The local on the floor of the exchange acts in the same way, buying from long-term sellers and selling to long-term buyers, who only enter the market when they feel price is away from value. We will refer to the long-term market participants as the "other" timeframe, for long term is a highly subjective concept and can represent a trade that spans anywhere from several days (sometimes called a swing trade) to several months. "Other" separates the traders whose participation spans more than one day from the locals, who operate solely in the shortest timeframe. The importance of the other timeframe participants will be discussed at greater length throughout the book, for it is the other timeframe activity that moves and shapes the market, just as General Motors and the consumer shape the automotive market. Understanding what the other timeframe is doing is vital in successfully trading the futures market.

2. In D period, the other timeframe seller enters the market and extends the range down to 96 $^{25}/_{32}$. Any movement in price beyond the initial balance set up by the local in the first hour of trading is called *range extension*, and signifies that something has changed because of other timeframe buyer or seller presence. The local is not responsible for any major moves in the market. It is the other timeframe that can move price substantially.

    Again, in D period, it is evident that the other timeframe seller entered the market and extended the range on the down side. Either the other timeframe buyer will respond to these lower prices, or the other timeframe seller will continue to auction price lower in search for buyers.

3. The responsive buyer did enter the market around 96 $^{24}/_{32}$, and price balanced around the lower portion of the day's range until K period. An hour before the market's close, the other timeframe seller probed downward once again beginning with the K print at 96 $^{25}/_{32}$ and extending down to 96 $^{17}/_{32}$, but was met by the buyer responding to lower prices, forcing price back to close in the middle of the range.

4. The *range* refers to the entire height of the Profile—from the high to the low. On this day range was 96 $^{17}/_{32}$ to 97 $^{10}/_{32}$.

5. All activity *below* the initial balance is other timeframe seller *range extension* (just as all activity above the initial balance is

other timeframe buyer range extension). Any activity above 97 $^{10}/_{32}$ or below 96 $^{29}/_{32}$ is range extension on this day.

6. The area where 70 percent of the day's business is conducted (roughly one standard deviation) is called the *value area*. This is logical, for the middle part of the bell curve is where most activity occurs and indicates two-sided trade took place in the day timeframe. Similarly, in a teacher's grading curve, most students score in the middle ranges, which is reflected in the wider middle area of the bell curve. If both buyer and seller are actively participating in an area, then that area is accepted as value by both parties. On July 25 in the bonds, value was accepted between 96 $^{24}/_{32}$ and 97 $^{3}/_{32}$. The value area can be easily calculated using TPOs or actual price/volume figures. A sample calculation of the value area is shown in Appendix 1.

7. The single "K" TPOs at the lower extreme of the Profile are called a *single-print buying tail*. This is an important reference point, for it indicates that the other timeframe buyer responded strongly to price advertised below value, rejecting price out of the lower range in one time period (K). Competition among buyers for contracts causes price to move quickly. Therefore, the longer the tail, the stronger the other timeframe activity. A tail occuring during the last period of the day is not technically a tail, for it cannot be validated by rejection in subsequent time periods. In addition, a tail must be at least two TPOs long to have any real significance.

8. The four single A prints at the top of the day's range are a *single-print selling tail*. This tail shares the same significance as the other timeframe buying tail in K period. The other timeframe seller reacted to higher prices, quickly moving price lower. Attempts to auction beyond the single-print tail by trading up into that price range in subsequent time periods (C and D) met strong resistance, showing seller strength at those prices.

9. The longest line of TPOs closest to the center of the range is called the *point of control*. This is the price where the most activity occurred during the day, and it is therefore the fairest price in the day timeframe. The greatest amount of time was spent trading at that price, signifying greatest value. This concept will be further developed later, for it is of great importance in monitoring other timeframe activity in the day timeframe.

10. M period denotes the *closing range*, which is the market's last
indication of overall sentiment for the day. It is used as a reference point against the following day's open to see if the underlying market sentiment has changed.

Challenging the Rules

You should now have a feel for reading the basic indicators of the
Market Profile. Many concepts were introduced, some undoubtedly
foreign to the opinions you were taught and the rules you learned about
the futures market. Roger von Oech, author of *A Whack on the Side of the
Head*, challenges the power of "the rules."

> . . . there is a lot of pressure in our culture to *follow the rules.*
> This value is one of the first things we learn as children. We
> are told, "Don't color out-side the lines," and "No orange
> elephants." Our educational system encourages further rule-
> following. Students are usually better rewarded for regurgitat-
> ing information than for playing with ideas and thinking of
> original uses for things. As a consequence, people feel more
> comfortable following rules than challenging them.
>   Challenging the rules is a good creative thinking strategy,
> but that's not all. Never challenging the rules brings with it . . .
> potential dangers.[1]

Understanding the Market Profile requires more than the regurgitation of a list of concepts; it requires the ability to challenge the rules and
look beyond the restricting confines of popular opinion. Look over the
basics we just covered again. David had to know the basics of the music
score before he could successfully play "Amazing Grace."

The Role of the Marketplace

Consider the purpose of the market for a moment. Most traders don't
take the time to understand the very foundation of the market they are
trying to master. The carpenter could not build a functional bird house if
he never stopped to ask himself "Just what is the purpose of a bird
house?" The reason for this basic oversight is directly related to von
Oech's challenge of the rules. Most people do not want to know the pur-

---

[1] Roger von Oech, *A Whack on the Side of the Head* (New York: Warner Books,
1983), p. 49.

pose of the market. They do not want to have to think rationally and objectively about the bigger picture. Most market participants, in fact most people in general, would rather be given a set of rules to blindly follow than to have to use personal insight and innovative thought. Again, the majority of the people who trade futures do not make money.

The purpose of the futures market is similar to any other market. It exists solely to *facilitate trade*, and it does so by auctioning from high to low and low to high, in order to find an area where trade can best be facilitated.

Think of trade facilitation in terms of your corner grocery store. If the price of peanut butter is too high, shoppers will refrain from buying, and the grocer will realize that price is too high. He will then move price lower until the buyer responds by purchasing the product. If the grocer moves price too low, however, his inventory will be quickly depleted as buyers take advantage of price below value. Finally, the price will balance somewhere in between the two extremes, where value is established and two-sided trade can take place. Price must move too high or too low before both the grocer and the shopper know it has gone far enough. The same is true in the futures market. The market auctions up until the buyer will buy no more, and down until the seller will sell no more, in the process establishing extremes of price, shown in the profile as the tapering ends of the bell curve.

Now imagine that Figure 2–3 is a profile of the grocer's peanut butter sales over the period of several months, instead of Treasury bond sales (in theory, not actual price and individual TPOs). Initially, the price was set too high, and there were no buyers to generate sales. The grocer then quickly lowered the price to move his inventory, as shown in the A period single print selling tail (see point #1 in Figure 2–3). Price went too low in that same period and buyers bought heavily, allowing the grocer to move prices back up in B and C period. The extremes of price seemed to have been established in A period, and value was accepted somewhere in the middle. In D period, however, another seller entered the market, a supermarket chain two blocks away. The larger store could afford to charge lower prices, so the local grocer had to cut costs to stay in business. In the following weeks, value was established near the bottom of the previous lower extreme—value was accepted lower because of stronger sellers. Finally, the local grocer decided to do a promotional "peanut butter extravaganza" and substantially lowered price to attract shoppers. The ploy worked, as shown by the strong buying tail in K period. The buyers responded to lower prices, allowing the grocer to raise them to a profitable level once again.

This comparison is intended to bring home the similarity of the trade facilitation process in all markets. The futures market is a constant auction looking for a balance between the two major forces behind market movement: the other timeframe buyer and seller.

Let us look at the role of the other timeframe within the marketplace from another perspective for a moment. Looking at something in a different light often brings valuable insight. If Gutenberg had never looked at a wine press as something entirely different, we might not have the printing press today and you would be reading a manual hand-written by a scrivener (and paid a lot more for it). Imagine the other timeframe seller and the other timeframe buyer as two distinct personalities, two separate entities who stand on opposite sides of a gameboard in the shape of an exchange pit. They both have their fingers on big buttons, one says "sell" and the other "buy." In the pit are miniature locals, yelling and gesturing as they do their trades. Other timeframe participants are battling for market control, and they enter the market when they feel price has gotten away from value or some external information convinces them to act. For example, a significant news event might cause the other timeframe buyer to enter the market and drive price upward for the entire day.

This example is obviously only an imaginative idea, but the other timeframe participants often do act as if they were individuals, and it is not always possible to tell why they enter the market. The point is, *to successfully trade the futures market, you must understand what the other timeframe is doing and position yourself with them.*

Going with the Crowd

In a classic "Candid Camera" TV show, a man waits for an elevator. When it arrives, everyone on it is facing the back of the elevator, so he gets on and faces backwards also. If you *blindly* follow the majority, *you will usually be going the wrong way.* As we said before, the majority of market participants do not make money.

This is a pretty bold statement, but if you stop and think about how many times the big name analysts have been plain wrong, it doesn't seem so far fetched. Nonetheless, when the big movers on the Street talk, most everybody listens—it is much easier to dogmatically rely on an "expert" than to be a rugged individualist who makes his own decisions. When you rely solely on yourself, you alone take pride in reaping the rewards of success—but there is also no one else to blame for defeat. The tendency to be a follower is not an easy thing to realize or admit. Not surprisingly, one of the primary reasons many traders use a technical (mechanical) trading system is to take themselves out of the decision making process.

These are but a few thoughts to keep in the back of your mind as we continue through the Novice stage and discuss more labels and terms. Again, the Market Profile is not a technical or mechanical system, and the discussion to follow should not be memorized for later "regurgitation." Remember, everything is a part of the larger whole, and "a little information is a dangerous thing."

Introduction to Day Timeframe Structure

When the local grocer priced his peanut butter below value in the "peanut butter extravaganza," the consumer bought in a frenzy, leaving in its wake a single print buying tail. Tails are an important piece of information in the anatomy of a Market Profile, for they indicate the presence of the other timeframe buyer or seller. A tail is an identifiable characteristic with definite implications. Whenever you see that particular pattern, you associate it with a specific set of facts, just as a linebacker learns, through experience, that certain formations indicate what the offense is going to do. On a bigger scale, the Market Profile as a whole tends to fall into readable patterns in the day timeframe, determined by the degree of involvement of the other timeframe participant. These patterns, when properly identified, can increase the day trader's success, as well as provide information regarding what the market is trying to do in the longer term.

The labels we will give these patterns are not as important as understanding how the day evolves in relation to the initial balance and the confidence with which the other timeframe has entered the market. Think of the initial balance as a base for the day's trading. The purpose of a base is to provide support for something, as the base of a lamp keeps the lamp from tipping over. The narrower the base, the easier it is to knock the lamp over. The same principle holds true for futures trading in the day timeframe. If the initial balance is narrow, the odds are greater that the base will be upset and range extension will occur. Days that establish a wider base provide more support and the initial balance is more likely to maintain the extremes for the day.

If you think of the other timeframe as a single personality, as in the game board analogy, it is possible to judge the activity of all the other timeframe buyers or sellers according to their level of "confidence." Each day type is the result of varying degrees and forms of other timeframe activity, and this activity tends to fall into certain patterns. Keep these broader concepts of base and confidence in mind as we examine the six day types.

Normal Day

Dynamics   The label "Normal day" is misleading, for in reality, "Normal" days are more the exception than the rule. Normal days are generally created by swift early entry of the other timeframe participant, which has the effect of establishing a wide initial balance. Thereafter, both the other timeframe buyer and seller auction price back and forth between them, as balanced, two-sided trade ensues.

Normal days are often caused by a news announcement early in the trading session that triggers a strong other timeframe reaction, driving price quickly in one direction. For example, suppose that a bearish economic indicator released shortly after the open causes the other timeframe seller to aggressively enter the market and drive price lower. Eventually, price moves low enough to attract other timeframe buying, thus cutting off the selling activity. For the remainder of the day, there is little strong directional conviction and price balances between the extremes. An example of a Normal day is shown in Figure 2–4.

Structural Characteristics   The primary characteristic of a Normal day is the wide initial balance, or "base," that is not upset throughout the day. In Treasury bonds in Figure 2–4, the initial balance was established in A and B periods from 96 $\frac{4}{32}$ to 97 $\frac{14}{32}$—well over a point wide. Other timeframe sellers entered on the upper extreme because price auctioned too high, creating a strong single-print selling tail, while other timeframe buyers entered on the lower extreme as price auctioned too low, creating a single print buying tail. Price spent the rest of the day auctioning within the extremes.

On the surface, Normal days might appear easy to trade. However, imagine the anxiety in placing an order to buy just after price has dropped over a point! The bottom appears to be literally dropping out of the market, and you have to pick up that phone and say "buy it." This is not to say that every time a market drops a point you should step up and buy—that would be financial suicide. But as we proceed through the more common day types and you observe them through your own experience, you will begin to develop an understanding of which day timeframe patterns and logical market situations will give you the confidence to buy against such a break. We bring this up primarily to touch on two key principles that you will no doubt grow tired of by the end of this book. They are:

The best trades often fly in the face of the most recent market activity, and never lose sight of the bigger picture.

Figure 2–4   Normal day.

97 14 /32	A
97 13 /32	A
97 12 /32	A
97 11 /32	A
97 10 /32	A
97 9 /32	A
97 8 /32	A
97 7 /32	A
97 6 /32	A
97 5 /32	A
97 4 /32	AG
97 3 /32	AG
97 2 /32	AG
97 1 /32	AG
97 0 /32	AG
96 31 /32	AGHK
96 30 /32	AFGHKL
96 29 /32	AFGHKL
96 28 /32	AFGHKL
96 27 /32	AFHKL
96 26 /32	AEFHKL
96 25 /32	AEFHKL
96 24 /32	AEFHKL
96 23 /32	ABEFHKL
96 22 /32	ABEFHIKL
96 21 /32	ABCDEFHIJKL
96 20 /32	ABCDEFHIJL
96 19 /32	ABCDEHIJL
96 18 /32	ABCDEHIJL
96 17 /32	ABCDEIJL
96 16 /32	ABCDEIJL
96 15 /32	ABCDEIJLM
96 14 /32	ABCDIJL
96 13 /32	ABCDIJL
96 12 /32	ABCDIJ
96 11 /32	ABCDIJ
96 10 /32	ACIJ
96 9 /32	ACIJ
96 8 /32	AC
96 7 /32	AC
96 6 /32	A
96 5 /32	A
96 4 /32	A
96 3 /32	

Normal Variation of a Normal Day

Dynamics   A Normal Variation of a Normal day is characterized by market activity early in the trading session that is less dynamic than that of a Normal day. As the day progresses, however, the other timeframe enters the market and substantially extends the range. It is as if the other timeframe participant had watched the auctions for a while, then decided price was opportune and entered aggressively. The other timeframe's conviction is more evident, due to range extension on this type of day (compared to a Normal day). In Figure 2–5, the other timeframe seller auctioned price downward in D period until the other timeframe buyer responded to lower prices and cut off the selling. For the remainder of the day, trade is two-sided and a new area of balance is established.

Structural Characteristics   Normal Variations typically do not have quite as wide of an initial balance as Normal days (Point 1 in Figure 2–5). The initial balance, or base, is upset on one side by other timeframe range extension, usually early in the day. In Figure 2–5, the other timeframe seller extended the range down in D period, "tipping over" the base to the downside (Point 2). For the duration of the day, the market's auction process involves the other timeframe buyer, other timeframe seller, and the local (referred to as two-timeframe trade). On this day, selling range extension causes value to be established lower (Point 3).

Trend Day

Dynamics   There are two types of Trend days: the "standard" Trend day and the Double-Distribution Trend day. The most important feature of a standard Trend day is the high level of directional confidence that is evident throughout the day. The other timeframe buyer or seller remains in control of the auction process virtually from the day's open to its close. In addition, as a Trend auctions higher or lower, it continues to draw new business into the market, thus creating unidirectional, sustained price movement fueled by higher volume.

Structural Characteristics   On a Trend day, the open forms the upper or lower extreme in the large majority of cases (Point 1 in Figure 2–6), because the other timeframe is usually in control from the opening bell. In the Trend day example in Figure 2–6, the other timeframe seller ex-

---

Figure 2–5 Normal variation of a normal day.

	①	②	③
	.	.	.
100 12 /32	A	A	A
100 11 /32	A	A	A
100 10 /32	A	A	A
100 9 /32	A	A	A
100 8 /32	AB	AB	AB
100 7 /32	AB	AB	AB
100 6 /32	AB	AB	AB
100 5 /32	AB	AB	AB
100 4 /32	AB	AB	AB
100 3 /32	AB	AB	AB
100 2 /32	AB	ABC	ABC
100 1 /32	AB	ABC	ABCL
100 0 /32	AB	ABCD	ABCDL
99 31 /32	AB	ABCD	ABCDL
99 30 /32	AB	ABCD	ABCDFL
99 29 /32	AB	ABCD	ABCDFGKL
99 28 /32	B	BD	BDFGKLM
99 27 /32	B	BD	BDFGHJKLM
99 26 /32	.	D	DEGHJKLM
99 25 /32	.	D	DEFGHJKLM
99 24 /32	.	D	DEFGHJKLM
99 23 /32	.	D	DEFGHJKLM
99 22 /32	.	D	DEFHIJKL
99 21 /32	.	D	DEFHIJK
99 20 /32	.	D	DEFHIJK
99 19 /32	.	.	FHIJ
99 18 /32	.	.	HI
99 17 /32	.	.	HI
99 16 /32	.	.	.
	A-B	A-D	A-L

Figure 2–6 Trend day. "O" designates the open.

	1	2	3
	.	.	.
99 24 /32	O	O	O
99 23 /32	A	A	A
99 22 /32	A	A	A
99 21 /32	ABD	ABD	ABD
99 20 /32	ABCD	ABCD	ABCD
99 19 /32	ABCD	ABCDE	ABCDE
99 18 /32	ABCD	ABCDE	ABCDE
99 17 /32	ABCD	ABCDE	ABCDE
99 16 /32	ABC	ABCE	ABCE
99 15 /32	BC	BCE	BCE
99 14 /32	BC	BCEFG	BCEFG
99 13 /32	B	BEFG	BEFG
99 12 /32	B	BEFG	BEFG
99 11 /32	.	EFG	EFG
99 10 /32	.	EFGH	EFGH
99 9 /32	.	EFGH	EFGH
99 8 /32	.	EGH	EGH
99 7 /32	.	EGH	EGH
99 6 /32	.	GH	GH
99 5 /32	.	GH	GH
99 4 /32	.	H	HIJ
99 3 /32	.	H	HIJ
99 2 /32	.	H	HIJ
99 1 /32	.	H	HIJ
99 0 /32	.	H	HIJK
98 31 /32	.	H	HIJK
98 30 /32	.	H	HIJK
98 29 /32	.	H	HJK
98 28 /32	.	H	HJK
98 27 /32	.	H	HJKL
98 26 /32	.	.	JKL
98 25 /32	.	.	JKL
98 24 /32	.	.	JKL
98 23 /32	.	.	KL
98 22 /32	.	.	KL
98 21 /32	.	.	KL
98 20 /32	.	.	KL
98 19 /32	.	.	KL
98 18 /32	.	.	KL
98 17 /32	.	.	L
98 16 /32	.	.	.
	A-D	A-H	A-L

tends the range downward during multiple time periods, remaining in control for the entire day (Points 2 and 3). Such unidirectional activity is referred to as a "one-timeframe" market. During a one-timeframe buying Trend day, each time period will auction to a higher (or equal) price level without auctioning below the previous time period's lows. Conversely, in a one-timeframe selling Trend day, each additional time period will equal or extend below previous periods without auctioning above the previous period's highs. For example, in Figure 2–6, E period extended below D on the downside, thus extending the range to begin the trend day. Then G auctioned lower than E (without auctioning above the E period high), H lower than G, J lower than L, and so on. One-timeframe conditions are a good indication of other timeframe control and a potential Trend day.

A Trend day differs from a Normal Variation day in that the Trend day's Profile is generally thinner and more elongated, usually no more than four or five TPO's wide at any point. Failure to recognize and accept that one is in a Trend day is one of the most costly mistakes a trader can make. Several days of trading profits can be lost in one trading session if you are positioned against the trend. It is important to identify early that either the other timeframe buyer or seller is in clear control and position yourself with them.

Double-Distribution Trend Day

Dynamics The second type of Trend day, the Double-Distribution Trend day, is relatively inactive during the first few hours of the trading session. Market participants possess a low level of conviction, resulting in a narrow base. Later in the session, a change in events causes the other timeframe to perceive price to be unfair at current price levels, enter the market aggressively, and substantially extend the range. This later entry by the other timeframe drives price to a new level, where a second balance region develops. The Double-Distribution Trend day does not possess the steady confidence of a typical Trend day and must stop and "reassure" itself after a substantial move.

Structural Characteristics A very small initial balance is the first indication of a potential Double-Distribution Trend day. Again, the more narrow the base, the easier it is to overwhelm this area and auction quickly to a new level (Point 1 in Figure 2–7). In Figure 2–7, the other timeframe seller extends the range down in F and G periods (Point 2). Lower prices are accepted as value forms below the original value area in a new distribution, separated by single TPO price prints (Point 3). This

---

Figure 2–7 Double-distribution trend day.

97 25 /32		A	. A	. A
97 24 /32		A	A	A
97 23 /32		A	A	A
97 22 /32		A	A	A
97 21 /32		AD	AD	AD
97 20 /32		ACD	ACD	ACD
97 19 /32		ACDE	ACDE	ACDE
97 18 /32	①	ACDE	ACDE	ACDE
97 17 /32		ABCDE	ABCDE	ABCDE
97 16 /32		ABCE	ABCEF	ABCEF
97 15 /32		ABE	ABEF	ABEF
97 14 /32		ABE	ABEF	ABEF
97 13 /32		BE	BEF	BEF
97 12 /32		B	BF	BF
97 11 /32		B	BF	BF
97 10 /32		.	F	F
97 9 /32		.	F	F
97 8 /32		.	F	F ④
97 7 /32		.	F	F
97 6 /32		.	F	F
97 5 /32		.	F ②	F
97 4 /32		.	FG	FG
97 3 /32		.	FG	FG
97 2 /32		.	G	GK
97 1 /32		.	G	GKL
97 0 /32		.	G	GHKL
96 31 /32		.	G	GHKL
96 30 /32		.	G	GHKL
96 29 /32		.	G	GHIKL
96 28 /32		.	G	GHJKL
96 27 /32		.	G	GHJKL
96 26 /32		.	G	③ GHIJKL
96 25 /32		.	.	HIJKL
96 24 /32		.	.	HIJKL
96 23 /32		.	.	HIJLM
96 22 /32		.	.	HIJLM
96 21 /32		.	.	HIJLM
96 20 /32		.	.	HIJL
96 19 /32		.	.	HIJ
96 18 /32		.	.	H
96 17 /32		.	.	H
96 16 /32		.	.	.
		A-E	A-G	A-L

new trading range generally holds throughout the day, often providing useful reference points and good trading opportunities for day traders.

The single prints separating the two distributions in a Double-Distribution Trend day become an important reference point near the end of the day. If price auctions back into the single prints during the latter time periods, in effect making them double prints, something has changed, and the second distribution is no longer accepted as value. For example, in the Double-Distribution Trend in Figure 2–7, a price probe into the F period single prints (Point 4) would indicate that a strong other timeframe buyer had entered, or that the other timeframe seller conviction that caused the initial range extension is no longer present.

Nontrend Day

Dynamics   A Nontrend day is characterized by a complete lack of directional conviction. Nontrend days often occur before the release of a big economic number, news event or a holiday. Market participants balance their positions in expectation of the market's reaction to the external stimuli—there is simply no activity. Trade is not being facilitated in any direction, for there is little market participation and no confidence.

Structural Characteristics   A Nontrend day starts out looking as if it might be a trend day, for the initial range is narrow. However, the other timeframe never surfaces and there is no range extension. The market is waiting for new information before making its next directional move. A typical Nontrend day in Treasury bonds is shown in Figure 2–8.

Neutral Day

Dynamics   When a Neutral day occurs, it means that the other timeframe buyer and seller are not far apart in their view of value. When they have similar views of value, the market balances, auctioning back and forth between them. During a Neutral day, both other timeframe participants are present (if only one were active, there would be an imbalance and a Trend or Normal Variation type of day would occur).

It is important to keep in mind that while the other timeframe buyer and seller may be close in their perception of value, they rarely agree on the same price, just as the automobile producer rarely agrees with the long-term car buyers. Therefore, the other timeframe buyer and seller do not trade with each other, they trade with the local—the middleman.

Figure 2–8   Nontrend day.

```
100  4 /32 A
100  3 /32 A
100  2 /32 AL
100  1 /32 AL
100  0 /32 AL
 99 31 /32 AL
 99 30 /32 AL
 99 29 /32 AL
 99 28 /32 ACGKL
 99 27 /32 ABCGK
 99 26 /32 ABCGHK
 99 25 /32 ABCDEFGHIK
 99 24 /32 ABCDEFGHIJK
 99 23 /32 BCDEFHIJK
 99 22 /32 BCDEHIJ
 99 21 /32 BCDJ
 99 20 /32 BCD
 99 19 /32 BC
 99 18 /32 B
 99 17 /32 B
 99 16 /32 .
 99 15 /32 .
```

Structural Characteristics   On a Neutral day, the base width is somewhere between a trend and normal day. It is not so small as to be easily
upset and not wide enough to hold the day's extremes (Point 1 in Figure
2–9). The salient feature on a Neutral day is the fact that both the other
timeframe buyer and the other timeframe seller are active, as is
evidenced by range extension on both sides of the initial balance (Points
2 and 3). This indicates a market in balance (Point 4), for all timeframes
are involved.

There are two types of Neutral days: Neutral-center and Neutral-extreme. On a Neutral-center day, the day closes with price in the middle
of the range, indicating a lack of confidence and a balance between the
other timeframe buyer and seller. On a Neutral-extreme day, price closes
on either the high or low extreme for the day, indicating a hypothetical
"victory" in the day timeframe battle for control between the other
timeframe buyer and seller. If the day closes on the upper extreme on a
Neutral day, then the other timeframe buyer has higher directional conviction. Conversely, if the close is on the lows, the other timeframe seller
has exhibited greater confidence.

Day Type Summary

The chart in Figure 2–10 displays the type of day on the horizontal axis
and the level of directional conviction that the day exhibits on the vertical axis. The result is a gradually ascending line from lowest conviction
to highest; from a Nontrend day to a Trend day. Again, the labels we
have given the day types are not carved in stone, but are used only for
learning purposes. What should become clear is that by monitoring a
day's conviction very early in the trading session, traders can quickly
begin to understand and visualize how the day will develop.

At this point you know the basic "objective facts and features"
about the Market Profile. Like David the novice piano player, you have
learned the foundation for further learning, but there is a long way to go.
In the following sections, the concepts you have learned as a novice will
serve as the foundation for understanding the market, like the staff and
notes are the foundation for understanding music.

Remember to actively interpret and combine your new knowledge
with your experience in the market. Do not put the facts you have
learned as a novice away and say, "OK, what's next." The learning
process is an ongoing synthesis, each part fitting into the next like a puzzle. Trying to become an expert trader without a continuum between the
stages is like trying to put together a puzzle with all the pieces the same
color. Look for the big picture.

Figure 2–9   Neutral Day.

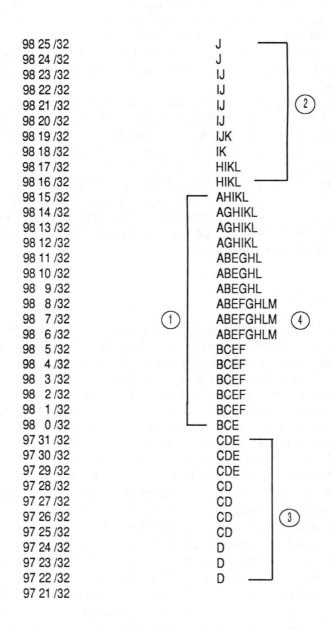

98 25 /32	J
98 24 /32	J
98 23 /32	IJ
98 22 /32	IJ
98 21 /32	IJ
98 20 /32	IJ
98 19 /32	IJK
98 18 /32	IK
98 17 /32	HIKL
98 16 /32	HIKL
98 15 /32	AHIKL
98 14 /32	AGHIKL
98 13 /32	AGHIKL
98 12 /32	AGHIKL
98 11 /32	ABEGHL
98 10 /32	ABEGHL
98 9 /32	ABEGHL
98 8 /32	ABEFGHLM
98 7 /32	ABEFGHLM
98 6 /32	ABEFGHLM
98 5 /32	BCEF
98 4 /32	BCEF
98 3 /32	BCEF
98 2 /32	BCEF
98 1 /32	BCEF
98 0 /32	BCE
97 31 /32	CDE
97 30 /32	CDE
97 29 /32	CDE
97 28 /32	CD
97 27 /32	CD
97 26 /32	CD
97 25 /32	CD
97 24 /32	D
97 23 /32	D
97 22 /32	D
97 21 /32	

Figure 2–10 Directional conviction according to day type.

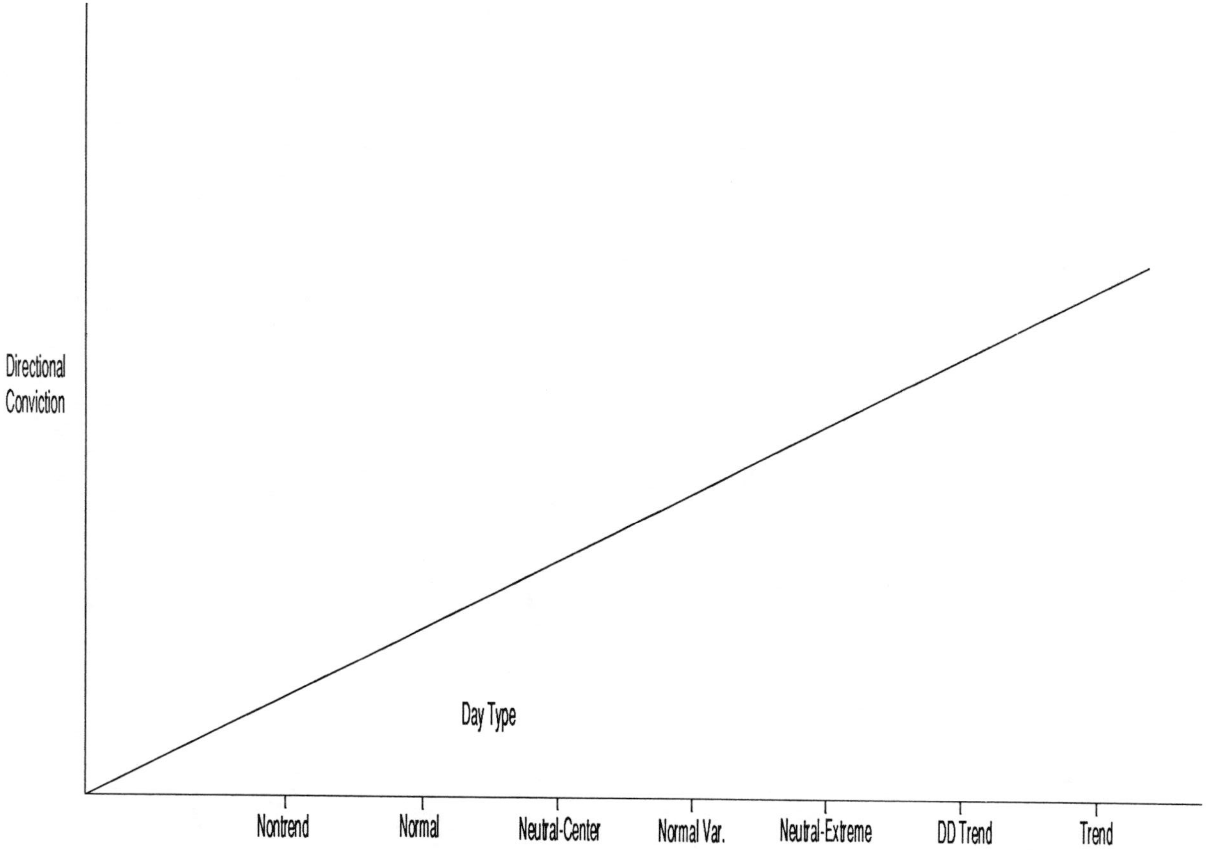

Directional
Conviction

Nontrend   Normal   Neutral-Center   Normal Var.   Neutral-Extreme   DD Trend   Trend

Day Type

CHAPTER 3

ADVANCED BEGINNER

When David reached the advanced beginner stage, he could play a few simple songs all the way through. Then his instructor gave him a new song to learn that was in a different key signature, explaining that certain notes are raised and must be played on the black keys. When David tried to play it, he became frustrated and exclaimed, "This song doesn't work."

He was playing every note as it was written, the way he had learned as a novice. The instructor calmly explained that in any key signature besides C major, certain notes must be played differently.

David fell victim to tunnel vision, for he was thinking only of the limited rules he had memorized and was not incorporating the new information in his playing. He then blamed the written music to explain his failure and frustration. The musical score is not right or wrong, it is only a passive medium that communicates a certain piece of music.

Tunnel vision is an easy trap to fall into, especially when learning large amounts of new information. It is not uncommon to hear beginning Market Profile traders comment, "The Profile doesn't work." There is nothing about the Profile that does or does not work. It is only a passive gauge of market-generated information—a way to organize the data, much like the musical score. What fails to work is the trader's ability to see the "big picture" objectively and realize that everything is a series of facts surrounded by other circumstances. Only when all the circumstances are interpreted together and a holistic image develops will successful trading occur.

Building the Framework

In Advanced Beginner, we will begin to build upon the foundation established in the Novice. You will learn many of the broad concepts that will serve as tools for building a framework for understanding the marketplace through the Market Profile.

The Big Picture: Market Structure, Trading Logic, and Time

The "big picture" is made up of three broad categories of information: market structure, trading logic, and time. As a novice you learned the basics of market structure, the most tangible information offered by the Market Profile in the unique bell curve graphic. Very short-term structure is reflected through TPOs and the market's half-hour auctions. As the day progresses, the market begins to form one of the day types through range extension, tails, etc. We can see, measure, and name the physical aspects of the Profile. By the day's end, structure shows not only what happened, but also when it happened and who was involved. In short, market structure provides visible evidence of the actions and behavior of the market's participants. In this section, this structural evidence will be built upon and combined with time and trading logic.

Time is the market's regulator. In its broadest sense, time sets limitations on the day's trading by imposing a certain framework, i.e., the number of hours from the open to the close. Most traders see time only in its function of the "closing bell," and do not consider its influence on price and opportunity. Without considering time, there is no way to judge value, and trading becomes a 50–50 gamble on price movement.

In the day timeframe, time validates price. The areas of the Market Profile's bell curve showing the greatest depth indicate the prices where trading spent the most *time*, thus establishing value for that day (price × time = value).[2] Understanding value and value area will become more and more important as we progress through the learning process.

[2] J. Peter Steidlmayer and Kevin Koy, *Markets and Market Logic* (Chicago: The Porcupine Press, 1986), p. 66.

Time also regulates opportunity. Consider an every day life example. You are in the market to buy a pair of snow skis. You shop around long enough to get a good feel as to how much skis normally cost or what you consider value. You don't need the skis right away, so you wait for a chance to buy them under value—you are a long term buyer.

You know that after the ski season ends, most stores will have "summer ski clearance sales," when price will temporarily drop below value. You also know that these prices will not last long, for time regulates opportunity. The stores could not afford to sell at such low prices all year and still make a profit. They are merely clearing excess inventory in preparation for new stock. To take advantage of the low price, you must act quickly.

The same principle is true in the futures market. Good opportunities to buy below value or sell above value will not last long, for price will move quickly with increased competition. If price stays below value for a long time, for example, it is no longer a good opportunity. Something has changed, and value is being accepted lower.

The third and most difficult category is trading logic. Trading logic is largely a product of experience, but it is more than just careful observation and practice; it is an understanding of *why* the market behaves the way it does. This understanding is best gained over time and through a conscious effort to understand the forces behind market movement. Certain aspects of trading logic can be taught in relation to structure and time, by derivative learning. For example, you know that a tail is an indicator of strong other timeframe activity on the extremes. If the tail is "taken out" by a price rotation back into the tail and TPOs build over time, trading logic says that something has changed, and the other timeframe buyer or seller that moved price quickly is no longer present or is less willing to respond to the same price levels.

The only way to really understand the market and its logic is to observe, interpret, and trade. Remember, much learning does not teach understanding. We will be integrating trading logic throughout the remainder of the book.

A Synthesis: Structure, Time, and Logic

Imagine two children, each racing to complete a giant jig-saw puzzle. Both are working on the same puzzle with an equal number of pieces (the same structure), but one child has a picture of the finished puzzle and one does not. Obviously, the child with a knowledge of the whole picture will finish first.

The Profile graphic is much like an intricate puzzle. Its structure reveals more and more as the day nears completion. But, like the child with a picture of the finished puzzle, traders with an understanding of the "big picture"—those that can see the market develop before it is revealed by structure—are generally the first to put together the pieces of the market. Market time and trading logic are the two *big picture* components of a whole market understanding. Only through a synthesis of all three components will a trader successfully put together the puzzle. We will now discuss market structure, time, and trading logic according to five general criteria:

1. Ease of Learning
2. Amount of Information
3. Recognition Speed
4. Trade Location
5. Confidence Level

Ease of Learning   Ironically, the order in which structure, time, and logic are usually learned is opposite from their order of occurrence in the marketplace—not because they are taught incorrectly, rather, because market structure is learned more quickly and easily than the roles of time and logic. Market structure is the finished product, and it is always easier to see the finished product than to identify the stages of its assembly. Mastering market structure is largely a matter of successfully recognizing and interpreting the Profile graphic. Understanding the role of time, however, requires a much deeper understanding of the market's auction process. Trading logic is the hardest to learn, particularly from a book or instructor, for logic is the ultimate outcome of trading practice and experience. *Trading logic is the raw human instinct of the marketplace.* True trading logic comes only through intensive participation and careful examination of real market situations.

Amount of Information   While market structure is clearly the most tangible information offered by the Profile, it also contains the greatest amount and variety of information. Why, then, is it so difficult to interpret market structure in real trading situations? It is relatively simple to recognize and interpret the day's final structure. The difficulty lies in recognizing what is transpiring as the structures are building.

The inability to identify a developing structure does not necessarily mean that the information is lacking. It is simply not conveyed in an easily readable format. In addition, it is possible to monitor the *wrong* information. Market time and trading logic provide very little in terms of visible, tangible information—but the information *is in the market*. Successful trading requires the ability to find and interpret the more subtle clues found in time and logic, and integrate them with the developing structure.

Recognition Speed It takes time to build structure. Thus, while the Profile structure reveals a lot, the sheer fact that *time* must transpire suggests that fundamental changes occur in the market before they are revealed by structure. Structure acts as the market's translator, and translated information is second-hand information. *The market has already spoken in the form of time and logic.* Traders who rely exclusively on structure without integrating time and logic will be late in entering and exiting the market, just as a catcher who holds his throw until he sees how fast a man stealing second base can run will never make the out.

Trade Location Later recognition leads to later entry and exit, which in turn leads to less desirable trade location. For example, range extension (structure) confirms that other timeframe buyers have entered the market. But *when* did they enter the market? If we rely solely on structure, we do not realize the other timeframe buyer's point of entry until the point of range extension, that is, when price is on the day's high. Buying the high results in poor day timeframe trade location, at least temporarily. In many cases, it is possible to know that buyers are assuming control before the actual structural confirmation (range extension) through an understanding of market time and trading logic.

Confidence Level Trading based on structure provides the greatest level of comfort and confidence, for there is obvious proof on which to base a decision. The more information we have in our favor, the more comfortable we are with a trade. Unfortunately, *visible* information and opportunity are inversely related. The more structural information present, the less an opportunity still exists. Thus, if a trader waits for too much information, chances are good that the real opportunity has been missed. If all the evidence is present and visible, then you are far from the first to have acted on it and probably have poor trade location.

Market time, followed by trading logic, provides the least amount of visible evidence. To the advanced beginner trader, trades based on time and logic offer a lower level of confidence, for the trader is not yet comfortable outside the realm of structure. Seasoned traders with a whole-market understanding, on the other hand, trade using logic and time and then monitor activity for the additional information (structure) necessary to increase their confidence in the trade.

Summary: *Logic creates the impetus, time generates the signal, and structure provides the confirmation.*

The preceding discussion delineates the many differences between structure, time, and logic, but the answer to a practical sense of their synthesis must be developed through time and experience. Such coordination is gained only through observing and acting on market-generated information every day (doing the trade). Although the Market Profile is best known for the Profile graphic, or structure, experience has shown that understanding the influence of time and trading logic is more important to reaching a holistic view of the marketplace. Putting in the extra effort to fully understand the building blocks of structure—market time and trading logic—will better prepare traders to anticipate and take advantage of trading opportunities as they develop, not after they have passed.

Evaluating Other Timeframe Control

We have stressed in general terms the importance of determining who, if anyone, is in control of the market. Let us now enter into evaluating other timeframe control in a more detailed, conclusive discussion. The elements that signify other timeframe control are perhaps the most deceptive of all market-generated information we will cover. Often, information that we believe we are interpreting objectively is presented in such a way that its actual nature is misinterpreted.

An example of such an "illusion" often occurs when a market opens exceptionally above the previous day's value area. The other timeframe seller responds to the higher open, enters the market aggressively and auctions price lower all day. However, at the conclusion of the trading session, the day's value is ultimately higher. In the day timeframe, other timeframe sellers dominated the market's auctions through their attempts to return price to previously accepted value. But the responsive selling was not strong enough to completely overpower the higher opening triggered by a strong other timeframe buyer. Day timeframe structure indicated weakness, while the market was actually very strong in the longer term.

As illusions go, the preceding example is relatively easy to detect and evaluate. Unfortunately, the information generated by the market is not always so clear. In most cases, a more analytical approach is needed to effectively gauge who is winning the battle for control between the other timeframe buyer and seller.

To evaluate other timeframe control, we will examine range extension, tails, activity occurring in the "body" of the Profile, and value area placement in relationship to the previous day. In addition, each of these factors will be studied further, based on whether the participants are acting on their own initiative or are willing to act only in response to an advantageous market movement. Another timeframe participant who acts on his own initiative is usually more determined than one who merely "responds" to a beneficial opportunity.

This section will deal with evaluating who has control in the day timeframe. The ability to process information via the Profile structures enables a trader to recognize attractive day timeframe trades. Longer-term traders must also be able to read and interpret day timeframe structure, for a longer-term auction is simply a series of day auctions moving through time. Longer-term auction evaluation and value area placement requires far more analysis and will be detailed in Chapter 4. We mention it here to avoid creating the illusion that day timeframe control is all-conclusive—it merely reflects activity occurring during one day in the life of a longer-term auction.

Learning to read and interpret day timeframe structure is beneficial to all market participants at one time or another. This understanding most obviously influences the individual who trades only in the day timeframe, in other words, one who begins and ends each day with no position. However, all longer-term traders are also day traders on the day that they initiate or exit a trade. The concept of longer timeframe participation in the day timeframe is best expressed through two examples.

Imagine a food company that purchases a large amount of corn for its cereal processing plant. The food processor has an opinion that corn prices will rise but also wants to be appropriately hedged against loss. Thus, as the price of corn rises, the company gradually sells grain futures against its inventory, in effect "scaling in" a hedge. On one particular morning, corn opens far above the previous day's value, but early Profile structure indicates weakness. The processor takes advantage of the higher open and expands the size of its hedge (by selling more futures). However, as price auctions lower over the course of the day, the processor may partially close out its shorts, seeking to replace them later at higher prices. The food company's hedging goals are clearly longer term. However, when the market created an opportunity in the day timeframe, the food company elected to "trade" a portion of the hedge.

In a second example, a futures fund manager with a bullish bias may elect to "trade around" his long-term positions by taking advantage of day timeframe structure. If market structure indicates that the market is likely to break, he may sell a percentage of his position, reestablishing it later in the day. In fact, if there is enough volatility in the market, he may reposition a portion of his inventory more than once on the same day.

Putting aside the longer term for a later section, we will now begin the discussion of other timeframe control in the day timeframe.

Other Timeframe Control on the Extremes

Tails (or Extremes)   Tails are created when an aggressive buyer or seller enters the market on an extreme and quickly moves price. Generally, the longer the tail, the greater the conviction behind the move (a tail must be at least two TPOs long to be significant). A tail at the upper extreme of a day's profile, for example, indicates a strong other timeframe seller entered the market and drove price to lower levels. In terms of other timeframe control, no tail may also be significant. The absence of aggressive other timeframe activity on an extreme indicates a lack of buyer or seller conviction.

Range Extension   Range extension is another structural feature that identifies control and helps gauge buyer/seller strength. Multiple period range extension is generally the result of successively higher or lower auctions. The stronger the control, the more frequent and elongated the range extension, resulting in a more elongated Profile (an elongated Profile is an indication of good trade facilitation). In a Trend day, for example, the other timeframe's dominance is clearly evident through continued range extension and price movement throughout the day.

Other Timeframe Control in the Body of the Profile

The role of the larger institutions and commercial participants in the marketplace is much greater than merely seeking to take advantage of price as it moves away from value (evidenced by tails and range extension). Many of the longer-term commercial users of the futures exchange have a certain amount of business they must conduct every day. For example, General Mills must put boxes of cereal on millions of breakfast tables every morning. Therefore, they are constantly in the market as part of their daily business.

This more subtle, involuntary other timeframe activity generally takes place within the body of the Profile. Nonetheless, it plays an important part in our evaluation of the competition that goes on between the other timeframe participants. The TPO count provides a means of measuring the activity of the other timeframe within the body of the day's Profile.

TPO Count   The Time Price Opportunity is the smallest unit of market measurement. As mentioned earlier, TPO stands for Time, the market's regulator, and Price, the market's advertiser, together creating the Opportunity to buy or sell at a given price at a particular time. Monitoring the TPO count helps evaluate other timeframe control within the developing value area. Specifically, the TPO count measures the level of imbalance (when such an imbalance exists) between the other timeframe participant and the day timeframe (mostly local) trader.

The key to understanding how an imbalance can occur is to recognize that the other timeframe buyer does not deal directly with the other timeframe seller. Recall that the local, or scalper, acts as a middleman between these two longer-term participants. Thus, the other timeframe buyer generally buys from a local, and the other timeframe seller typically sells to a local. Imbalance occurs when there are more other timeframe buyers than sellers or more other timeframe sellers than buyers, leaving the local with an imbalance. Before we can learn how to measure this imbalance, we must first gain a better understanding of how the locals conduct their business.

The locals position themselves between the flow of outside buy orders and outside sell orders (orders placed predominantly by off-floor, other timeframe participants). For example, suppose that a floor broker receives an order to sell 100 contracts at, say, $5.00 per contract. The locals would buy the contracts from the broker and then turn around and sell them to another floor broker who has an order to *buy* 100 contracts at $5.02. In this situation, the locals perform their role of facilitating trade and, in return, receive a small margin of profit.

The trade facilitation process is seldom so ideal, however. Often there are more other timeframe buyers than sellers—causing the local's inventory to become overloaded. For example, if an usually large number of sell orders enter the pit, the local's inventory begins to accumulate to a point where he gets "too long." In other words, the local has purchased too much from the other timeframe seller. If the other timeframe buyer does not appear relatively quickly, the local must bring his inventory back into balance in some other way. One's first thought would be that the local simply needs to sell off his excess inventory. However, this is not so easy, for reversing and selling would only serve to accentuate the selling that is already flowing into the market. Therefore, his first priority is to stop the flow of outside sell orders by dropping his bid in hopes that the market will stabilize and he can balance his inventory. If lower prices do not cut off selling, the local may then be forced to "jump on the bandwagon" and sell (liquidate) his longs at a lower price.

Viewed from another perspective, suppose you decided to try to make extra spending money by scalping football tickets. A month before the chosen game you purchased twenty tickets from the box office at $10 each. In this case, the box office is the other timeframe seller and you are the day timeframe buyer. Over the ensuing month, your team loses every game and slips from first to fifth place. Not surprisingly, the attendence is dismal on the day of the game at which you intend to sell your tickets. Few other timeframe buyers (fans) show up. In order to get rid of your inventory and recover at least part of your costs, you are forced to sell your tickets at $8 instead of $12 or $15. In this example, there were more other timeframe seller than buyers. Consequently, price had to move lower to restore balance.

The same concepts apply to the futures marketplace. If we can identify imbalance before it corrects itself, then perhaps we can capitalize on it, too. Tails and range extension are more obvious forms of other timeframe presence, but on a volatile or choppy day, much of the imbalance occurs in more subtle ways within the value area. The TPO count is an excellent method for evaluating day-to-day imbalance that occurs within the developing value area.

The "TPO count" is found by isolating the point of control (the longest line closest to the center of the range), summing all the TPOs above it and comparing that number to the total number of TPOs below it. Single print tails are excluded from the count, because their implications are clear and have already been considered when examining activity on the extremes. Remember, the point of control is significant, because it indicates the price where the most activity occurred during the day and is, therefore, the fairest price in the day timeframe (price × time = value). Figure 3–1 illustrates the TPO count.

The total TPO figure above the point of control represents other timeframe traders willing to sell and stay short above value, while total TPOs below the point of control represent other timeframe traders willing to buy and stay long below value. The resulting ratio is an estimate for buyer/seller imbalance in the value area. For example, a ratio of 32/24 breaks down to 32 selling TPOs above the point of control, and 24 buying TPOs below. Note that a value area is not specifically calculated. Rather, the methodology of the TPO count, i.e., single-print rejections are not counted, implies value.

Portrayed in Figure 3–2 are three developing versions of the treasury bond Profile of January 29, 1988. Profile A displays time periods A–F of the day. The 29th saw an opening substantially higher than the

Figure 3–1 Calculation of the TPO count.

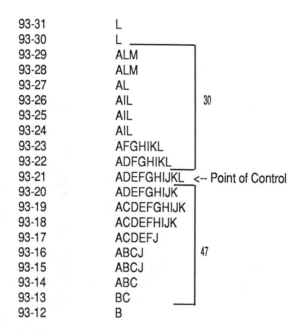

93-31	L
93-30	L
93-29	ALM
93-28	ALM
93-27	AL
93-26	AIL	30
93-25	AIL
93-24	AIL
93-23	AFGHIKL
93-22	ADFGHIKL
93-21	ADEFGHIJKL	<-- Point of Control
93-20	ADEFGHIJK
93-19	ACDEFGHIJK
93-18	ACDEFHIJK
93-17	ACDEFJ
93-16	ABCJ	47
93-15	ABCJ
93-14	ABC
93-13	BC
93-12	B

Total TPO's Above Point of Control:	Total TPO's Below Point of Control:
2 ALM*	9 ADEFGHIJK
2 ALM*	10 ACDEFGHIJK
2 AL	9 ACDEFHIJK
3 AIL	6 ACDEFJ
3 AIL	4 ABCJ
3 AIL	4 ABCJ
+ 7 AFGHIKL	+ 3 ABC
8 ADFGHIKL	2 BC
--------------	-----------------
30	47

Figure 3–2 TPO's in a developing market for Treasury Bonds, January 29, 1988. "O" designates the open.

	A-F		A-H		A-Close	
94 0 /32	.		.		.	
93 31 /32	.		.		L	
93 30 /32	.		.		L	
93 29 /32	A		A		ALM	
93 28 /32	A		A		AL	
93 27 /32	A		A		AL	
93 26 /32	A		A		AIL	
93 25 /32	A		A		AIL	
93 24 /32	O		O		OIL	
93 23 /32	AF		AFGH		AFGHIKL	30
93 22 /32	ADF		ADFGH		ADFGHIKL	
93 21 /32	ADEF	13	ADEFGH	21	ADEFGHIJKL <	
93 20 /32	ADEF		ADEFGH		ADEFGHIJK	
93 19 /32	ACDEF <		ACDEFGH <		ACDEFGHIJK	47
93 18 /32	ACDEF		ACDEFH		ACDEFHIJK	
93 17 /32	ACDEF		ACDEF		ACDEFJ	
93 16 /32	ABC	21	ABC	22	ABCJ	
93 15 /32	ABC		ABC		ABCJ	
93 14 /32	ABC		ABC		ABC	
93 13 /32	BC		BC		BC	
93 12 /32	B		B		B	
93 11 /32	.		.		.	
93 10 /32	.		.		.	
93 9 /32	.		.		.	
93 8 /32	.		.		.	
	Profile A		Profile B		Final Profile	

close of the previous day, followed by an early morning sell-off as price attempted to auction down.

As the trading day proceeds, however, our concern is with discovering exactly who is more aggressive (who is in control) within the developing value area. Occasionally, activity reflected by range extension and tails will give us some clues regarding which participant is more aggressive on the extremes. But the value area battles are more subtle and often much slower to develop. Monitoring the TPO count through time helps us measure how the wins and losses are stacking up and gives some indication of who will be the victor in the battle for control in the body of the Profile.

Examine Profile A again. A–F period registers a 13/21 TPO count, which favors the other timeframe buyers. Consider what this 13/21 TPO count logically means: the fact that the TPO count below the point of control is growing larger indicates that, although price is spending time below the point of control, *price is not going anywhere.*

Had other timeframe sellers been aggressive within the value area, there would have been downside range extension. Range extension would have lowered the point of control (and the perception of value), therefore balancing the TPO count and quite probably shifting it in favor of the sellers. With a TPO count building in the bottom half of the value area (buyers) and no selling range extension, chances are that it is the floor traders, or locals, who are selling to the other timeframe buyers.

Profile B in Figure 3–2 shows the TPO count through H period moving back into balance at 21/22. This temporary return to balance indicates that the locals' inventories became too short—in essence, *they had sold too much*—and were forced to cover (buy back) some of their shorts to bring their inventories back into line. Consequently, price rotated up in G and H periods, as the locals restored balance to their inventories.

Again, in the final Profile, other timeframe sellers were not present as price continued to rotate toward the day's upper extreme. The L period TPO print at 93 21/32 (Bonds trade in 32nds of $1000), and subsequent L period range extension pulled the point of control higher, confirming a final TPO tally in favor of buyers, 30/47. This end-of-the-day imbalance often provides momentum into the following day.

Initiative versus Responsive Activity

Knowing whether the other timeframe participants are acting on their own *initiative*, as opposed to *responding* to opportune prices is also important to understanding their influence. Traders can determine if activity is initiative or responsive by comparing the relationship of the day's structure to the previous day's value area. The previous day's value area acts as the truest, most recent indication of a level where price has been accepted over time. Four types of potential activity may emerge:

1. Initiative Buying
2. Initiative Selling
3. Responsive Buying
4. Responsive Selling

Briefly, initiative buying is any buying activity occurring within or above the previous day's value area. Conversely, initiative selling is any selling activity that takes place within or below the previous day's value area. Initiative activity indicates strong conviction on the part of the other timeframe.

Responsive activity is the obverse of initiative activity. Buyers respond to price below value, and sellers respond to price above value. Figures 3–3 and 3–4 illustrate these concepts in detail. Looking first at the lower right-hand side of Figure 3–3, the upward range extension in C period and the E period buying tail represent responsive buying. Buyers are responding to price considerably below the area of recent price acceptance. In other words, buyers have responded to the opportunity to buy cheap. *Keep in mind that if price auctions down and finds buyers, that alone is not responsive. It is the fact that price is below value that makes the buying responsive.*

A responsive buying tail is also initiative selling range extension. For example, when the grocer lowered prices in his "peanut butter extravaganza," it created initiative selling range extension. Buyers responded to this price below value, returning price to previous levels in a responsive buying tail. *The initiative range extension and the responsive tail were one and the same activity.*

Referring again to Figure 3–3, notice that the flip-side of the C period responsive buying range extension is a C period initiative selling tail. Similarly, the E period responsive buying tail was actually the outcome of a harsh rejection of E period initiative selling range extension. In Figure 3–4 we find the same thing: C period initiative buying range extension meets a responsive seller and eventually becomes a responsive selling tail. If range extension occurs in the last period of the day, however, it does not indicate a tail as well. A tail is only valid when confirmed by a rejection of price in at least one additional time period.

Range extension and tails occurring within the previous day's value area *are also considered initiative.* If people choose to buy or sell within the

Figure 3–3   Initiative vs. responsive activity.

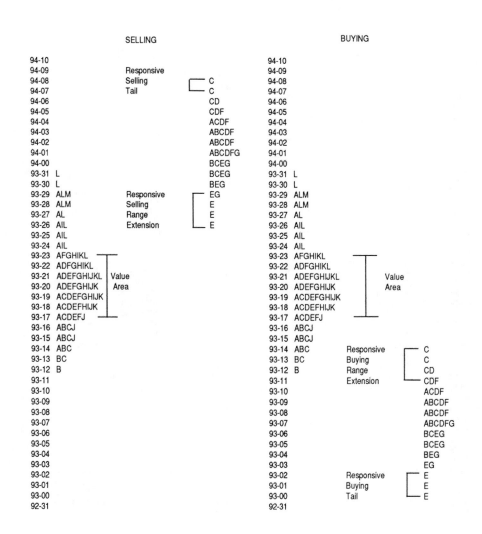

Figure 3–4. Initiative vs. responsive activity.

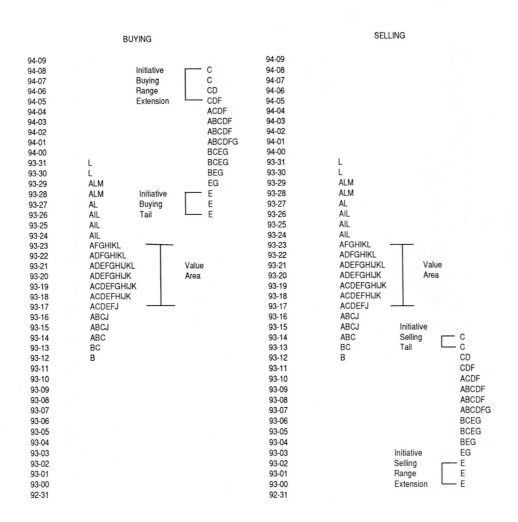

area of most recently perceived value, their free choice to "agree" with recent price levels is really an initiative decision in itself, for they are not responding to excess price. Like all the information you are learning, the concept of initiative and responsive action is not just a random designation that should be committed to memory, but rather a logical characterization of price's relationship to value.

The entire day's value area can be classified as either initiative or responsive as well. As noted before, this identification is important because it gives the trader an indication of market conviction and confidence. In short, initiative buying and responsive selling TPOs occur above the previous day's value area, while responsive buying and initiative selling TPOs occur below the previous day's value area. Any TPO activity occurring within the previous day's value area is considered initiative, although it does not carry as much confidence as initiative activity that takes place outside of the value area. Figures 3–5 and 3–6 illustrate these concepts.

Trending versus Bracketed Markets

Understanding the dynamics of trending and bracketed markets, and the transition from one to the other, is one of the most difficult auction market concepts to grasp. In a very real sense, this could be due to the fact that such an understanding requires a firm grasp of overall market behavior, as well as the synthesis of a large part of all Profile knowledge. For this reason, we lay the groundwork of trending and bracketed markets here, with a more detailed discussion to follow in the Competent section.

Let us begin with a few common dictionary definitions of a trend and a bracket in order to form a basic mental image of the two. *Webster's New Collegiate Dictionary* defines a trend: (a) "to extend in a general direction: follow a general course . . . to show a tendency," or (b) "the general movement in the course of time of a statistically detectable change; also: a statistical curve reflecting such a change." Unfortunately, there is no *absolute* way to define a trend, for it is a function of the market and your trading timeframe. A trend, put simply, is a divergence of price away from value. For our purposes, the price divergence in a trend is characterized by a series of day auctions (value areas) moving in a clear direction over a long period of time. An example of such a long-term trend is illustrated between Points 1 and 2 in the daily bar chart for Crude Oil in Figure 3–7. Figure 3–8 displays another trend occurring in the S&P 500 (between Points 1 and 2) that ends in a "bracket."

Figure 3–5   Initiative vs. responsive TPO's.

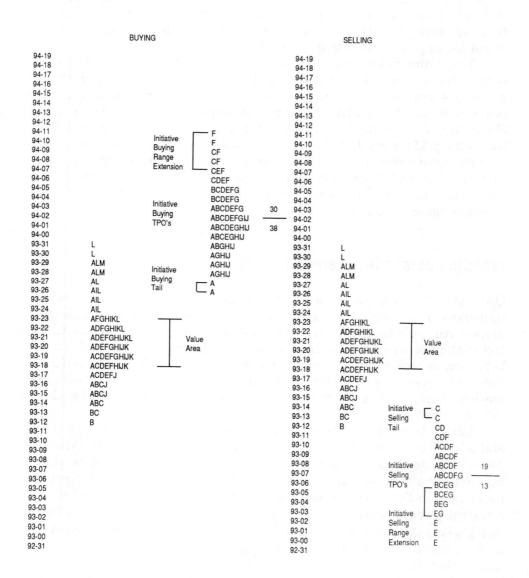

Figure 3–6 Initiative vs. responsive TPO's

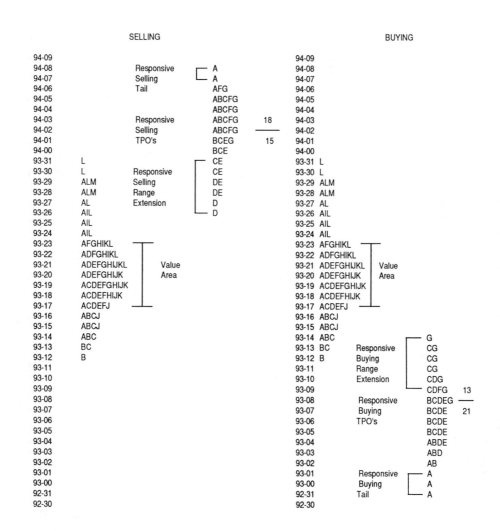

Figure 3-7 A trend occurring in June Crude Oil. Data courtesy of Commodity Quote Graphics.

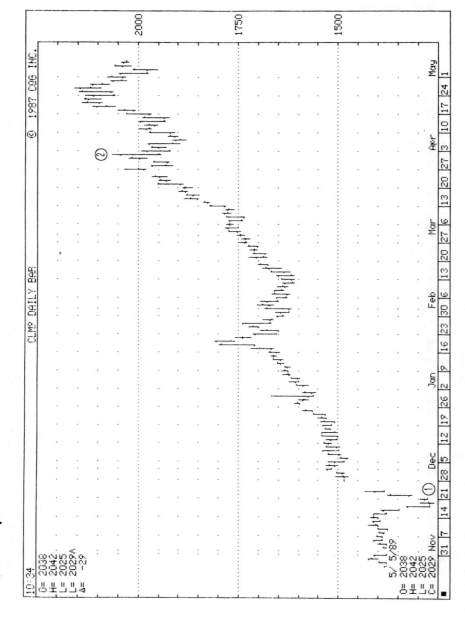

Figure 3–8   Trend to bracket in the June S&P 500. Data courtesy of Commodity Quote Graphics.

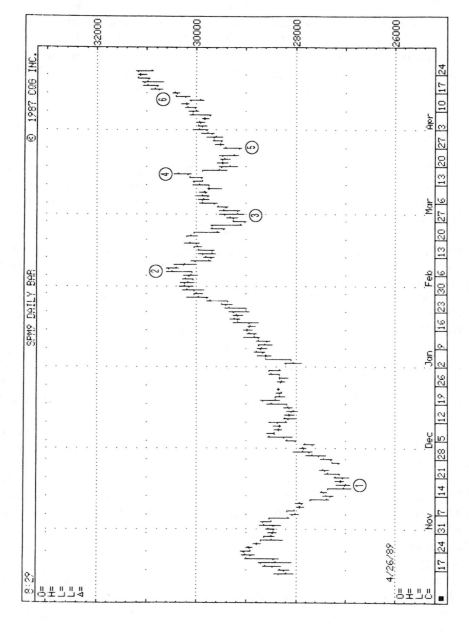

Webster's defines bracket: (a) "to place within or as if within brackets," or (b) "to establish a margin on either side of." A bracketed market is a series of price movements contained "as if within brackets." The market auctions back and forth between two price levels that serve as a margin on either end of the range. Referring to Figure 3–8 again, the S&P market began the bracketing process at Point 2, then auctioned back and forth within the bracket enclosed by Points 2 through 6.

Key Elements—A Brief Discussion

We have defined a trend as a divergence of price away from value. While the divergence may last for an extended period of time, it will not continue indefinitely—eventually price and value will reach an equilibrium.

A trending market ends when price begins to auction back and forth between two known reference points, forming a bracket or trading range. A new trend begins when price leaves the bracketed area and is accepted over time.

Many knowledegable professionals estimate that markets trend only 20 to 30 percent of the time. Failure to recognize this fact is one of the main reasons why a large number of traders don't make money. Many of the popular technical systems are trend following systems that require sustained price movement to be successful. As many traders are painfully aware, bracketed markets often move just fast and far enough to trigger these trend following systems, then the potential move stalls and the market heads the other way.

It is evident by now that the trader colloquialism "the trend is your friend" is a misleading expression. It is true that during a trending market, a trader can make a substantial profit if positioned with the trend. However, if a trader constantly employs a trend following system, his chances of success during a bracketing market are greatly reduced. Therefore, as the market evolves from trend to bracket and back to trend again, your trading strategy should change dramatically. Trends require a less active type of strategy; they need to be left alone. Because of their strong convictional nature, profit expectations are relatively high. In a trending market, you put the trade on and then let the market do the rest of the work. Brackets, however, require a closer, more hands-on approach. The market moves in erratic spurts with no real longer term directional conviction. The prices that form the bracket's extremes provide significant reference points by which to monitor future change, i.e., the start of a new trend, continuation of the bracketing process, and so forth. To successfully trade a bracketed market, you need to learn how to identify the outer reaches of the bracket and then take gains quickly instead of "letting them ride." Monitoring how the market behaves around these points of reference helps you gauge your profit expectations and adjust your trading strategy.

Knowing if a market is in a trend or a bracket is an integral part of a holistic market understanding. It is vital to formulating, developing, and implementing your own trading timeframe and strategy.

Trending Markets   The key to capitalizing on a trend lies in the trader's ability to determine if the trend is *continuing*, that is, if the divergence of price is being accepted or rejected by the market. A good indication of trend continuation lies in observing value area placement. If a series of value areas is moving in a clear direction through time, then the new price levels are being accepted and the trend is finding acceptance. If value areas begin to overlap or move in the opposite direction of the trend, then chances are good that the trend is slowing and beginning to balance.

A trend is started by initiative action from the other timeframe participant, who perceives price to be away from value in the longer term. In an up trend, for example, price is perceived as below value by the other timeframe buyer and unfair to the other timeframe seller. As price auctions higher, the trend "draws in" market participants from many different timeframes until virtually *everyone* is a buyer. At that point, the whole world believes the trend will go on forever, but there is no one left to buy. The upward trend ends, for there are simply no more buyers, and the responsive seller enters and auctions price downward, beginning the bracketing process. The other timeframe buyer and seller's view of value has narrowed, producing a relatively wide area of buyer/seller equilibrium contained within the bracket "margins."

Bracketed Markets   As mentioned previously, a trend typically ends in a balanced area, otherwise known as a trading range or bracket. Markets do not trend up, then turn on a dime and begin a trend down. An upward-trending market auctions higher, balances, then either continues up or begins to auction downward. Similarly, a down trend ends in a bracketed market, then either continues down or begins a trend to the up side.

In a bracket, both the other timeframe buyer and seller become responsive parties. As price nears the top of the perceived bracket, the seller responds and auctions price downward through the bracket or equilibrium range. In turn, the responsive buyer enters and rotates price back to the upside. This bracketing process indicates that the market is in balance and waiting for more information. Therefore, when price is accepted above or below a known bracket extreme, the market could be cepted above or below a known bracket extreme, the market could be coming out of balance. Monitoring such a break-out for continuation and acceptance can alert the observant trader to the beginning of a new trend.

To better illustrate the concept of balance and the dynamics of price rotation within a bracket, consider an everyday example—the car buyer. Imagine five different people who go to Rawley's car dealership to purchase a car during the same week. They all have the same ultimate goal in mind: the purchase of the new Series Magma 8.9 automobile. However, the similarities end there, for chances are good that each is focusing on different aspects of the same car. One of the five wrecked his car on the day before and needs transportation immediately for business purposes. A wealthy college student likes the style of the Magma and wants all the extras—sun roof, stereo, power windows, and racing stripes. A suburban middle-income family has been pricing cars for several weeks and has been to the Rawley dealership several times negotiating price. A woman who commutes to a nearby city is interested in the Magma because of its excellent gas mileage. The last of the five is a salesman who simply decides it is time he purchased a new car. All five view the same market from vastly different perspectives, and each has a certain price range in mind that he or she believes is value. The car dealer, too, has a perception of value that acts as a bracket in the negotiating process. His idea of value ranges from the lowest markup that will still clear a profit to the highest price he can get a buyer to pay. When dealing with each customer, price moves back and forth within his bracket until an agreement is reached. The college student would probably pay the most, for he is not worried about price and wants all the added luxuries. The family would probably get the best deal, for they are longer term buyers who have researched and bargained over a period of time. The point is that all five market participants will purchase the same car, but they will each pay a different price. The car dealer fulfills the status of middleman, facilitating trade at different price levels in his bracket by making the necessary deals to move the cars off his lot.

A bracketed market acts in a similar fashion. When the market is in a balancing mode, participants consider different factors in their perception of value. Price auctions back and forth as they respond to the changing factors that give rise to differing opinions. Technicians, for example, may monitor stochastic indicators, while fundamentalists look at economic figures and news. Still other traders may evaluate open interest, previous highs and lows, yield curves, and activity in other commodities. Because of this segmentation, one group of market participants may "rule" for a short period of time, accentuating the bracketing process.

A bracket provides less obvious information than a trend, where price movement and market sentiment are relatively easy to understand. In a strong trend, the direction of the trend is clear and all market opinion is generally geared with the trend. Except for entry and exit, a trader does not need the Market Profile, or any other system for that matter, to determine which way the market is trying to go. In a bracket, however, there is no clear indication regarding longer-term market sentiment. Because of the varied and often conflicting mixture of opinions that surface in a bracketed market, a trader must look harder to find directional clues. The diversity of these clues brings about the danger of overweighting any one piece of information and thus getting an incomplete (and often incorrect) view of the market. When market-generated information is organized using the Market Profile, otherwise segmented market opinions are brought together in one composite information source. In a sense, the Market Profile is a filter for all market opinions. By observing and understanding the Market Profile, it is possible to differentiate short-term bracketing activity from a potentially strong, sustained price movement. In other words, the Market Profile conduit is a powerful tool in evaluating bracket activity and control.

This concludes the basic concepts of trending and bracketed markets. A more detailed discussion that builds on these concepts will follow in Chapter 4.

The Two Big Questions

We have covered a large amount of material: Profile structure, day types, other timeframe control, initiative and responsive activity, trending and bracketed markets—and all of the subtleties that accompany each of them. It is as if we have been rubbing away at a large fogged-over window, each concept revealing a slightly larger view of the whole picture. Learning how markets operate and how to interpret them through the Market Profile is an evolving process that involves learning an enormous number of facts and concepts that are all interrelated. Bringing it all together is a challenge that combines knowledge, dedication, and experience as more of the window is exposed. Let us attempt to look at what we have uncovered so far in a way that will help unify what you have learned in the Novice and Advanced Beginner chapters.

Successful implementation of the Profile depends on being able to answer just two basic, sweeping questions that stem from the market's ultimate purpose in facilitating trade:

Which way is the market trying to go?
and
Is it doing a good job in its attempt to go that way?

Understanding these two questions together is in essence the equation for determining trade facilitation. As we continue through the more advanced portions of the learning process, these two questions will become the cornerstones for understanding the market through the Market Profile.

CHAPTER 4

COMPETENT

L et us think back for a moment to David, the aspiring pianist. David reached the third level of learning and became a *competent* pianist after many months of study and practicing the basics. He began to see each song as a whole, a certain expression to be performed with a definite goal in mind. He still played by reading the notes but achieved continuity in his playing.

In this chapter, we will complete the study of the basic concepts and theories behind evaluating market-generated information through the Market Profile. We will give a thorough discussion of practical applications to day and longer timeframe trading. By the close of Competent, more of the "big picture" will be revealed as the basics merge together to make you a competent trader.

Doing the Trade

"All reasonings concerning the matter of fact seem to be founded on the relation of Cause and Effect . . . I shall venture to affirm that the knowledge of this relation is not in any instance attained by learning a priori, but arises entirely from Experience."

—David Hume

Knowledge arises from experience. Just as a musician practices diligently to become a concert pianist and an athlete spends uncounted hours on the court to become a great tennis player, a trader must gain experience through actual trading to become an expert trader.

Any effective performance is a combination of knowledge, skill, and instinct. With each trade, you put your knowledge, your understanding, and your *experience* on the line to be judged by the market. Clearly, it is necessary to "do the trade" to learn. Experience provides the confidence to overcome such barriers as fear, hesitancy, and inflexibility.

We introduce the psychological side of trading here for good reason. By the end of the Advanced Beginner stage you should be incorporating what you have learned and will continue to learn into your trading technique. We will continue the discussion of the "You" portion of trading once all the mechanical aspects of the Market Profile have been covered. Remember: trading is the link to experience and knowledge.

Section I: Day Timeframe Trading

Mike Singletary of the Chicago Bears was the National Football League's defensive player of the year during the 1988–89 football season. Considered by many to be the finest linebacker to play the game, Singletary's all-pro ability transcends his physical strength and agility.

As captain of his defensive team, he attempts to, in effect, "read" the offense. As simple as this may sound, it is a complex process that involves both long- and short-term analysis. Singletary spends hours preparing for each game, studying play charts, game films, and player statistics. When the game starts, he knows exactly which plays the opponent has used in every possible situation, what formations these plays have involved, and who the key players are in each play. In other words, Singletary has done his long-term homework and, based on the opponent's past performances, enters each game with specific defensive plans in mind.

After the opening kickoff, however, Mike Singletary does not actively think about the charts and playbooks—he doesn't have time. It is here that Singletary's expertise shines. The game films and technical information are, in a sense, a holistic image in his mind. He acts intuitively, recognizes patterns, and quickly directs the defense. His expectations coming into the game serve as guidelines, but he actively assimilates his play to the evolving offense.

The opposing team's offensive coach changes his strategy and composition of plays with every game in an attempt to throw players such as Singletary off guard. The ability to recognize such changes in time to stop the play is what makes an expert linebacker.

An experienced day timeframe trader and Mike Singletary follow the same sort of evaluation process. He or she begins each day with a set of expectations that serve as guidelines, based on the market's past performance. The trader studies factors such as longer-term market direction, recent value area placement, and the opening call (all topics to be discussed in this section). Once the market opens, the trader switches to a more intuitive mindset, molding expectations to the developing structure, such as the opening type, the open's relationship to the previous day's value, and the auction rotations. Like Mike Singletary, the experienced trader knows that the market will seldom develop patterns identical to those that have happened in the past. The ability to recognize these subtle changes as they occur in the marketplace is what makes an expert trader.

In this section, we will study important structural reference points in the order that they occur in the unfolding market, beginning with the open and ending with the close.

Day Timeframe Directional Conviction

Recall for a moment the two big questions introduced at the end of Chapter 3. The first was, "Which way is the market trying to go?" The second was, "Is it doing a good job in its attempt to go that way?" Both of these questions relate directly to the concept of market confidence and directional conviction. *The sole purpose behind interpreting other timeframe activity is to find out which way the market is trying to go.*

If you know which other timeframe participant is in control in the day timeframe (or that neither is in control) and with what level of confidence they have entered the market, then you can successfully answer the two big questions and position your trade accordingly. We will now discuss how to evaluate market confidence and directional conviction, emphasizing their effect on estimating the day's range. We will start with the first available measure of market sentiment, the opening call.

Opening Call   During one of our advanced trading seminars, a successful floor trader asked an intriguing question: "If the opening exceeds or fails to make its opening call, can that also be considered recordable initiative or responsive activity, even though the market never actually traded there?" The answer, as you will see, is clearly "yes."

Day timeframe trading strategy begins with the succession of early morning calls that indicate where the market will open. Opening calls can occur at any time—from two hours before, to just a few minutes prior to the actual opening. Observing the succession of calls as the market nears its open and the call closest to the opening bell is one of the first important pieces of information available to the day timeframe trader.

In the last few minutes before the day's actual open, the largest and most active accounts have direct access to the trading floor through on-floor telephone clerks. The telephone lines to these large accounts are often left open during this period, providing continuous and almost instant communication with the trading pit. As early indications of price ranges are relayed to off-floor accounts around the world, they often attract the attention of the longer timeframe traders, leading them to place orders. As these orders are signaled into the pit, they are seen and communicated to other off-floor accounts, which in turn may stimulate additional orders. In a sense, the auction is actually underway before the market opens. This pre-opening auction process, although invisible to most, is often as important to evaluating market direction as the day's actual trade, for it is composed almost exclusively of other timeframe participants.

If the early call is perceived as too high or too low, opening call price levels and the eventual opening price can change quickly. What the astute floor trader at the seminar recognized is that the information available before the opening is often as valuable as looking at a tail on the Market Profile graphic. For example, if the first call is an expected opening around 87–19, but the actual opening takes place at 87–12, there is, in a sense, a seven-tick "hidden selling tail." That tail will be responsive or initiative depending on where it is located in relation to the previous day's value area (just like a visible tail).

The Open   Experienced day timeframe traders start each trading day with a firm knowledge of recent market activity, much like Mike Singletary studies films and playbooks before each game. They have done their homework and watched the opening call to develop some idea of what to expect during the day's trading.

When the market opens, less experienced traders may wait for the initial balance to develop, thinking that there is little information or little to do prior to the development of structure. Seasoned traders, however, know that the first half hour of trade establishes one of the day's extremes in the large majority of cases. As accurate as this fact may be, it is of little value unless a trader can identify which extreme will hold throughout the day. The activity occurring during the formation of the initial balance (many times, just the first few minutes) often enables a trader to identify which extreme has the greatest holding potential. This knowledge alone can play a large part in forming a trader's day timeframe strategy.

The Open as a Gauge of Market Conviction   After the opening call, the first few minutes of the open provide an excellent opportunity to observe and evaluate the market's underlying directional conviction. With an understanding of market conviction, it is possible to estimate very early on where the market is trying to go, which extreme is most likely to hold (if any), and even what type of day will evolve. In other words, the market's open often foreshadows the day's outcome.

Four distinct types of opening activity provide a good indication of the level of directional conviction and which extreme is most likely to hold throughout the day. These labels are not carved in stone, however, and should be used only as a guideline for learning. Like the day types discussed in Chapter 2, the importance is not in the labels but in the level of market directional conviction that is displayed. The four types of opens are:

1. Open-Drive
2. Open-Test-Drive
3. Open-Rejection-Reverse
4. Open-Auction

Open-Drive   The strongest and most definitive type of open is the *Open-Drive*. An Open-Drive is generally caused by other timeframe participants who have made their market decisions before the opening bell. The market opens and aggressively auctions in one direction. Fueled by strong other timeframe activity, price never returns to trade back through the opening range. Figure 4–1 illustrates the Open-Drive.

On April 10, copper opened above the previous day's value area and promptly trended upward. The strong, driving activity on the part of the buyer indicated a high level of market confidence. Figure 4–1 shows an aggressive 12-tick initiative buying tail in "A" period that ignited a Double-Distribution Buying Trend day. In the majority of cases, the extreme left behind after an Open-Drive will hold for the entire day.

The market's behavior during an Open-Drive open can be compared to a thoroughbred racehorse just as the bell sounds and the gates swing open. Both the market and the racehorse explode with confidence running high—their goals are obvious and their direction clear. If a trader expects to trade such a market, he must act quickly or be left in the dust.

Figure 4–1   Open-drive in Copper, April 7 and 10, 1989.

	April 7	April 10
	.	.
14040	.	IJ
14020	.	IJ
14000	.	IJ
13980	.	IJ
13960	.	I
13940	.	HI
13920	.	HI
13900	.	HI
13880	.	DHI
13860	.	DHI
13840	.	DEFHI
13820	.	CDEFH
13800	.	CDEFGH
13780	.	CDEFGH
13760	.	CEGH
13740	.	CGH
13720	.	CG
13700	.	C
13680	.	C
13660	.	C
13640	.	C
13620	.	C
13600	.	C
13580	.	C
13560	.	C
13540	.	C
13520	.	C
13500	.	AC
13460	.	ABC
13440	.	AB
13420	.	A
13400	.	A
13380	.	A
13360	.	A
13340	.	A
13320	.	A
13300	IJ	A
13280	IJ	A
13260	IJ	A
13240	IJ	A
13220	I	A
13200	I	O
13180	I	.
13160	BI	.
13140	ABCHI	.
13120	ABCEHI	.
13100	ABCDEH	.
13080	ACDEFGH	.
13060	CDEFGH	.
13040	C	.
13020	.	.

Open-Drive activity sends clear signals to the trader regarding the type of day to expect—a Trend or Normal Variation day. It also enables the trader to enter positions earlier, before confirmation by structure. Examine Figure 4–1 again. Notice the difference between the trade location for longs entered during the A period tail or the B period pullback, versus longs entered with range extension in C period. On this day, both would probably have resulted in profitable trades; however, A and B period longs gained much better trade location. *Understanding Open-Drive activity helps traders stay one step ahead of structure.*

The extreme established by the Open-Drive remains a reliable reference point throughout the day. If the market eventually returns to trade through the open and erase the tail, the trader is alerted to the fact that conditions have changed and trades should be exited.

Open-Test-Drive   An *Open-Test-Drive* is similar to an Open-Drive, except that the market lacks the initial confidence necessary to drive immediately after the opening bell. During this type of open, the market generally opens and tests beyond a known reference point (previous day's high or low, bracket top or bottom, etc.) to make sure there is no new business to be done in that direction. The market then reverses and auctions swiftly back through the open. This activity, a "failed" initial test followed by a drive in the opposite direction, often establishes one of the day's extremes. An Open-Test-Drive provides the second most reliable type of extreme after the Open-Drive. Figure 4–2 illustrates an Open-Test-Drive occurring in Soybeans.

The Open-Test-Drive is a classic example of how the human elements so often influence market behavior. In Figure 4–2, Soybeans had been balancing (as is evidenced by the successive days of narrowing, overlapping value), following a sharp break to the downside on April 3 that established a new long-term low at 708. When a market is in balance, there is little directional conviction among the participants. Traders need confidence if they are to participate in a sustained move in either direction. Thus, in the case of the soybean market on this day, before other timeframe buyers could begin an up auction with any degree of confidence, they needed to test below the 708 longer term low to "see" if lower prices attracted new activity (new other timeframe sellers, in this case). When the test below actually discouraged activity, buyers could then probe to the upside with conviction. The result was an Open-Test-Drive that brought in increased activity as soybeans auctioned higher. As the saying goes, sometimes markets need to "break to rally" and "rally to break." *Often times participants need the security of knowing what is below the lows or above the highs before they can move the market with confidence.*

Figure 4–2 Open-test-drive in July Soybeans, April 3-10, 1989.

	April 3	April 4	April 5	April 6	April 7	April 10
7300	D	.	.	.	.	.
7295	D	.	.	.	.	.
7290	D	.	.	.	.	.
7285	D	.	.	.	.	.
7280	D	.	.	.	.	.
7275	D	.	.	.	.	.
7270	D	.	.	.	.	.
7265	D	.	.	.	.	.
7260	D	.	.	.	.	.
7255	D	.	.	.	.	.
7250	D	.	.	.	.	.
7245	D	.	.	.	.	J
7240	D	.	.	.	.	J
7235	D	.	.	.	.	J
7230	D	.	.	.	.	FGIJK
7225	D	.	.	.	.	FGIJK
7220	D	.	.	.	.	FGHIJK
7215	D	.	.	.	.	FGHIJK
7210	D	.	.	.	.	FGHIJK
7205	D	.	.	.	.	FGHIK
7200	DE	.	.	.	.	FGHIK
7195	DEF	J	I	.	.	FGK
7190	DEF	J	I	.	.	EFK
7185	DEFG	DJ	HI	.	.	EFK
7180	DEFG	DEIJ	DGHIK	G	.	EFK
7175	DEFG	DEIJK	DEGHIJK	GH	.	EF
7170	DEFG	DEIJK	DEGHIJK	DGH	.	EF
7165	DEFG	DEFGIJK	DEFGHIJK	DEGHK	D	EF
7160	DEFG	DEFGIJK	DEFGHIJK	DEGHJK	D	EF
7155	DEFG	DEFGHIK	DEFGIJK	DEGHJK	DE	E
7150	DEFGH	DFGHK	DEFGJK	DEGHIJK	DEFHJK	E
7145	DEGH	DFGHK	DEFGJK	DEFGHIJK	DEFHIJK	E
7140	DEGHI	DFGHK	DEFK	DEFGHIJK	DEFHIJK	E
7135	DEGHI	.	DK	DEFGHIJK	EFGHIJK	E
7130	DEGHI	.	DK	EFGHIJK	EFGHIJK	E
7125	DEHI	.	DK	EFGHIJK	EFGHIJK	E
7120	DEHI	.	DK	EFHIJ	FGHIK	DE
7115	DEHI	.	D	EFHIJ	FGHIK	DE
7110	DEIK	.	D	EFHIJ	FGIK	DE
7105	DEIK	.	D	EFH	GI	DE
7100	DEIJK	.	D	EFH	.	OE
7095	DIJK	.	D	EFH	.	D
7090	DIJK	.	D	EF	.	D
7085	DIJK	.	.	F	.	D
7080	DJK	.	.	.	.	D
7075	.	.	.	.	.	D
7070	.	.	.	.	.	D
7065	.	.	.	.	.	D
7060	.	.	.	.	.	D
7055	.	.	.	.	.	D
7050	.	.	.	.	.	D
7045	.	.	.	.	.	D
7044	.	.	.	.	.	D
7043	.	.	.	.	.	.
7042	.	.	.	.	.	.
7041	.	.	.	.	.	.
7040	.	.	.	.	.	.

In hindsight, the soybean market activity on April 10 and the ideal trades that should have been entered are relatively easy to see and understand. In reality, however, "pulling the trigger" and placing a trade was an extremely difficult task. Let us evaluate the situation confronting soybean traders on this day. First, the longer term auction was down. Second, the previous five days had recorded basically overlapping value areas, indicating balance. And third, on the 10th the initial "break-out" appeared to be to the downside. When the market opened and swiftly auctioned below the balance area lows, it was easy to assume that price was going to move substantially lower.

When price stalled around 704½, it was difficult to remain objective. The break-out to the downside was initiative activity, which should have brought in new activity and displayed immediate continuation—but there was no follow-through. When the break-out failed and price began to auction higher, longs should have been placed with the knowledge that the price probe below the balance area lows had actually shut off activity (longs should have been entered when price returned to the region of the previous day's value area, if not sooner).

This trade was extremely difficult to execute because it flew in the face of the most recent market activity. Even if a trader possesses a sound enough market understanding to recognize such an opportunity, the ability to execute still depends on the power of his or her own self-understanding. The anxiety created by the thought of placing a trade against strong opposing activity often influences a trader's ability to trade rationally. This is where the power of experience takes over. As you begin to personally witness and then experience more and more of these unique opportunities, you will gradually build the self confidence required to become a player, instead of a spectator.

The strategy for Open-Test-Drive days is similar to that of the Open-Drive, with the understanding that the tested extreme has a slightly lower probability of holding. Again, look for a Normal Variation or Trend day to develop. The odds favor placing trades in the direction of the driving activity, as close as possible to the tested extreme. However, during this type of open (like the Open-Drive), placing the trade early is more important than the immediate trade location. If you wait to buy a pullback or wait to get perfect trade location, you will often miss the opportunity altogether.

Once price has driven in one direction, it should not return to the point where the drive began, because the participants who initially drove price should still be willing to act in that area. A return through the opening range often indicates that conditions have changed and the Open-Test-Drive extreme is no longer a reliable trading reference point.

In the Open-Drive and Open-Test-Drive, the initial extreme is established by the early entry of an aggressive other timeframe buyer or seller. Extremes created by such conditions are useful day timeframe reference points and indicate which way the market is trying to go. Unfortunately, these openings are not nearly as common as the Open-Rejection-Reverse and the Open-Auction, which lack clear-cut conviction. These final two types of openings are, however, equally important to day timeframe strategy.

Open-Rejection-Reverse   The *Open-Rejection-Reverse* is characterized by a market that opens, trades in one direction, and then meets opposite activity strong enough to reverse price and return it back through the opening range. The initial extreme is established when buying or selling in one direction dies out, the auction stalls, and opposite activity begins to auction price in the other direction. An Open-Rejection-Reverse type of open is less convinced of its direction when compared to the Open-Drive and Open-Test-Drive. Because of the lower level of directional conviction, initial extremes generally hold less than half of the time. This is not to say that opposite activity strong enough to return price back through the opening is insignificant. However, in terms of gauging the strength of an extreme and assessing the day type that will develop, the early entry of the other timeframe in the Open-Drive is stronger than the late entry of the Open-Rejection-Reverse. Figure 4–3 illustrates the Open-Rejection-Reverse.

In this example, the Swiss franc opened below the previous day's value area, traded lower and eventually found responsive buyers below .6630. Buyers returned price up and through the opening range in Z period. Such activity provided the trader with three important pieces of information:

1. Lower directional conviction indicates that this will be a two-sided trading day, balancing between the other timeframe buyer and seller. The probability of a Trend day is low.
2. A Normal or Normal Variation type of day should be expected.
3. Since the Y period initial extreme has a relatively low chance of holding, there is a strong possibility that the market will return to retest the opening range.

The key to trading an Open-Rejection-Reverse type of day is *patience*. As is shown by early trade in Figure 4–3, shortly after the "Rejection-Reverse" the Swiss Franc quickly auctioned higher. This is often the case following Open-Rejection-Reverse type of activity.

Figure 4–3 Open-rejection-reverse in the Swiss Franc, August 29, 1987.

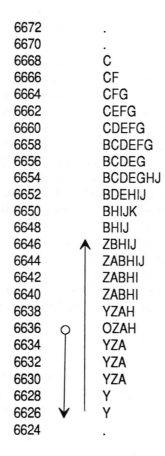

6672	.
6670	.
6668	C
6666	CF
6664	CFG
6662	CEFG
6660	CDEFG
6658	BCDEFG
6656	BCDEG
6654	BCDEGHJ
6652	BDEHIJ
6650	BHIJK
6648	BHIJ
6646	ZBHIJ
6644	ZABHIJ
6642	ZABHI
6640	ZABHI
6638	YZAH
6636	OZAH
6634	YZA
6632	YZA
6630	YZA
6628	Y
6626	Y
6624	.

Through C period the market appeared strong and well on its way to a big move to the upside. Less experienced traders often get so caught up in the swift price movement that they "jump on board," thinking that a prime buying opportunity might be slipping away. It is important to remember, however, that Open-Rejection-Reverse activity conveys a much lower level of conviction. Understanding this lack of conviction, combined with the patience and discipline to wait for the market to rotate back to you, will come through experience.

Open-Auction   At first glance, *Open-Auction* activity reflects a market with no apparent conviction at all. The market appears to open and randomly auction above and below the opening range. In reality, the conviction reflected by an Open-Auction largely depends on where the market opens relative to the previous day. An Open-Auction open that occurs *inside* the previous day's range conveys a different opinion regarding potential day timeframe development than an Open-Auction that occurs *outside* the range. In general, if a market opens and auctions within the previous day's value area and range, then a nonconvictional day will usually develop. If, however, a market opens outside the previous day's range and then auctions around the open, the conditions are markedly different. Here, the market has opened *out-of-balance*. In this case, while early Open-Auction structure may suggest nonconviction, *the fact that the market is out of balance means that there is good potential for a dramatic price move in either direction.* This type of Open-Auction activity often gives rise to Double-Distribution Trend days. We follow with a discussion on both types of Open-Auction activity.

Open-Auction In Range   If a market opens within the region of the previous day's range and auctions, market sentiment has probably not changed. Initial extremes formed by Open-Auction activity are not established by aggressive other timeframe activity. Rather, the market auctions in one direction until activity slows, then auctions in the other direction. The other timeframe is not present with any large degree of confidence. Figure 4–4 illustrates Open-Auction in range activity.

An Open-Auction in range generally sets the stage for a Nontrend, Normal, or Neutral type of day. The low market conviction suggests that any extreme established early on has a low probability of holding throughout the day. Referring to the Treasury bond market for June 30th in Figure 4–4, after opening within June 29th's value area, price auctioned above and below the open with ease in B and C periods. Such seemingly random trade indicated that the bond market was in balance and that its participants held little directional conviction. Without this knowledge, however, a trader could have been fooled into selling with the C period selling range extension, thinking it meant that strong other timeframe sellers were present. The Open-Auction within range made it clear early on that a "big day" would be unlikely.

Open-Auction in range strategy is straightforward. Patiently wait for the market to establish its extremes and perceived value area, and then look to trade the value area extremes. If a good trading opportunity does not develop and a Nontrend type of day occurs, it is often wise to simply stand aside and wait for new activity.

Open-Auction Out Of Range   When a market opens outside of the previous day's range and then auctions around the open, one's first impression is that there is no directional conviction present. In reality, the mere fact that the opening is beyond the previous day's range suggests that new other timeframe activity has caused price to seek a higher or lower level. Given that the market has opened out of balance, there is a greater chance that directional conviction will develop than if the market had opened and auctioned within the range. On March 22 in Figure 4–5, for example, the Treasury bond market opens and auctions substantially above the value area and range for the previous day. In comparison to the Open-Auction in range example in Figure 4–4, the activity up to the first three time periods in Figure 4–5 (up to the point of range extension) appears very similar:

June 30—Figure 4–4	*March 22—Figure 4–5*
A	B
AB	B
AB	AB
AB	ABC
AB	OBC
OBC	ABC
BC	ABC
BC	AC
BC	AC
C	C
C	C
C	C

(O designates the opening)

Figure 4–4 Open-auction (in range) in September Treasury Bonds, June 29 and 30, 1988.

	June 29	June 30	
	.	.	.
88 26 /32	.	.	L
88 25 /32	.	.	L
88 24 /32	.	.	LM
88 23 /32	E	.	L
88 22 /32	DEF	.	L
88 21 /32	CDEF	A	ADL
88 20 /32	CDEF	AB	ABDKL
88 19 /32	CDEFG	AB	ABDEKL
88 18 /32	CDEFG	AB	ABDEHJKL
88 17 /32	CDEFG	AB	ABDEHIJKL
88 16 /32	ACEFG	OBC	OBCDEFGHIJKL
88 15 /32	OCEFG	BC	BCDEFGHIJK
88 14 /32	ACFGI	BC	BCEFGHIJK
88 13 /32	ACFGHI	BC	BCEFGHIJK
88 12 /32	ABCGHI	C	CFGHIJ
88 11 /32	ABCGHI	C	CFGH
88 10 /32	ABCGHI	C	CF
88 9 /32	ABCGHI	C	C
88 8 /32	ABHIJ	.	.
88 7 /32	BIJL	.	.
88 6 /32	BIJL	.	.
88 5 /32	BIJL	.	.
88 4 /32	IJLM	.	.
88 3 /32	JL	.	.
88 2 /32	JL	.	.
88 1 /32	JKL	.	.
88 0 /32	JKL	.	.
87 31 /32	JKL	.	.
87 30 /32	JKL	.	.
87 29 /32	JKL	.	.
87 28 /32	JK	.	.
87 27 /32	JK	.	.
87 26 /32	K	.	.
87 25 /32	.	.	.
	A-C	A-Close	

Figure 4–5   Open-auction (out of range) in June Treasury Bonds, March 21 and 22, 1988.

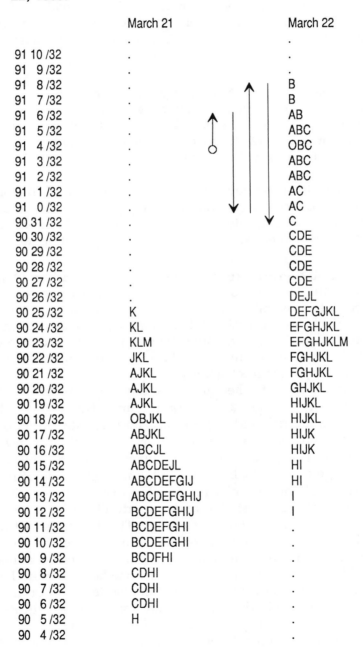

	March 21	March 22
	.	.
91 10 /32	.	.
91 9 /32	.	.
91 8 /32	.	B
91 7 /32	.	B
91 6 /32	.	AB
91 5 /32	.	ABC
91 4 /32	.	OBC
91 3 /32	.	ABC
91 2 /32	.	ABC
91 1 /32	.	AC
91 0 /32	.	AC
90 31 /32	.	C
90 30 /32	.	CDE
90 29 /32	.	CDE
90 28 /32	.	CDE
90 27 /32	.	CDE
90 26 /32	.	DEJL
90 25 /32	K	DEFGJKL
90 24 /32	KL	EFGHJKL
90 23 /32	KLM	EFGHJKLM
90 22 /32	JKL	FGHJKL
90 21 /32	AJKL	FGHJKL
90 20 /32	AJKL	GHJKL
90 19 /32	AJKL	HIJKL
90 18 /32	OBJKL	HIJKL
90 17 /32	ABJKL	HIJK
90 16 /32	ABCJL	HIJK
90 15 /32	ABCDEJL	HI
90 14 /32	ABCDEFGIJ	HI
90 13 /32	ABCDEFGHIJ	I
90 12 /32	BCDEFGHIJ	I
90 11 /32	BCDEFGHI	.
90 10 /32	BCDEFGHI	.
90 9 /32	BCDFHI	.
90 8 /32	CDHI	.
90 7 /32	CDHI	.
90 6 /32	CDHI	.
90 5 /32	H	.
90 4 /32		.

However, it is evident in the two examples that an Open-Auction outside of range has the potential to be a big day, while an Open-Auction within value usually lacks conviction. This is evidenced in the fact that March 22 developed into a Selling Trend day, while June 30 resulted in a narrow Normal Variation day. This concept is discussed at further length in the next section of this chapter.

Summary   The labels we have given the four types of openings are designed only to make them easier to learn and remember. In reality, two openings will seldom look alike, and textbook examples are rare. What is important about the market's open is the notion that it is possible to evaluate market directional conviction very early in the trading session.

The analysis of the day's open should not be used in isolation, but as an integral part of understanding the big picture that gradually emerges as you learn and develop experience using the Market Profile. As a refresher, Figure 4–6 is a summary of the four types of opening activity.

Opening's Relationship to Previous Day—Estimating Daily Range Potential   In the large majority of cases, activity during any given day has direct and measurable implications on the following day. It is only on the relatively rare occasion when a market moves extremely out of balance that there is no correlation between two consecutive days. Understanding these implications enables a trader to more successfully visualize developing market activity.

The simple fact of whether a new day opens within or outside of the previous day's range helps a trader gauge two key day timeframe elements: (1) trade risk and opportunity, and (2) estimating, or visualizing, the day's potential range development. The salient concept here is market *balance*. The relationship of the open to the previous day's value area and range gives valuable clues to the market's state of balance and what kind of risk/opportunity relationship to expect on a given trading day. In short, the greatest risk and opportunity arise when a market opens outside of the previous day's range. This indicates that the market is out of balance. When a market opens out of balance, the potential for a dynamic move in either direction is high. Conversely, a market that opens and is accepted (auctions for at least one hour) within the previous day's value area embodies lower risk, but also less opportunity. The acceptance of price within the previous day's value area indicates balance, and therefore reduces the potential for a dynamic move.

We will discuss three different opening/previous day relationships, highlighting the potential trade risk, opportunity, and range development for each. The three relationships are:

Figure 4–6 Opening type summary.

① Open Drive	② Open Test Drive	③ Open Rejection Reverse	④ Open Auction
O	A	A	A
A	A	A	A
A	O	A	AB
A	A	A	ABC
A	A	A	ABC
A	A	O	OBC
AB	AB	ABC	ABC
AB	AB	AB	ABC
AB	AB	AB	AC
BC	BC	BC	C
BC	BC	BC	C
BC	BC	BC	
C	C	C	
C	C	C	

Market
Conviction

High   Low

* "O" designates the open.

1. Open within previous day's value area.
   —Acceptance/Rejection
2. Open outside previous day's value, but within range.
   —Acceptance/Rejection
3. Open outside previous day's range.
   —Acceptance/Rejection

Open Within Value

Acceptance   When a market opens within value and is accepted (overlapping TPOs signify value, or acceptance), this generally indicates that the market is in balance and that market sentiment has not changed dramatically from the previous day. Trade risk and opportunity are both relatively low. The day's range usually will be contained within the previous day's range or overlap one of the previous day's extremes slightly to one side. It is a trader's dream to know ahead of time what the day's range will be. When a market opens and builds value within the previous day's value area, it is possible—very early on—to make a rough estimate of the developing day's range potential.

As mentioned before, the mere fact that a market opens and auctions within value indicates market sentiment has not changed significantly. Thus, generally, the developing range will rarely exceed the length of the previous day's range. If you are confident that one of the day's extremes will hold, to estimate the day's range potential you simply superimpose the length of the previous day's range from that extreme. For example, suppose that after several time periods on a day that opened within value, a buying tail supports the lower extreme and appears secure. The tail indicates other timeframe buyer presence and will probably hold throughout the day, thus forming the bottom of the day's Profile. If the previous day's range was 15 ticks, count up 15 ticks from the bottom of the tail to find an approximate limit for the day's high. While this is by no means a fool-proof rule, it does provide a consistent approximation and contributes to the visualization needed to successfully trade in the day timeframe.

Before we proceed to an actual example, let us first present a few guidelines for estimating range potential:

1. Determine the opening's relationship to the previous day's value and range.

2. If an estimate is possible (acceptance in range), identify the initial extreme that has the greatest potential to hold. Then superimpose the length of the previous day's range to arrive at an estimate.

3. Allow roughly 10 percent in either direction, recognizing that this is just an estimate, not a prediction.

4. As the day develops, early extremes are erased or confirmed and buyer or seller directional conviction becomes more evident, adjust the estimate if necessary.

Figure 4–7 illustrates range estimation for markets that open and auction within the previous day's value area. The vertical line denoted by Point A represents a completed day's range, with the black bar in the middle designating the value area. On the following day, the market opens and auctions inside the previous day's value area, as is evidenced by the auction rotations back and forth through the open. (The arrows at Point B represent auction rotations, not necessarily half-hour time periods. The market may rotate several times in any given time period.) What is most important is that the market is indeed establishing acceptance within the previous day's range and value area through time. This indicates that conditions have not changed significantly from the previous day, and the market will probably demonstrate similar range development (not necessarily the same high and low).

Point C in Figure 4–7 denotes the initial estimation of the day's potential range. If the extreme left behind after the first auction down eventually forms an A period selling tail, it has the potential to be the day's high. If this is the case, the range is estimated to be the length indicated by the dotted line at Point C. The range potential is determined by super-imposing the length of the previous day's range downward, starting from the top of the selling tail. These early estimates, however, should be used only as a general guideline and must be monitored carefully for change. For example, as the day progresses in Figure 4–7, if the market auctions back up above the selling tail, a new range must be calculated. The probe to the upside in C period (denoted by Point D) creates the need to reestimate the range, for it extends above the initial high and leaves behind a B period buying tail on the low. Given the new extreme created by the up auction in C period, the new estimate would be about the length of the dotted line represented by Point E.

Let us now look at a real market example. Figure 4–8 shows S&P activity on September 23, 1988. The market opened within value, which suggested that conditions for the S&P had not changed overnight. However, immediately following the open in B period, price "drove out" of value to the downside, indicating a potential change in market sentiment. If early seller conviction had been genuine, the selling auction should have continued below the previous day's value area, and ultimately the previous day's low. However, other timeframe sellers did not successfully challenge the low of the 22nd, an important day timeframe reference point. In fact, in C period, the S&P market rotated back up into the value area and *above* the open, thus negating the apparent confidence that was reflected by the early Open-Drive selling activity. The fact that the market was spending *time* auctioning within the region of the previous day's value area (building multiple TPO prints) indicated that market sentiment had changed and that, at best, overlapping value would develop. Moreover, based on the information generated through C period, it was unlikely that the day's trade would bring significant movement in either direction. For, while the seller was

Figure 4–7   Open within value—acceptance. "O" designates the open.

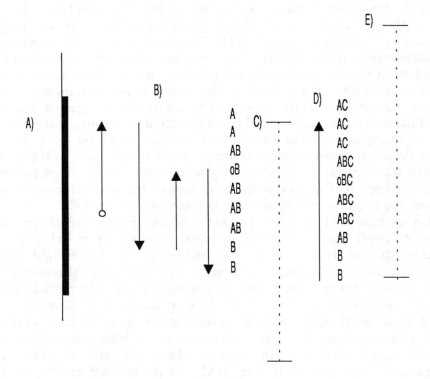

Figure 4–8 Open within value-acceptance in the December S&P 500, September 22 and 23, 1988. "O" designates the open.

	Sept. 22	Sept. 23		
273.30	.	.	.	.
273.15	.	.	.	L
273.00	B	.		L
272.85	B	.		L
272.70	B	.		KLMN
272.55	BC	.		JKLMNP
272.40	BC	.		JKMNP
272.25	CEF	.		IJKMNP
272.10	CEFGHP	.		IJKMNP
271.95	CDEFGHIP	.		IJK
271.80	CDEFGHIJP	.		GIJ
271.65	CDEGHIJP	.		DFGHI
271.50	CDIJNP	.		DFGHI
271.35	CDIJNP	C		CDEFGHI
271.20	CDIJMN	OC		BCDEFGH
271.05	CDJMN	BC		BCDE
270.90	CJKMN	BC		BC
270.75	JKLMN	BC		BC
270.60	KLM	BC		BC
270.45	KLM	BC		BC
270.30	KLM	B		B
270.15	KL	.	.	.
270.00	.	.	.	.
	Previous Day	Open/ 1st Hour	Initial Range Estimate	Final Day's Profile

unable to sustain the opening drive, the buyer did not have the confidence of knowing what was below the 22nd's lows.

Having already visualized eventual overlapping value, and given the development of a B period buying tail, the trading opportunities in day timeframe longs should be visible. The rejection of the B period selling probe indicated the probable formation of a day timeframe low at 270.30. By adding the length of the 22nd's range (285 points) to the B period lower extreme, it was possible to estimate that the high on the 23rd would be in the area of 273.15. In this case, the range estimate proved to be exact (not a common occurrence). Longs placed during the slowing of price in D, E, and F periods had good potential to be successful trades.

Rejection (Break-out)   When a market opens within the previous day's value area and drives out during the first half-hour of trade (does not build double TPOs to signify acceptance within value), the market could be breaking out of balance. If the early break-out drives price completely beyond the limits of the previous day's range, then both risk and opportunity are high and range estimation is unlimited in the direction of the initiative drive (Figure 4–9).

A market that opens and is accepted within the previous day's value area is like a rubber ball bouncing along a level sidewalk. As long as the surface remains flat (or the market continues to open in balance) the ball will rebound off the pavement much like it did during the previous bounce. In contrast, if the sidewalk is cracked and broken (not "balanced"), it is impossible to determine how far or in which direction the ball will bounce (Figure 4–10). Similarly, if the market opens out of balance, it is difficult to tell which way the market will auction and with what force it will move. Over the next several pages we briefly discuss the remaining opening/previous day relationships and the potential range development for each. The guidelines introduced earlier for estimating range potential apply to these discussions as well.

Open Outside of Value but Within Range

Acceptance   A market that opens outside of the previous day's value area but within range is not as balanced as an open within value, but the market is still "bouncing on flat pavement." It is as if the ball simply bounced over a curb to land in the street. The ball will bounce about the same net distance, but the height will be reduced by the distance from the sidewalk to the street (Figure 4–11). Similarly, a day that opens within range but outside of value will generally produce a range that is similar to the previous day, but overlapping to one side. The risk on this type of day is slightly greater than the previous open relationship, but the opportunity is greater as well. Openings outside of value but within range indicate a market slightly out of balance and usually result in value that overlaps to one side.

The method for range estimation used for "Openings Within Value" applies equally well here. The resulting range development will usually extend beyond the previous day's high or low, for the market opens closer to one of the previous day's extremes.

Rejection (Break-out)   On this type of day, the market opens above or below the previous day's value area but still within the previous day's range. If the market subsequently breaks-out beyond the extremes of the

Figure 4–9   Open within value—rejection.

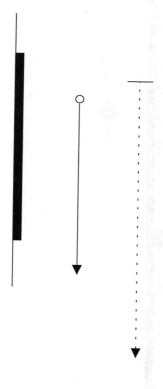

Figure 4-10 Opening's relationship to previous day—market balance.

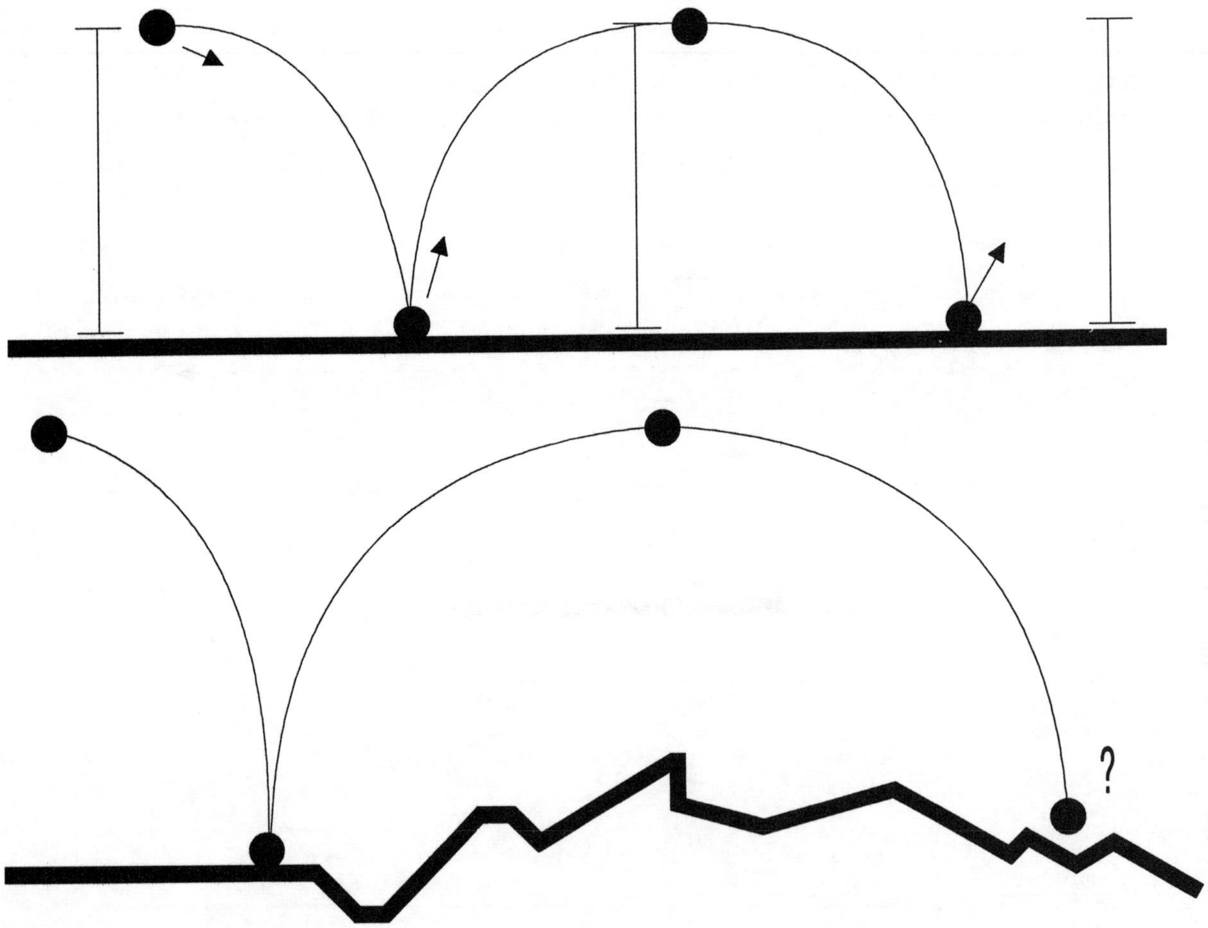

Figure 4–11 Open outside of value but within range—acceptance, ball off curb.

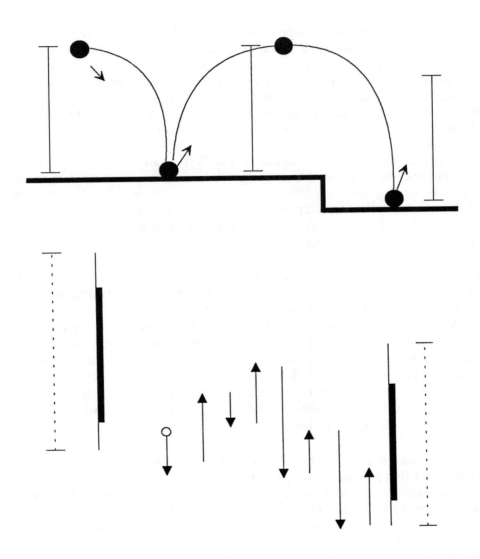

previous day's range, then the market is coming out of balance and range potential is unlimited in the direction of the break-out (Figure 4–12).

Open Outside of Range

Acceptance   When a market opens outside of the previous day's range and is accepted, conditions have changed and the market is out of balance. At this point, one of two scenarios are possible: (1) the market will continue to drive in the direction of the break-out; or (2) the market will begin to auction back and forth at the new price levels (Figure 4–13 illustrates these two relationships). In both cases, as long as price does not return to the previous day's range, the market has accepted the break-out.

The greatest imbalance occurs in the first scenario, when a market opens beyond the previous day's range and continues in the direction of the break-out (Figure 4–13). The movement away from value is initiative and the other timeframe often moves price with great speed and conviction. Range potential is unlimited in the direction of the break-out, and a trend day is usually the result.

This type of open offers the greatest potential to the trader who recognizes the opportunity early and positions him- or herself with the break-out. However, it also poses the greatest risk to the trader who attempts to trade against the driving initiative auction.

A market out of balance is like a ball that ricochets off a piece of jagged concrete—there is no way to estimate how far it will bounce. Potential range development is unlimited and risk is extremely high for the trader who is positioned the wrong way. Accompanied by increased risk, however, is also the potential for greater opportunity. An open outside of range offers the potential for a highly successful and profitable trade if market direction is detected early.

Rejection   When a market opens beyond the previous day's range and is rejected *back into the range*, the potential for a dynamic price move in the direction opposite to the opening break-out is set into motion. A typical example would be a market that opens too far above the previous day's high, fails to follow through, and is quickly "corrected" by responsive sellers who return price to previously accepted value. The day's range potential is still unlimited, for the market opened out of balance and cculd move significantly in the opposite direction. Figure 4–14 illustrates the range estimation for a market whose opening break-out is rejected.

Figure 4–12 Open outside of value but within range—rejection.

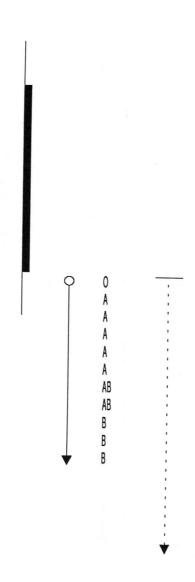

Figure 4–13   Open outside of range—acceptance

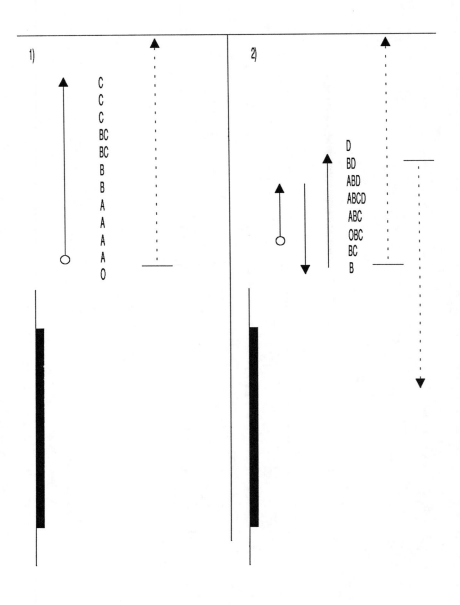

Figure 4–14   Open outside of range—rejection.

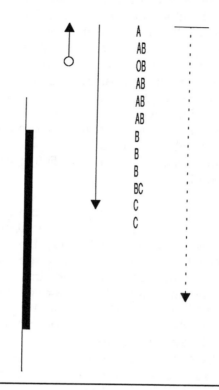

Summary   Simply keeping track of where the market opens in relation to the previous day's range and value area is valuable market-generated information. A market that opens within value is generally in balance and awaiting new information. A market that opens outside of value is out of balance, and carries with it greater opportunity and risk. By synthesizing the opening's relationship to the previous day with other market-generated elements, such as the opening type and initiative/responsive activity, it is possible to trade with a more objective understanding of the big picture.

While writing this segment of the book, a day developed in the market that exhibited many of the opening/value relationships we have just covered. April 13, 1989, will serve as a review and summation of the concepts introduced in this section.

April 13, 1989   Before the market opened on Thursday, April 13th, traders knew that the Retail Sales number would be announced at 7:30.

In addition, five major figures were to be released on the following day: Merchandise Trade, Producer Price Index, Business Inventories, Capacity Utilization and Industrial Production. And, as usual, a variety of predictions and contradicting speculations arose from all sides of the market. The anxiety among market participants was understandably high. To further complicate matters, Switzerland unexpectedly raised its interest rates soon after the foreign currency futures opened on the IMM. With all these external elements playing havoc in the market, it was difficult to remain calm and objective. However, traders with a firm understanding of the dynamics of opening/value relationships saw many good trading opportunities unfold on April 13. The following discussion focuses on the development of six markets: crude oil, S&P 500, gold, Japanese yen, soybeans and Treasury bonds.

Crude Oil   In Figure 4–15, crude oil opened substantially above the previous day's high. Any such opening that is clearly above or below the previous day's range is known as a "gap." A gap is the result of initiative other timeframe activity and indicates that the market is out of balance. In this example, however, the other timeframe buyer who caused the gap higher opening was unable to take control and continue the buying auction. In addition, the development of a narrow initial balance (Point A in Figure 4–15) alerted traders to the potential for a Double Distribution Trend day in either direction.

Given that crude oil was out of balance and carried the potential for a Double Distribution Trend day, traders should have been ready to enter trades with range extension on either side of the initial balance. Buying range extension would signal a potentially big day to the upside. Selling range extension would indicate that the market had opened too far out of balance and that responsive sellers had entered to return price to value. The day's range potential was unlimited in both directions because of the open out of balance.

Responsive sellers did, in fact, enter and extend the range down. Traders placing shorts with the selling range extension were well positioned to take advantage of a dynamic downside move that ultimately retraced the previous day's range and closed on its lows.

S&P 500   In Figure 4–16, the S&P "gapped" open below the 12th's range (out of balance), indicating the potential for a big move to the downside or an "outside day" if price should return up to trade through the gap and retrace the previous day's range. In either case, the potential range development could be very large. After C and D periods failed to trade back into the previous day's range, it became evident that the market was indeed out of balance. The day's range expectations became un-

Figure 4–15   Crude Oil, April 12 and 13, 1989.

	April 12	April 13
2096	.	.
2094	.	.
2092	.	.
2090	.	.
2088	.	.
2086	.	B
2084	.	OC
2082	.	BC
2080	.	BCD
2078	.	BCD
2076	.	BCD
2074	.	BCD
2072	.	DE
2070	.	DE
2068	.	DE
2066	.	DEI
2064	L	EHI
2062	L	EHIJ
2060	CHIL	EHIJ
2058	CGHIL	EFGHIJ
2056	CGHIKL	EFGHIJ
2054	BCGHIJKL	EFGHIJ
2052	BCFGHIJKL	EGJ
2050	BCFGHIJKL	GJK
2048	BCFGHJK	JK
2046	BCDEFGHJK	JK
2044	BCDEFJK	KL
2042	BCDEF	KL
2040	DE	KL
2038	DE	KL
2036	.	KL
2034	.	KL
2032	.	KL
2030	.	L
2028	.	L
2026	.	L
2024	.	.
2022	.	.
2020	.	.

Figure 4–16   June S&P 500, April 12 and 13, 1989.

	April 12	April 13
	.	.
303.20	C	.
303.10	C	.
303.00	C	.
302.90	CL	.
302.80	CDKL	.
302.70	BCDKL	.
302.60	BCDJKL	.
302.50	BDJKL	.
302.40	BDGIJKLMN	.
302.30	BDGHIJKLMN	.
302.20	BDFGHIJMNP	.
302.10	BDEFGHIJMNP	.
302.00	BEFGHIJMNP	.
301.90	BEFMNP	.
301.80	EN	.
301.70	E	.
301.60	E	.
301.50	.	.
301.40	.	C
301.30	.	CD
301.20	.	OCDE
301.10	.	BCDEF
301.00	.	BCDEF
300.90	.	BCDEFG
300.80	.	BCDEFG
300.70	.	BCDEFGH
300.60	.	BDEGHI
300.50	.	HI
300.40	.	HIJ
300.30	.	HIJK
300.20	.	HIJK
300.10	.	IJK
300.00	.	IJK
299.90	.	IJK
299.80	.	K
299.70	.	K
299.60	.	K
299.50	.	K
299.40	.	K
299.30	.	K
299.20	.	KM
299.10	.	KLMN
299.00	.	KLMN
298.90	.	KLMN
298.80	.	KLMN
298.70	.	KLN
298.60	.	K
298.50	.	.

limited to the downside, and optimal trade location could have been gained in the auction rotations of E, F, and G periods before the market broke swiftly in what resulted in a Double Distribution Selling Trend day.

The previous four days in the S&P had recorded successively higher highs. On the 13th, many traders had this fact so firmly implanted in their minds that they responded emotionally to the price break, thinking it was a prime opportunity to buy a strong market below value. Over weighting or focusing on just one or two facts can lead to tunnel vision and inhibit one's ability to see the bigger, developing picture. On the other hand, traders who understood day timeframe structure could have recognized the imbalance indicated by the opening out of range and entered the short side of the market.

Gold   Gold on the 13th provided an excellent example of the value of range estimation. In Figure 4–17, the market opened and drove out of the previous day's value area and range, suggesting a potentially big day on the upside. However, in Z period gold auctioned back down to build double TPO prints in the 12th's value area, thus establishing value and limiting the day's expectations. When Z period was unable to extend below the open, thus confirming the Open-Drive structure and Y period buying tail, it was possible to estimate the range for the 13th by adding the length of the 12th's range to the Y period low. The range potential for the 13th, then, was roughly 392.60 to 397.20, give or take 10 percent. Using this range, longs placed in the Z period pull-back could have been successfully exited near the day's highs.

The area around 393.00 in the gold market had been a support level in the past, and many traders were waiting for a break-out. The Open-Drive activity and quick buying auctions in Z and A periods might have inferred that a big move to the upside was developing, leading many traders to buy all the way up the range. However, traders who recognized that the day's range potential was limited due to acceptance within the 12th's value area could have curbed any high expectations and identified areas providing good trade location.

Japanese Yen   The activity in the Japanese yen on the 13th displays the significance of acceptance (or nonacceptance) within the previous day's range and value area. In Figure 4–18 the yen opened and auctioned just outside of the range of the 12th. In Z period, a selling auction into the previous day's range was flatly rejected, forming a buying tail. Despite the Z period price probe down, the base (initial balance) for the 13th remained relatively narrow. This fact, combined with the open out of value and the rejected attempt to auction down into the previous day's

Figure 4–17   June Gold, April 12 and 13, 1989.

	April 12	April 13
	.	.
3968	.	A
3966	.	A
3964	.	zA
3962	.	zA
3960	.	zA
3958	.	zA
3956	.	zAB
3954	.	zAB
3952	.	zABI
3950	.	yzBI
3948	.	yzBGHIJ
3946	.	yzBCGHIJK
3944	.	yzBCEGHIJK
3942	.	yzCDEFGHJK
3940	.	yzCDEFGJK
3938	.	yzCDEF
3936	.	yzCDEF
3934	B	yzC
3932	BC	yz
3930	BC	yz
3928	BC	O
3926	BC	y
3924	BCDEFHI .	
3922	BCDEFGHIJK	.
3920	BCDEFGHIJK	.
3918	BEFGHIJK	.
3916	BE	.
3914	B	.
3912	B	.
3910	B	.
3908	B	.
3906	B	.
3904	zAB	.
3902	zAB	.
3900	zAB	.
3898	zA	.
3896	z	.
3894	z	.
3892	yz	.
3890	y	.
3888	y	.
3886	.	.
3884	.	.
3882	.	.
3880	.	.

Figure 4–18 June Japanese Yen, April 12 and 13, 1989.

	April 12	April 13
	.	.
7664	.	.
7662	.	.
7660	.	C
7658	.	C
7656	.	C
7654	.	CJ
7652	.	CDJK
7650	.	CDJK
7648	.	BCDJKL
7646	.	BCDJKL
7644	.	BCDEIJKL
7642	.	BCDEFIJ
7640	.	BCDEFGI
7638	.	BDEFGHI
7636	.	ABDEFGHI
7634	.	ABEFGHI
7632	.	ABEFHI
7630	.	ABE
7628	.	A
7626	.	A
7624	.	A
7622	.	yzA
7620	.	yzA
7618	.	OzA
7616	.	yz
7614	D	yz
7612	CD	z
7610	CD	z
7608	zABCD	z
7606	yzABCDE	.
7604	yBCDE	.
7602	yEIJK	.
7600	EFGIJK	.
7598	EFGHIJKL	.
7596	EFGHIJKL	.
7594	EGHIKL	.
7592	EGHKL	.
7590	HKL	.
7588	.	.
7586	.	.
7584	.	.
7582	.	.
7580	.	.

range, confirmed that the yen was out of balance and that buyers were in control. Because value was not established in the 12th's range (except for one tick), the expectations for the day were unlimited to the upside. Longs placed after the Z period rejection or with the A period range extension resulted in excellent day timeframe trade location.

Soybeans   In soybeans on the 13th, the market opened in balance, immediately alerting the trader that sentiment had not changed significantly from the 12th. Figure 4–19 shows that in D period, soybeans were unable to auction price above the previous day's highs and subsequently returned down to trade through the open in E period. However, without the confidence provided by knowing what was beyond the 12th's highs, sellers could not be expected to auction price significantly lower. By superimposing the length of the 12th's range from the top of the D period selling tail, it was possible to estimate the developing range to be from roughly 723 ½ to 729 ½. Traders acting without this knowledge might have sold with the initiative range extensions in G and H periods. Shorts placed at these levels resulted in poor day timeframe trade location (near the day's lows), as was indicated early by the range estimate.

Treasury Bonds   Treasury bonds opened in range and were accepted within the previous day's value area in Z period (Figure 4–20). While just two ticks of double TPO prints within the 12th's value area might seem insignificant because of the narrow range on the 12th, two ticks actually accounted for a third of the value area. This day developed into a trading day with no real conviction. Due to the open within value, it was apparent early on that this day would be similar to the 12th—a day in which it would have been best to stand aside and wait for directional conviction to develop.

Summary   We have now completed our discussion of the market's open: from the opening call to the actual open and its relationship to the previous day. As we proceed farther into the day, remember to consider each new piece of learning in relation to the whole. The big picture continues to unfold and more of the fogged window is becoming clear as you move closer to becoming a competent trader.

Day Timeframe Auction Rotations   Based on information we have covered thus far, let us review the process a trader might go through in developing his or her day timeframe strategy. The first signs of underlying market sentiment are formed during the succession of opening calls, which alerts the trader to possible directional conviction before the markets opens. He or she then monitors the conviction demonstrated by

---

Figure 4–19　May Soybeans, April 12 and 13, 1989.

	April 12	April 13
	.	.
730.50	.	.
730.25	.	.
730.00	J	.
729.75	J	.
729.50	FIJ	D
729.25	FIJ	D
729.00	FGIJ	D
728.75	FGIJ	D
728.50	FGHIJK	DK
728.25	FGHIJK	DK
728.00	FGHIJK	DEJK
727.75	FGHJK	DEJK
727.50	EFGHJK	DEJK
727.25	EFK	DEJK
727.00	DEFK	DEFJK
726.75	DEK	DEFJK
726.50	DEK	OEFIJK
726.25	DEK	DEFIJK
726.00	DEK	DEFGIJK
725.75	DE	DGIJ
725.50	DE	DGIJ
725.25	DE	GI
725.00	DE	GHI
724.75	DE	GHI
724.50	DE	GHI
724.25	D	GHI
724.00	D	GHI
723.75	.	GHI
723.50	.	GHI
723.25	.	GHI
723.00	.	HI
722.75	.	HI
722.50	.	HI
722.25	.	H
722.00	.	.
721.75	.	.

Figure 4–20   June Treasury Bonds, April 12 and 13, 1989.

	April 12	April 13
	.	.
88 14 /32	.	.
88 13 /32	.	.
88 12 /32	y	.
88 11 /32	yKL	.
88 10 /32	yBCKL	.
88 9 /32	yzABCJKL	y
88 8 /32	yzABCDJKL	O
88 7 /32	yzACDHIJ	y
88 6 /32	zDEFGHIJ	yz
88 5 /32	DEFGHIJ	yz
88 4 /32	DEFGHI	yzEFG
88 3 /32	FGHI	zDEFGHJ
88 2 /32	HI	zACDEFGHIJ
88 1 /32	.	zABCDEHIJK
88 0 /32	.	ABCDJKL
87 31 /32	.	ABKL
87 30 /32	.	ABKL
87 29 /32	.	ABL
87 28 /32	.	L
87 27 /32	.	.

the opening, as well as the opening's relationship to the previous day's value area and range. At this point, which is generally within the first hour of trade, the trader should have a good feel for the confidence behind the market's initial activity and the likelihood of its continuation. The next step in the day's analysis develops as the market's auction rotations reveal other timeframe activity and control.

Think of the marketplace as a game in which the other timeframe buyer and seller are vying for control. In the simplest sense, when the buyer is in control, prices tend to rise. When the seller is in control, prices generally fall, like a vertical tug-of-war. When only one participant (usually either the other timeframe buyer or seller) is in control, the market is referred to as a "one-timeframe market." A one-timeframe market is characteristic of a Trend day. Interestingly, a Nontrend day is also a one-timeframe market. During a Nontrend day, control is also in the hands of just one participant—the local.

If neither party is in complete control, price fluctuates up and down as one side pulls and tires, then the other, and so on. When both the other timeframe and the day timeframe participants are sharing control, the market is in a "two-timeframe" mode. Two-timeframe market conditions are common during Normal, Normal Variation, or Neutral days. During a two-timeframe market, the trader must exercise greater patience, for more time is required before other timeframe control becomes evident (if at all).

Consistent off-floor trading results are most often achieved by trading with the control of the other timeframe participant. Obviously, this requires that one be able to determine *who* (if anyone) is in control, and second, *when* that control may be wavering or reversing altogether. Monitoring the development of the day's half-hour auction rotations helps identify which participant is in control of price at a given moment in time. Before examining how day timeframe auction rotations help discern other timeframe control, let us first discuss the two basic forms of other timeframe market control in greater detail.

Two-timeframe Markets   In a two-timeframe market, either the other timeframe buyer or seller (or both) share control with the day timeframe participant. Price rotates up and down without clear directional conviction, like a balanced tug-of-war. The resulting activity is similar to the formation of a day timeframe "bracket." The Profile graphic in Figure 4–21 provides a good example of two-timeframe activity.

During two-timeframe market conditions, examination of the individual half hour auctions (each time period viewed separately) does not generally reveal a dominance by either party. Notice from Figure 4–21 how successive time periods tend to rotate upon each other and fail to generate sustained price movement (B overlaps A on the low side, D overlaps C on the high side, etc.). *Neither other timeframe participant is in control.*

One-Timeframe Markets   In contrast, occasionally one participant gains the upper hand, causing price to auction (or trend) in one direction for a sustained period of time. The market is controlled almost entirely by either the other timeframe buyer or other timeframe seller. Such unilateral control is referred to as a one-timeframe market (a day timeframe *trending* market). A one-timeframe market is like an uneven tug-of-war in which one side is clearly stronger and steadily gains ground. The thin, elongated Trend day Profile, shown in Figure 4–22, is a good example of a one-timeframe market.

Trend days signify a high level of other timeframe conviction, are characterized by range extension occurring in one direction during several time periods. Referring to Figure 4–22, notice that the downward rotations (Z, C, D, F, G, H, and I) are generally stronger than the rotations up (A, B, and E). One-timeframe seller control is evidenced by the inability of the buyer to successfully rotate price upward beyond the previous time period's auction high during two or more successive time periods. Successively lower rotations translate into repeated selling range extension.

Using Auction Rotations to Evaluate Other Timeframe Control   Determining which other timeframe participant is in control within the half-hour auctions, once again, falls into the two familiar categories: market structure and market time. Both play an important role in understanding and evaluating other timeframe control.

Structure   In the Advanced Beginner chapter, we discussed how to monitor other timeframe control using structural features such as the TPO count, tails, range extension, and initiative and responsive activity. In this section we take a closer look at evaluating other timeframe control through the market's half-hour auctions and their offspring—tails and range extension. Our goal is not to simply identify control, but also to determine when it may be changing *intraday*. This concept, called "timeframe transition," will be illustrated following a brief discussion of *Time*.

Half-hour Auctions   By now, it should be clear that the half-hour auctions provide a vivid picture of the market's "composure" at any point in time. The half-hour auctions are illustrated in Figure 4–22.

Figure 4–21 A two-timeframe market.

Price															
6620															
6618															
6616							D								D
6614						D	E								DE
6612						D	E								DE
6610						D	E								DE
6608						D	E								DE
6606						D	E								DE
6604						D	E								DE
6602			A		C	D	E	F							CDEF
6600	Y		A	B	C	D	E	F			I	J			ACDEFIJ
6598	Y	Z	A	B	C		E	F		H	I	J			YZABCEFHIJ
6596	Y	Z	A	B	C		E	F	G	H	I	J	K		YZABCEFGHIJK
6594	Y	Z	A	B					G	H	I				YZABCGHI
6592	O	Z		B					G	H					OZBGH
6590	Y	Z		B					G	H					YZBGH
6588									G						G
6586									G						G
6584									G						G
6582															
6580															

Figure 4–22 A one-timeframe market.

Price													Summary
6728	.	.	.	.	.	.	.	.	.	.	.	.	.
6726	.	.	.	.	.	.	.	.	.	.	.	.	.
6724	Y	.	.	.	.	.	.	.	.	.	.	.	Y
6722	Y	Z	.	.	.	.	.	.	.	.	.	.	YZ
6720	O	Z	.	B	.	.	.	.	.	.	.	.	OZB
6718	Y	Z	.	B	.	.	.	.	.	.	.	.	YZB
6716	Y	Z	.	B	.	.	.	.	.	.	.	.	YZAB
6714	Y	Z	A	B	C	.	.	.	.	.	.	.	YZABC
6712	Y	Z	A	B	C	.	.	.	.	.	.	.	YZABC
6710	.	Z	A	B	C	.	.	.	.	.	.	.	ZABC
6708	.	Z	A	.	C	.	E	.	.	.	.	.	ZACE
6706	.	Z	.	.	C	.	E	.	.	.	.	.	ZCE
6704	.	.	.	.	C	.	E	.	.	.	.	.	CE
6702	.	.	.	.	C	D	E	.	.	.	.	.	CDE
6700	.	.	.	.	C	D	E	.	.	.	.	.	CDE
6698	.	.	.	.	C	D	E	.	.	.	.	.	CDE
6696	.	.	.	.	C	D	E	.	.	.	.	.	CDE
6694	.	.	.	.	C	D	E	.	.	.	.	.	CDE
6692	.	.	.	.	C	D	E	F	.	.	.	.	CDEF
6690	.	.	.	.	C	D	.	F	.	.	.	.	CDF
6688	.	.	.	.	C	D	.	F	.	.	.	.	CDF
6686	.	.	.	.	C	D	.	F	.	.	.	.	CDF
6684	.	.	.	.	C	D	.	F	G	.	.	.	CDFG
6682	.	.	.	.	.	D	.	F	G	.	.	.	DFG
6680	.	.	.	.	.	D	.	F	G	.	.	.	DFG
6678	.	.	.	.	.	.	.	F	G	H	.	.	FGH
6676	.	.	.	.	.	.	.	F	G	H	.	.	FGH
6674	.	.	.	.	.	.	.	F	G	H	.	.	FGH
6672	.	.	.	.	.	.	.	.	G	H	.	.	GH
6670	.	.	.	.	.	.	.	.	G	H	.	.	GH
6668	.	.	.	.	.	.	.	.	G	H	.	J	GHJ
6666	.	.	.	.	.	.	.	.	G	H	.	J	GHJ
6664	.	.	.	.	.	.	.	.	.	H	.	J	HJ
6662	.	.	.	.	.	.	.	.	.	H	I	J	HIJ
6660	.	.	.	.	.	.	.	.	.	H	I	J	HIJ
6658	.	.	.	.	.	.	.	.	.	H	I	J	HIJ
6656	.	.	.	.	.	.	.	.	.	H	I	J	HIJ
6654	.	.	.	.	.	.	.	.	.	H	I	J	HIJ
6652	.	.	.	.	.	.	.	.	.	H	I	J	HIJ
6650	.	.	.	.	.	.	.	.	.	H	I	J	HIJ
6648	.	.	.	.	.	.	.	.	.	.	I	J	K	IJK
6646	.	.	.	.	.	.	.	.	.	.	I	J	.	IJ
6644	.	.	.	.	.	.	.	.	.	.	.	J	.	J
6642	.	.	.	.	.	.	.	.	.	.	.	.	.	.
6640	.	.	.	.	.	.	.	.	.	.	.	.	.	.

Not only does the relationship of one auction (time period) to another reflect the ongoing status of control, but the auction is often one of the first structural features to signal when control may be shifting. Subtle changes occurring within the auctions are often the precursor to dramatic changes that do not appear until much later in the form of tails and range extension. As we noted earlier, if you wait to enter a trade until after the market commits itself, you generally will not gain the favorable trade location that is so important to making objective, rational trading decisions. Tails and range extension are strong indicators, but if you rely solely on them to judge timeframe transition, you will often be too late, for they are *by-products of the market's auctions.* Later, in the discussion entitled "Timeframe Transition," we detail one approach to evaluating subtle changes in the day timeframe auctions.

Extremes   The extremes, or tails, often provide the most obvious evidence of other timeframe control. Tails are created when the other timeframe buyer or seller enters the market aggressively when they feel that price is away from value. Generally, the longer the tail, the greater the conviction behind the move.

In terms of other timeframe control, no tail on the extreme is also significant. The absence of aggressive other timeframe activity on an extreme indicates a lack of buyer or seller conviction. In terms of practical trading applications, consider a rising market that shows no tail on the day's low. Such a scenario suggests that it may be wise to take gains earlier than one might if a tail were present, for the market is subject to a possible reversal.

Range Extension   Range extension is another structural feature generated by the market's auctions that identifies other timeframe control and helps gauge buyer/seller strength. Multiple-period range extension is the result of successively higher or lower auctions. The stronger the control, the more elongated the range extension. If the range is extended in multiple time periods to the upside, for instance, it is apparent that the market is trying to auction higher and the other timeframe buyer is exerting a relatively high degree of control. It is important to monitor this attempted direction for continuation to determine the success of the market's attempts to go that way. Like all structural features, range extension is most useful when taken into consideration with the rest of the big picture, such as the auction rotations and tails.

Time   The second, and perhaps most important ingredient in evaluating timeframe control is *time.* As we have noted before, time is the market's regulator and is responsible for creating the structures we later identify and interpret. Simply stated, the less time a market spends trading at a particular price level, the lower its acceptance of those prices. If the market moves very quickly through a particular price region, then there is strong other timeframe presence at those prices which they will generally serve as support or resistance in the future. For example, a selling tail is the result of swift rejection by the other timeframe seller at prices perceived to be above value. The quicker the rejection, the stronger the other timeframe presence at that price level.

Conversely, the more time spent at a particular price level, the greater the acceptance of that price. Greater time indicates that two-sided trade is occurring, and that both the other timeframe buyer and seller are probably active. It is important to note, however, that time can be a two-edged sword. If a market is not successful auctioning in one direction over time, control may reverse as the market seeks to facilitate trade in the opposite direction. If the market spends *too much time* at a given level, price will ultimately be rejected.

The ability to identify the difference between *enough time* and *too much time* is the key to anticipating a change in control. Understanding and interpreting market activity according to time—instead of relying solely on structure—improves one's recognition and execution speed. *Time provides the signal, structure provides the confirmation.* An understanding of time allows the trader to enter the market when control first begins to change, rather than waiting until it is confirmed by structure.

Time, however, is an intangible concept and is therefore very difficult to learn through a derivative source. Not until you personally observe the effect of time in the marketplace and gain experience through trading will you come to realize and respect the overwhelming power of time.

Identifying Timeframe Transition   Most trading days do not develop into a pure one-timeframe or two-timeframe market, just as most tug-of-wars are neither perfectly balanced nor a total upset. Day timeframe development generally involves a degree of give and take—one side rallies for a substantial gain, then the opponent responds with greater effort in order to balance the contest, followed by another rally, and so on. In a tug-of-war, it is possible to anticipate a change in control by listening to the participants on either team psyching themselves up for a new attack.

While varying noise levels on the exchange floor often signify change, it is not of much help to the off-floor trader. However, *the Market Profile is a conduit for "listening to the floor."* By observing the developing structure of the Profile, it is possible to identify timeframe transitions as they occur. The off-floor trader might even have an advantage over the floor traders who are right there in the action and apparent chaos, for the

Profile reflects *composite* market activity. In a crowded pit, traders may have access to only a portion of the total activity.

Although each day develops differently, there are a few general categories of timeframe transition that we can identify:

1. No transition; either one-timeframe or two-timeframe all day.
    Example: A Trend day (one timeframe) or most Normal days (two timeframe).

2. One-timeframe to two-timeframe trade.
    Example: A price probe beyond a known reference point (such as a previous day's high or a weekly high, etc.) does not attract new activity, causing the market to return to two timeframe trade.

3. Two-timeframe to one-timeframe trade.
    Example: A market that is in a trading range near a known reference point that provides resistance or support, then price breaks through and a trend situation results.

4. One-timeframe in one direction to one-timeframe in the opposite direction.
    Example: A Neutral day.

Not only do structure and time help determine who is in control, but they are also useful in identifying when control may be shifting. To demonstrate the interplay between time and structure when evaluating timeframe transition, refer to Figure 4–23 as we walk through the activity occurring in the Swiss franc on October 12, 1987.

December Swiss Franc, October 12, 1987   Activity on this day was characterized by early morning one-timeframe buying, a midmorning transition to one-timeframe selling, followed by a late return to one-timeframe buying. Using a "running Profile" helps traders visualize and monitor timeframe transition. A running Profile separates the day into selected time periods, starting with evidence of a change in control. The following points of discussion use Figure 4–23 to illustrate the changes in control that developed in the Swiss franc on October 12.

Y–E: *One-timeframe Buying*   One-timeframe buying control prevails during Y through E periods. Notice the successively higher (or equal) half-hour auction periods. Buyer control translated into buying range extension in A, B, and D periods. The lack of significant downward rotation shows a conspicuous absence of the other timeframe seller.

E: *Time*   In E period, price slows. Buyers spent better than a full period near the high and were unable to extend the range further. Time,

Figure 4–23 Timeframe transition. Segmented profile in the Swiss Franc, October 12, 1987.

	Y - E	Y - F	E - H	E - I	H - J	Entire Day
6732	.	.	.	.	.	.
6730	.	.	.	.	.	.
6728	.	.	.	.	J	J
6726	.	.	.	.	J	J
6724	.	.	.	.	J	J
6722	.	.	.	.	J	J
6720	.	.	.	.	J	J
6718	.	.	.	.	J	J
6716	DE	DE	E	E	JK	DEJK
6714	DE	DE	E	EI	IJ	DEIJ
6712	BCDE	BCDE	E	EI	IJ	BCDEIJ
6710	BCDE	BCDEF	EFH	EFHI	HIJ	BCDEFHIJ
6708	BC	BCF	FH	FHI	HI	BCFHI
6706	ABC	ABCF	FH	FHI	HI	ABCFHI
6704	A	AF	FH	FHI	HI	AFHI
6702	YZA	YZAF	FGH	FGHI	HI	YZAFGHI
6700	OZA	OZAF	FGH	FGHI	HI	OZAFGHI
6698	YZ	YZ	GH	GH	H	YZGH
6696	Y	Y	GH	GH	H	YGH
6694	.	.	H	H	H	H
6692	.	.	H	H	H	H
6690	.	.	H	H	H	H
6688	.	.	H	H	H	H
6686	.	.	H	H	H	H
6684	.	.	.	.	.	.
6682	.	.	.	.	.	.

in this case *too much time*, provides the first indication that control may be shifting.

Y–F: *Auction Test* F period sees the seller enter and rotate price down below the E period .6710 auction low. This deliberate opposite rotation is viewed as a "test" of buyer control. Markets, being controlled by people, often behave like people. Within any trend, markets need to pause, reflect on where they are, test in the opposite direction, and so on—all in an effort to determine if they have traveled too far, or have yet to probe farther. Temporary pauses amid strong price and value trends are a natural, logical part of the market auction process.

The question to be answered in succeeding time periods is: Does this initial rotation against the one-timeframe activity reflect a loss of buyer control, or is the buyer merely taking a "breather."

G: *Transition Confirmation* "Double prints" (two time period TPO prints) against a one-timeframe auction often confirm that the one-timeframe activity has ended. Double TPO prints indicate that the market has spent sufficient time rotating in one direction to justify a potential timeframe transition.

The "FG" double prints at .6702—double prints below the .6710 E period low—suggest that buyers were not just resting, but had relinquished control. The transition, in this case, is either to two-timeframe trade or one-timeframe selling. It is too early to tell, structurally, which will result.

Note, however, that even though timeframe control has apparently shifted, the seller was not aggressive enough to generate a selling tail on the high. The "DE" double TPO print on the day's high represents a high made by time, not aggressive opposite activity. This indicates a general lack of conviction on the part of the seller, and suggests that traders looking for an opportunity to sell this market should exercise caution.

E–H: *One-timeframe Selling* A running Profile starting with E period (when the one-timeframe upward rotation first slowed) indicates one-timeframe selling extending from E period to midway through H period.

H: *Auction Test* In H period, buyers rotated price above the G period auction high, this time testing the seller's strength. The strong H period buying tail reflects staunch rejection of lower prices, and stands as an indication of aggressive other timeframe buying.

I: *Transition Confirmation* Double "HI" prints at .6704 confirm yet another timeframe transition, this time from selling to buying.

H–J: *One-timeframe Buying* Following the double "HI" period prints, buyers tested and extended the range on the upside once again. Notice also that buyers had little difficulty extending the range beyond the .6716 "DE" previous high, an extreme established earlier by a non-conviction seller.

Summary Two-timeframe trade did occur during the periods of transition (F and H periods); however, the speed of the transition indicates a virtual immediate transfer of control, rather than a tug-of-war scenario.

Auction Failures We have mentioned the term "follow-through" quite frequently—in our discussions of trends, break-outs, initiative activity, during the open, and so on. In fact, follow-through is essentially the answer to the question, "How good of a job is the market doing in its attempts to auction in a certain direction?" Without follow-through to the upside during a bull trend, the market, in effect, fails to auction higher. Without follow-through in a golf swing, the golfer fails to successfully hit the ball. And without follow-through in a business negotiation, even the most promising deal will likely fail. The point is that failure to follow through is just as significant as successful follow-through when monitoring market activity.

When a market auctions above or below a known reference point, one of two scenarios will develop: (1) new initiative activity will fuel continuation beyond the reference point; or (2) the auction will fail to follow through. After an auction failure, price is often rejected in the opposite direction with speed and conviction. The magnitude of this movement depends on the significance of the tested reference point. Known reference points exist in many forms: daily high/low, weekly high/low, monthly high/low, a break or rally point caused by an important news announcement, bracket top/bottom, and so forth. The greater the variety of other timeframe participants who are present at the tested reference point, the greater the potential magnitude of the auction failure. For example, if a selling auction fails to continue below a bracket low that has held for several months, day, swing, and other timeframe buyers will all be "brought into" the market en masse, causing a high level of volatility. The resulting rejection of such a long-term bracket extreme could trigger a substantial rally and have a significant impact on the direction of the longer-term auction.

Let us consider this example in greater detail. When price nears a bracket bottom, many traders wait to see if the previous support level will hold before entering the market. If the market should "fail" to break-out below the bracket bottom, these traders often respond quickly, causing the market to rally. Conversely, if price auctions through the bracket low and is accepted, the same traders may enter the market on the sell side, driving price lower and adding fuel to a strong initiative selling auction. Such longer-term auction failures are as important to the day trader as they are to the longer-term participant. If a day trader is aware of longer-term support levels and reference points, he or she is better prepared to capitalize on (or protect him- or herself from) the dramatic day timeframe price movement common during a longer-term auction failure. In fact, the longer the timeframe that the failure represents, the greater the profit potential (and risk) that is often present in the market.

Figure 4–24 illustrates a longer-term auction failure in soybeans. On April 3, 1989, soybeans recorded a new long term low at 708. The soybean market then came into balance, as is evidenced by the four consecutive days of overlapping value that followed. Figure 4–25, on April 10th, shows the activity that occured shortly thereafter. Soybeans opened in balance at 710 ½, then quickly drove below the low created on the 3rd (708). However, the selling auction *failed to generate new selling*. Two events generally happen after such a significant failure: (1) the participants who auctioned price lower (generally the short timeframe or local) cover their shorts and reverse their position; and (2) other traders become aware of the lack of selling below a known reference point and enter the market with confidence (the opposite applies to a probe *above* a significant reference point). On April 10, after the auction below the balance area lows stalled, buyers responded and drove the soybean market higher. The result was a Double Distribution Buying Trend day. Traders who monitored the balance-area lows and the longer-term reference point at 708 could have used the auction failure to secure excellent day timeframe trade location.

Auction failures at shorter timeframe reference points are generally more subtle and result in smaller price movements when compared to auction failures at longer timeframe reference points. However, the price rejection that follows a short-term auction failure can still be swift and substantial relative to normal day timeframe structure. Figure 4–26 shows a typical day timeframe auction failure occurring in the Treasury bond market. On May 16, 1989, bonds auctioned below the previous day's low (90.22) in Y period, but failed to follow through to the downside. The market auctioned lower looking for more selling business, but there were no sell stops or new activity to sustain the downward price movement. Armed with the knowledge that there was no new selling below the short-term lows, bonds traded higher for the remainder of the day and eventually closed on the highs.

Placing a trade after an auction failure is an incredibly challenging task. In the previous example, the most recent Treasury bond activity had been down, and the "crowd" was selling. When price slowed, indicating potential failure, it was not easy to enter the market as a responsive buyer. Again, the best trades often fly in the face of the most recent market activity.

**Figure 4–24 Long-term auction failure occurring in May Soybeans. Data cour-
tesy of Commodity Quote Graphics.**

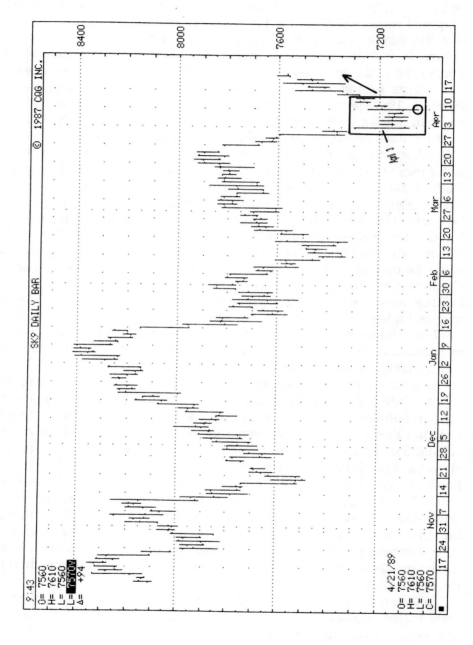

Figure 4–25 **Auction failure occurring in May Soybeans, April 7-11, 1989. "O" designates the open.**

	April 7	April 10	April 11
725.00	.	.	.
724.50	.	J	.
724.00	.	J	.
723.50	.	J	.
723.00	.	FGIJK	.
722.50	.	FGIJK	.
722.00	.	FGHIJK	K
721.50	.	FGHIJK	DK
721.00	.	FGHIJK	DFJK
720.50	.	FGHIK	OEFIJK
720.00	.	FGHIK	DEFGIJK
719.50	.	FGK	DEFGHIJK
719.00	.	EFK	DEGHIJK
718.50	.	EFK	DEHIJK
718.00	.	EFK	DHIJ
717.50	.	EF	H
717.00	.	EF	H
716.50	D	EF	.
716.00	D	EF	.
715.50	DE	E	.
715.00	DEFHJK	E	.
714.50	DEFHIJK	E	.
714.00	DEFHIJK	E	.
713.50	EFGHIJK	E	.
713.00	EFGHIJK	E	.
712.50	EFGHIJK	E	.
712.00	FGHIK	DE	.
711.50	FGHIK	DE	.
711.00	FGIK	DE	.
710.50	GI	OE	.
710.00	.	DE	.
709.50	.	D	.
709.00	.	D	.
708.50	.	D	.
708.00	.	D	.
707.50	.	D	.
707.00	.	D	.
706.50	.	D	.
706.00	.	D	.
705.50	.	D	.
705.00	.	D	.
704.50	.	D	.
704.00	.	.	.

Figure 4–26 Day timeframe auction failure occurring in September Treasury Bonds, May 15 and 16, 1989.

	May 15	May 16
	.	.
91 9 /32	.	.
91 8 /32	.	.
91 7 /32	.	.
91 6 /32	yA	N
91 5 /32	yA	N
91 4 /32	yA	MN
91 3 /32	yzAEFG	MN
91 2 /32	yzBDEFG	LM
91 1 /32	zBCDEG	LM
91 0 /32	zBCDG	yLM
90 31 /32	zCDGHI	yHL
90 30 /32	zCHIJKLMN	yGHJL
90 29 /32	zHIJKLMN	yGHJL
90 28 /32	zJKL	yDFGHJK
90 27 /32	zJK	yCDEFJK
90 26 /32	z	yCDEJK
90 25 /32	z	yzABC
90 24 /32	z	OzAB
90 23 /32	z	yzAB
90 22 /32	z	yzA
90 21 /32	.	y
90 20 /32	.	.

Excess To achieve its primary goal of trade facilitation, the market auctions lower to find buyers and higher to attract sellers. Ideally, the market finds a value range where both the other timeframe buyer and seller perceive price to be fair so that two-sided trade can take place. However, the market is effective, not efficient.[1] Consequently, in its attempt to generate trade with all participants, the market occasionally creates excess by auctioning too far in a given direction.

[1] J. Peter Steidlmayer and Kevin Koy, *Markets & Market Logic*, The Free Press, Chicago, 1986.

Suppose that a local baker produces 1,000 loaves of bread daily, which he sells for 50 cents each. Business is good at this price, and he consistently sells every loaf he bakes. Because the demand for his home-made bread seems to have been on the rise, one morning the baker raises his price to 55 cents a loaf and still sells every one. Pleased with the results, he decides to charge 60 cents the next week, but finds he sells just 800 loaves—*higher prices began to discourage buying.* The baker quickly lowers the price back to 55 cents a loaf due to decreasing sales volume and shrinking profits. The point is, he had to raise prices *too far* above value to be sure that he had found a price that both he and the consumer perceived to be fair. The baker's pricing method created an excess of 5 cents, the difference between the 60 cent extreme and 55 cent value.

Similarly, the market must auction too high to know when prices are perceived to be above value and too low to know which prices are considered to be below value. The potential for market excess occurs any time price trends significantly out of balance, or away from value. *Excess is created when the other timeframe recognizes an opportunity and aggressively enters the market, returning price to the perceived area of value.* Evidence of the resulting excess, in both the day and longer timeframe, can be identified through market structure.

Signs of Excess   By definition, excess is useful only in hindsight analysis, for it is not identifiable until it has already formed. While this is, in fact, true, many of the structural characteristics reflected by the Profile help identify excess quickly. Tails, for example, are simply day timeframe auction excess. Day timeframe excess is illustrated in Figure 4–27.

In Figure 4–27, the other timeframe was active on both ends of the range, entering aggressively and creating day timeframe excess on both extremes. Price auctioned lower in A period and was met by a strong other timeframe buyer, establishing a buying tail. Conversely, an E period buying price probe was rejected by the other timeframe seller, creating a selling tail. Tails are perhaps the most common manifestation of excess, and they occur in a similar way in the longer-term auction process. Longer term excess is covered later in "Long-Term Trading."

Let's take a moment to look at excess from another, more conceptual, perspective. Any time a given price level is rejected quickly by the market, excess is formed. The single prints separating the two areas of a Double Distribution Trend day are a variety of excess. Just like a tail, they represent prices perceived as away from value by the other timeframe. A gap is also a form of market excess, for it is, in effect, an "invisible tail."

The importance of any type of excess is that it represents an area that should serve as support or resistance to price in the future. As long

Figure 4–27 Day timeframe excess. Japanese Yen, March 8, 1988.

7882	.	.	.	.	.	.	.	.	.	.	.	.
7880	.	.	.	.	.	.	.	.	.	.	.	.
7878	.	.	.	.	.	.	E	.	.	.	.	E
7876	.	.	.	.	.	.	E	.	.	.	.	E
7874	.	.	.	.	.	.	E	.	.	.	.	E
7872	.	.	.	.	C	.	E	.	.	.	.	CE
7870	.	.	.	.	C	D	E	.	.	.	J	CDEJ
7868	.	.	.	.	C	D	E	F	.	.	I	J	CDEFIJK
7866	Y	.	.	.	C	D	E	F	G	.	I	J	YCDEFGIJ
7864	Y	.	.	.	C	D	E	F	G	.	I	J	YCDEFGIJ
7862	Y	Z	.	.	C	.	.	F	G	H	I	J	YZCFGHIJ
7860	Y	Z	.	B	C	.	.	.	G	H	I	.	YZBCGHI
7858	Y	Z	.	B	C	.	.	.	G	H	I	.	YZBCGHI
7856	O	Z	.	B	.	.	.	.	G	H	I	.	OZBGHI
7854	.	Z	A	B	.	.	.	.	G	H	I	.	ZABGHI
7852	.	Z	A	B	.	.	.	.	.	H	.	.	ZABH
7850	.	Z	A	B	.	.	.	.	.	.	.	.	ZAB
7848	.	.	A	.	.	.	.	.	.	.	.	.	A
7846	.	.	A	.	.	.	.	.	.	.	.	.	A
7844	.	.	A	.	.	.	.	.	.	.	.	.	A
7842	.	.	.	.	.	.	.	.	.	.	.	.
7840	.	.	.	.	.	.	.	.	.	.	.	.

as conditions have not changed markedly, the other timeframe participant that drove price so vehemently should react similarly at those same price levels. This is why a tail can be used to estimate range potential, for it is a reliable benchmark by which to gauge future activity.

The Rotation Factor   As we near the end of Day Timeframe Auction Rotations, we again address the question *"Which way is the market trying to go?"* Thus far, we have discussed concepts such as directional conviction, initiative and responsive activity, and other timeframe control—all of which provide bits and pieces of the answer to the first of the two Big Questions. In the day timeframe, however, we have yet to provide a finite, objective answer to the question of market direction. We present here a simple, objective means for evaluating day timeframe attempted direction based on the markets half-hour auction rotations. It is called the Rotation Factor.

At any point in time within the day, segmenting the Profile into half-hour auctions helps determine which other timeframe participant is *currently* in control (or that neither is in control). However, it is not always easy to determine which participant is exerting greater overall influence. The Rotation Factor objectively evaluates a day's attempted direction. Each auction rotation is measured step-by-step, allowing the trader to discern overall daily directional attempts. Figure 4–28 provides reference for the following discussion on how to calculate the Rotation Factor.

The method for assigning a value to each time period's auction rotation is relatively simple. If the high of the current time period is higher than the previous period's high, then the rotation is given a +1. If the high is lower than the previous period's high, then it is assigned a -1. Similarly, if a time period's low is higher than the previous period's low, then a value of +1 is added. An auction bottom that is lower than the previous period's low receives a -1. And, if both periods highs or lows come out even, then no value, or 0 is assigned. The same process is performed for each subsequent time period, ultimately resulting in a number that can provide a good indication of day timeframe sentiment. Figure 4–29, for instance, shows the Rotation Factor for a day in Treasury Bonds. The cumulative rotation numbers across the time period tops totaled +3, as did the figures across the auction bottoms. The net total for this day is +6, which exhibits consistent buyer attempts throughout the day.

It is important to keep in mind, however, that the Rotation Factor only answers one of the two "Big Questions"—that is, which way the market is trying to go. Before any conclusions can be drawn, you must also determine if the market is "doing a good job" in its attempts to auction in that direction. The answer to this second Big Question requires a much more sweeping analysis than that which can be provided by a simple measure of the auction rotations. As we proceed through this chapter, we will thoroughly detail the methods necessary for determining a market's directional success.

TPO Trading   The TPO count is used to measure other timeframe activity within day timeframe structure. The theory behind TPO trading is based on the fact that the other timeframe buyer and seller do not deal directly with each other—they conduct trade through the local, or middleman. Any imbalance that develops between the longer-term participants is measurable in the TPO count (for a complete discussion of the mechanics of the TPO count, refer to Chapter 3, Advanced Beginner).

Figure 4–28 The Rotation Factor.

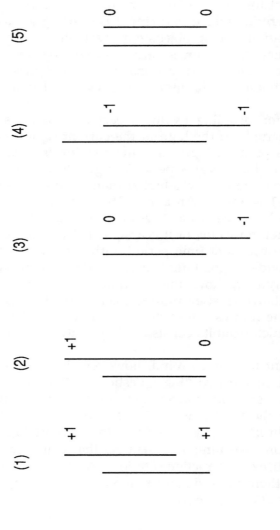

Figure 4–29 The Rotation Factor. Application in Treasury Bonds.

Price	A	B	C	D	E	F	G	H	I	J	K	L
90-20												L +1
90-19												L
90-18												L
90-17						F +1						L
90-16						F		H +1			K +1	L
90-15						F		H			K	L
90-14						F		H	I -1		K	L
90-13						F		H	I		K	L +1
90-12					E +1	F	G -1	H	I	J -1	K	
90-11					E	F	G	H	I	J	K	
90-10				D +1	E	F +1	G	H	I	J	K	
90-09				D	E		G	H	I	J	K	
90-08				D	E		G -1	H 0	I 0	J	K	
90-07				D	E					J	K +1	
90-06				D	E					J		
90-05				D	E +1					J		
90-04				D						J -1		
90-03		B +1		D								
90-02		B	C -1	D								
90-01		B	C	D								
90-00	A	B	C	D +1								
89-31	A	B	C									
89-30	A	B	C									
89-29	A	B +1	C									
89-28	A		C -1									
89-27	O											
89-26	A											
89-25	A											
89-24	A											
89-23	A											

Top Total = +1-1+1+1+1-1+1-1-1+1+1 = +3
Bot Total = +1-1+1+1+1 -1+0+0-1+1+1 = +3
Overall RF = (Top + Bot) = +6

For example, a TPO count of 16/25 indicates buyers (25) are more active below the point of control (the fairest price in the day timeframe) than sellers (16) trading above the point of control. If buyers continue to be more aggressive, the point of control will gradually rise as value migrates higher. If the point of control remains constant, price will auction back and forth between the buyer and seller in balanced, two-sided trade.

In order for the TPO count to be effective, then, the market must be in a two-timeframe, rotational mode. Again, two-timeframe conditions occur when the other timeframe and day timeframe participants are sharing control. In a one-timeframe market, generally one other timeframe participant is dominant, and each successive time period extends the range with clear unidirectional conviction. The TPO count is not needed on Trend days, for example, because it is clear who is in control. Monitoring TPO imbalances is necessary (or effective) only when there is a two-timeframe struggle brewing within the value area.

Occasionally, a market will start the day in a two-timeframe mode but then develop into a one-timeframe market. The Profile structure might appear to be rotational when, in fact, either the other timeframe buyer or seller has subtly taken control. This is often a difficult situation to identify quickly. Thus, the trader must learn to recognize the underlying conditions that often preclude such activity, and then monitor those conditions closely. This sort of activity often occurs when price auctions near or beyond the day's extremes and fails to follow through, causing the market to reverse and auction aggressively (one-timeframe) in the opposite direction. A running Profile starting with the time period of potential structural change (a tail or break-out) is an effective means for monitoring intraday transition.

Futures markets that are controlled almost exclusively by the other timeframe, such as the municiple bond market and to a lesser extent the foreign currency market, are best interpreted by using directional indicators other than the TPO count—tails, range extension, the Rotation Factor, and so forth. Municiple bonds are traded mostly by longer term money managers and off-floor professionals. Because the local does not act as "middleman," the TPO count is not as effective in measuring other timeframe control. Treasury Bonds, on the other hand, are traded by a wide variety of participants and the local plays an integral part in the trade facilitation process. The TPO count has also been found to be effective in Crude Oil, Gold, grains, and other markets that are not so heavily influenced by off-floor professionals.

The most important aspect of TPO trading is the ability to visualize potential change in the TPO count. A chess champion can visualize the huge complexity of potential moves to be made, by both him and his opponent, far in advance. Similarly, a successful day trader can visualize how different market activity will affect the evolving TPO structure. Using Figures 4–31 through 4–35, let us closely examine a day in Treasury Bonds, discussing the visualization process that occurs as the trading session progresses.

9:30 AM   Figure 4–30: TPOs favor the buyer, 13/16. The point of control is actually between 99–00 and 98–31, for both prices have equal lengths and the center of the range is between them. (There is also the option of choosing either the upper or lower price, as long as you are consistent in your choice.) Range extension to either side will change the point of control (the longest line closest to the center of the range). Any amount of buying range extension will raise the point of control to 99–00. One tick of selling range extension will lower it to 98–31. Additional selling range extension will lower point of control.

10:00 AM   Figure 4–31: At the end of D period, the point of control moves up to 99–00, due to the single tick of buying range extension at 90–08 (the point of control is now actually in the middle of the range). The TPO count is basically balanced, although slightly in favor of the seller. If price should continue to auction at higher levels without trading down to 99–00, the point of control in E period will rise, turning TPOs in favor of the buyers once again. A second rise in the point of control would indicate strong other timeframe buyer presence in the value area.

10:30 AM   Figure 4–32: The point of control moves higher in E period. TPOs are 16/24 in favor of the buyer. It may seem improbable that the point of control can move so quickly and cause such a dramatic swing in implications, but consider the character of the futures market. Inventory can be liquidated in a minimal amount of time, creating control shifts within a single time period.

After E period, it is possible to start visualizing potential auction rotations. If F period trades at the point of control (99–03) and auctions downward, it will add buying TPOs. A long position placed around 98–29 would offer relatively good trade location, as long as price does not spend too much time at the lower prices. If F and G periods trade at lower prices without printing at 99–03, the point of control will move lower, indicating stronger sellers. If this situation arises, longs should be exited immediately, for the buyer is no longer in command.

Noon   Figure 4–33: Auction rotations in F, G, and H periods raise the point of control once again, reflecting a strong imbalance (17/38) and

Figure 4–30 TPO trading in Treasury Bonds—9:30 AM (The point of control, shown here to be at 99-00, is actually between 98-31 and 99-00).

```
                              9:30
                               .
            99 15 /32          .
            99 14 /32          .
            99 13 /32          .
            99 12 /32          .
            99 11 /32          .
            99 10 /32          .
            99  9 /32          .
            99  8 /32          .
            99  7 /32          A
            99  6 /32          A
            99  5 /32          AC
            99  4 /32          AC
            99  3 /32          AC
            99  2 /32          AC
            99  1 /32          AC
            99  0 /32          ABC <
            98 31 /32          ABC
            98 30 /32          ABC
            98 29 /32          ABC
            98 28 /32          ABC
            98 27 /32          AB
            98 26 /32          AB
            98 25 /32          A
            98 24 /32          A

            TPO'S           13/16
```

Figure 4–31 TPO trading in Treasury Bonds—10:00 AM.

	9:30	10:00
	.	.
99 15 /32	.	.
99 14 /32	.	.
99 13 /32	.	.
99 12 /32	.	.
99 11 /32	.	.
99 10 /32	.	.
99 9 /32	.	.
99 8 /32	.	D
99 7 /32	A	AD
99 6 /32	A	AD
99 5 /32	AC	ACD
99 4 /32	AC	ACD
99 3 /32	AC	ACD
99 2 /32	AC	ACD
99 1 /32	AC	AC
99 0 /32	ABC <	ABC <
98 31 /32	ABC	ABC
98 30 /32	ABC	ABC
98 29 /32	ABC	ABC
98 28 /32	ABC	ABC
98 27 /32	AB	AB
98 26 /32	AB	AB
98 25 /32	A	A
98 24 /32	A	A
TPO'S	13/16	18/16

Figure 4–32 TPO trading in Treasury Bonds—10:30 AM.

	9:30	10:00	10:30
	.	.	.
99 15 /32	.	.	.
99 14 /32	.	.	.
99 13 /32	.	.	.
99 12 /32	.	.	.
99 11 /32	.	.	.
99 10 /32	.	.	.
99 9 /32	.	.	E
99 8 /32	.	D	DE
99 7 /32	A	AD	ADE
99 6 /32	A	AD	ADE
99 5 /32	AC	ACD	ACDE
99 4 /32	AC	ACD	ACDE
99 3 /32	AC	ACD	ACDE <
99 2 /32	AC	ACD	ACD
99 1 /32	AC	AC	AC
99 0 /32	ABC <	ABC <	ABC
98 31 /32	ABC	ABC	ABC
98 30 /32	ABC	ABC	ABC
98 29 /32	ABC	ABC	ABC
98 28 /32	ABC	ABC	ABC
98 27 /32	AB	AB	AB
98 26 /32	AB	AB	AB
98 25 /32	A	A	A
98 24 /32	A	A	A
TPO'S	13/16	18/16	16/24

Figure 4–33 TPO trading in Treasury Bonds—Noon.

	9:30	10:00	10:30	12:00
99 15 /32	.	.	.	.
99 14 /32	.	.	.	.
99 13 /32	.	.	.	.
99 12 /32	.	.	.	.
99 11 /32	.	.	.	.
99 10 /32	.	.	.	F
99 9 /32	.	.	E	EFG
99 8 /32	.	D	DE	DEFG
99 7 /32	A	AD	ADE	ADEFG
99 6 /32	A	AD	ADE	ADEFG
99 5 /32	AC	ACD	ACDE	ACDEFGH <
99 4 /32	AC	ACD	ACDE	ACDEGH
99 3 /32	AC	ACD	ACDE <	ACDEH
99 2 /32	AC	ACD	ACD	ACDH
99 1 /32	AC	AC	AC	ACH
99 0 /32	ABC <	ABC <	ABC	ABCH
98 31 /32	ABC	ABC	ABC	ABC
98 30 /32	ABC	ABC	ABC	ABC
98 29 /32	ABC	ABC	ABC	ABC
98 28 /32	ABC	ABC	ABC	ABC
98 27 /32	AB	AB	AB	AB
98 26 /32	AB	AB	AB	AB
98 25 /32	A	A	A	A
98 24 /32	A	A	A	A
TPO'S	13/16	18/16	16/24	17/38

confirming the continuing buyer dominance. Longs placed below the point of control in H period offer excellent trade location, for any additional activity below the point of control will add buying TPOs. The market still needs to auction higher to find balance.

At this point, the point of control can only be lowered if I period trades below 99–04 without trading at 99–05. Even so, the TPO count would favor buyers. This is an excellent time to buy below value (the point of control), for buyers are clearly in control of this market.

The large imbalance favoring the buyers is also evident in the day's structure. Notice how the Profile appears incomplete to the upside. This is part of the visualization process that develops through time and experience.

2:00 PM   Figure 4–34: Once Treasury bonds traded at 99–05 in K period, the point of control can not change. Any market break will simply add buying TPOs. The odds favor a close on the highs due to the buying imbalance. A break early in L period provides another buying opportunity.

The Close   Our progression through a typical trading session has uncovered many of the processes that a day trader can employ to evaluate day timeframe confidence and directional conviction. The last indication of day timeframe market sentiment is embodied in the day's close. Given no overnight news events, the activity that takes place during the close sometimes has direct implications on the following session's open.

The fact that the market is closing literally forces participants that still have business to conduct in the day timeframe to make a decision and execute quickly. This type of forcing action generally flushes out two types of activity that can send misleading signals to a trader who is unaware of their implications.

First, the close represents the last opportunity for other timeframe participants with an opinion regarding market direction to establish new positions. Second, the close is also the final opportunity for traders who do not want to hold a trade overnight to balance their inventory. Obviously, the first type of activity has definite implications on the following day, while the latter has no lasting effect—but both can have a significant impact on price movement.

Unfortunately, it is sometimes difficult to differentiate between the two forms of closing activity. When available, monitoring movement near the close for continuation into the evening session (as in Treasury bonds) or in the cash and futures overnight markets (bonds, currencies, and gold) will provide clues regarding which type of participant was responsible for the closing activity. Otherwise, the next day's opening

Figure 4–34 TPO trading in Treasury Bonds—2:00 PM.

	9:30	10:00	10:30	12:00	2:00
	.	.	.	.	.
99 15 /32	.	.	.	.	L
99 14 /32	.	.	.	.	L
99 13 /32	.	.	.	.	JL
99 12 /32	.	.	.	.	JL
99 11 /32	.	.	.	.	JKL
99 10 /32	.	.	.	F	FJKL
99 9 /32	.	.	E	EFG	EFGJKL
99 8 /32	.	D	DE	DEFG	DEFGIJKL
99 7 /32	A	AD	ADE	ADEFG	ADEFGIJKL
99 6 /32	A	AD	ADE	ADEFG	ADEFGIJKL
99 5 /32	AC	ACD	ACDE	ACDEFGH <	ACDEFGHIKL <
99 4 /32	AC	ACD	ACDE	ACDEGH	ACDEGHIKL
99 3 /32	AC	ACD	ACDE <	ACDEH	ACDEHIKL
99 2 /32	AC	ACD	ACD	ACDH	ACDHL
99 1 /32	AC	AC	AC	ACH	ACH
99 0 /32	ABC <	ABC <	ABC	ABCH	ABCH
98 31 /32	ABC	ABC	ABC	ABC	ABC
98 30 /32	ABC	ABC	ABC	ABC	ABC
98 29 /32	ABC	ABC	ABC	ABC	ABC
98 28 /32	ABC	ABC	ABC	ABC	ABC
98 27 /32	AB	AB	AB	AB	AB
98 26 /32	AB	AB	AB	AB	AB
98 25 /32	A	A	A	A	A
98 24 /32	A	A	A	A	A
TPO'S	13/16	18/16	16/24	17/38	43/45

call, actual open, and early auction rotations reveal the strength of the previous trading session's close.

Figure 4–35 contains three consecutive days in the sugar market that illustrate the difference in continuation exhibited by the two forms of closing activity. Late in the day on May 31, sugar auctioned substantially below established value and closed on the low. However, the following day opened above the weak close and immediately auctioned higher, indicating that the 31st's closing activity was probably caused by traders balancing their positions. On this day, the buying continued through to the end of the day, as Sugar closed significantly above the day's established value following an aggressive buying probe in J period. When sugar then opened and accepted value above the previous day's close, traders were alerted that the previous session's bullish close was probably the result of other timeframe directional conviction, not forcing action.

The reader should note that most days do not close with such extreme price movement as exhibited on May 31 and June 1. These days were chosen because they clearly exhibited the difference in continuation following the two forms of closing activity. Usually the close is more subtle, occurring within the body of the Profile.

Day Timeframe Visualization and Pattern Recognition

Garri Kasparov, the world chess champion, once challenged 59 schoolchildren in separate games of chess—*all at once*. The competition took place in a Bronx gymnasium with the chess tables set up in the form of a large square. The expert strolled from board to board, selecting his moves. He spent very little time making decisions, while each of his opponents had all the time they needed. While a child is no match for the skilled Kasparov, taking on 59 children at once is a challenge to any one individual, regardless of skill level. Yet, he handily beat 57 of the students, while two proud young chess players managed to take him to a draw. How did Kasparov do it, particularly in such a short amount of time? Playing—not to mention winning—57 matches simultaneously requires something more than skill alone.

Over the course of his chess career, Kasparov has probably experienced nearly every conceivable arrangement of the game's playing pieces. There are a variety of known and recognizable chess strategies, openings, and so on. Quite possibly, Kasparov was relying on *pattern recognition*. He was speed-reading, or *visualizing*, the board, recognizing patterns and making decisions based on past experience in similar situations.

Figure 4–35   Two types of closing activity in Sugar, May, 31- June 2, 1989.

	May 31	June 1	June 2
	.	.	.
1158	.	.	H
1156	.	.	HIJ
1154	.	.	DHIJ
1152	.	.	DEHIJ
1150	.	.	DEHIJ<
1148	.	.	CDEFGHIJ
1146	.	J	ODEFGIJ
1144	.	J<	CDFGIJ
1142	.	J	CDFIJ
1140	.	J	CDJ
1138	.	J	CD
1136	.	J	D
1134	.	J	.
1132	.	IJ	.
1130	.	IJ	.
1128	.	DIJ	.
1126	.	DEIJ	.
1124	.	DEI	.
1122	.	DEFHI	.
1120	.	DEFHI	.
1118	C	DEFHI	.
1116	C	DEFHI	.
1114	CDFG	CDFGHI	.
1112	ODEFG	CDFGHI	.
1110	CDEFG	CDGHI	.
1108	CDEFGH	CDGH	.
1106	CGH	CGH	.
1104	GH	CGH	.
1102	H	CG	.
1100	HI	CG	.
1098	HI	C	.
1096	HI	C	.
1094	HI	O	.
1092	IJ	.	.
1090	J	.	.
1088	J	.	.
1086	J	.	.
1084	J<	.	.
1082	.	.	.

Pattern recognition, or visualization, begins to materialize after extensive practice and experience in practically any endeavor, whether it be playing chess, predicting the weather, diagnosing a patient, or trading.

As a trader gains more and more experience observing and trading via the Market Profile, a number of recognizable patterns begin to surface in day timeframe structure. Virtually every structural feature of the Profile involves pattern recognition in one form or another, and most play a part in visualizing the developing day timeframe structure. For example, an Open-Drive outside of the previous day's range is a pattern that allows a trader to immediately visualize a Trend day scenario and sustained price movement throughout the day. Conversely, an Open-Auction in value is usually a good indication of a more balanced, trading type of day. This information enables a trader to visualize and estimate the potential extremes of the day's range.

Successful trading is assisted by successful visualization. Monitoring the opening call and open activity allows a trader to visualize the formation of the day's auction rotations. In turn, observing the evolving auctions makes it possible to visualize the type of day pattern that might emerge. Recognizing certain day types and structural patterns allows the visualization of trade facilitation and attempted market direction. All these factors contribute to the ongoing visualization process and make up the big picture for the day timeframe.

We will discuss here three distinctive patterns that have particularly interesting implications for day timeframe visualization: short covering rallies, long liquidation breaks, and ledges.

Short Covering Rallies   Probably one of the market's most deceptive and misunderstood behaviors is known as short covering. Almost all rallies start with "old business" covering their short positions, which at least temporarily causes price to auction higher. If this rally is not accompanied by new buying, it is usually due solely to short covering.

Short covering often follows a day (or several days) of strong selling activity. As the market moves farther out of balance, participants simply become "too short." A sharp rally, generally occurring on or soon after the open, follows as participants enter to cover (buy back) their short positions. The need to cover may be a result of: (1) locals simply selling so much that their inventories become too short; (2) profit-taking after an extended down move; or (3) other timeframe participants with short positions who are forced to exit. Like a kettle that whistles when too much steam has built up inside, a short covering rally is a short-term event that relieves temporary market pressure.

After recent strong selling activity, the swift rally that is characteristic of short covering can be easily misinterpreted as aggressive other timeframe buying. However, if the rally is truly caused by short covering and not new buying interest, the market will often resume its prior course once the selling imbalance has been neutralized. Unfortunately, such quick and erratic activity can easily heighten market anxiety and cause traders to exit a trade far too early, or even exit shorts and enter longs. When identified and interpreted properly, however, short covering often generates a market-created opportunity to sell.

As illustrated in Figure 4–36, a short covering rally (that is not accompanied by new buying) resembles the letter "P," or a half-completed Profile. Once the covering diminishes, price usually recedes and corrects itself, in effect, filling in the lower half of the range. The trader's first alert to potential short covering is the swift, excited rally that is immediately followed by the virtual disappearance of the buyer. The rally stalls almost as quickly as it got started. *Short covering is caused by old business, not by new participants entering the market.*

This is not to say that every time a market rallies quickly and stalls it is the result of short covering. There are situations in which the market will rally, stall, then rally further. For example, the top of a bracket can offer sufficient resistance to slow price after a strong rally. Once price "breaks through" the bracket, however, the rally will generally resume with renewed force. Figure 4–37 demonstrates this scenario. How, then, can a trader tell the two apart? Let us refer to Figure 4–38 for illustration.

In Figure 4–38, the "P" formation is evident through E period in the S&P market. The individual half-hour auctions for B through E periods are separated to show the short covering rotations, followed by the Profile for the same period, the B–H Profile, and finally the completed day. It is evident that after the initial rally in B period, each subsequent half-hour auction did a worse job of facilitating trade with the buyer. Nearly every successive higher auction was *lower* than the previous auction high. Compare this formation closely to the formation in Figure 4–37. In Figure 4–37, the buyer successfully managed to hold his ground, while in Figure 4–38 the buyer gradually *lost* ground.

Figure 4–38 projects the waning buyer strength. Through E period, the half-completed Profile is apparent, looking as if the market needs to rotate downward and fill in the other half. By F period, the short covering begins to dissipate, sellers reenter and the day's structure begins to close in on itself. In addition, Figure 4–38 illustrates a unique phenomenon not uncommon during short covering rallies. After the initial rally, the S&P actually switched to a one-timeframe selling mode beginning with the formation of the high during C period (each successive auction was equal to or lower than the previous half-hour auction without extending beyond the high).

Figure 4-36   Day timeframe short covering occurring in three markets: Gold, February 24, 1988; Treasury Bonds, February 19, 1988; Japanese Yen, February 18, 1988.

April COMEX Gold

Price	February 24	February 19
4400	·	·
4398	·	·
4396	YA	·
4394	YZAB	·
4392	YZABC	·
4390	YZABC	·
4388	YZAB	·
4386	·	DEF
4384	·	DEFG
4382	·	EFGH
4380	·	EFGH
4378	·	EFH
4376	·	EFH
4374	·	EH
4372	·	HI
4370	·	HI
4368	·	I
4366	·	IJ
4364	·	IJ
4362	·	IJ
4360	·	IJ
4358	·	IJK
4356	·	IJK
4354	·	IJK
4352	·	JKL
4350	·	K
4348	·	·
4346	·	·
4344	·	·
4342	·	·
4340	·	·
	Y-C	D-K

March Treasury Bonds

Price	February 19	February 18
94 0/32	·	·
93 31/32	·	·
93 30/32	·	·
93 29/32	·	·
93 28/32	D	·
93 27/32	DE	·
93 26/32	BDE	G
93 25/32	BCDE	GL
93 24/32	BCDEF	GLM
93 23/32	BCEF	GL
93 22/32	BCEF	GL
93 21/32	BEF	GHIL
93 20/32	BE	GHIL
93 19/32	B	HIL
93 18/32	AB	HIKL
93 17/32	AB	IJKL
93 16/32	AB	IJKL
93 15/32	A	JK
93 14/32	A	JK
93 13/32	A	JK
93 12/32	O	JK
93 11/32	·	JK
93 10/32	·	J
93 9/32	·	·
93 8/32	·	·
93 7/32	·	·
93 6/32	·	·
93 5/32	·	·
93 4/32	·	·
93 3/32	·	·
93 2/32	·	·
	A-F	G-K

March Japanese Yen

Price	February 18	February 18
7740	·	·
7738	·	·
7736	·	·
7734	·	·
7732	·	·
7730	·	·
7728	A	·
7726	ABC	·
7724	ABCD	·
7722	ZABCD	·
7720	ZABCD	·
7718	ZABD	·
7716	YZBD	·
7714	YZB	·
7712	YZB	·
7710	YZ	·
7708	Y	E
7706	Y	E
7704	O	E
7702	·	E
7700	·	E
7698	·	E
7696	·	EFGH
7694	·	EFGH
7692	·	EFGH
7690	·	FGHIJ
7688	·	FGHIJ
7686	·	FGHIJK
7684	·	FGHIJ
7682	·	FJ
7680	·	·
	Y-D	E-J

Figure 4–37   Exception to short covering occurring in the Japanese Yen, March 7, 1988.

7840	.	.
7838	.	.
7836	.	.
7834	.	J
7832	.	JK
7830	.	J
7828	.	IJ
7826	.	IJ
7824	.	HIJ
7822	.	HIJ
7820	.	HI
7818	.	H
7816	.	GH
7814	.	EFGH
7812	.	EFGH
7810	.	EFG
7808	.	DEF
7806	.	DEF
7804	ZAC	D
7802	ZABC	D
7800	ZABC	D
7798	ZABC	.
7796	YZABC	.
7794	YZ	.
7792	YZ	.
7790	YZ	.
7788	Y	.
7786	Y	.
7784	Y	.
7782	Y	.
7780	O	.
	Y-C	D-J

Figure 4–38   Short covering occurring in the March S&P 500, January 20, 1988.

250.00	.	.	.	.	.	.	.
249.80	.	.	.	.	.	.	.
249.60	.	.	.	.	.	.	.
249.40	.	C	.	.	C	C	C
249.20	.	C	D	.	CD	CD	CD
249.00	.	C	D	.	CD	CD	CD
248.80	.	C	D	.	CD	CD	CD
248.60	B	C	D	E	BCDE	BCDE	BCDE
248.40	B	C	D	E	BDE	BDEG	BDEG
248.20	B	C	D	E	BCDE	BCDEFG	BCDEFG
248.00	B	C	D	E	BCDE	BCDEFGH	BCDEFGH
247.80	B	C	D	E	BCDE	BCDEFGH	BCDEFGH
247.60	B	.	.	.	B	BFGH	BFGHI
247.40	B	.	.	.	B	BFGH	BFGHI
247.20	B	.	.	.	B	BFGH	BFGHI
247.00	O	.	.	.	O	O	OI
246.80	B	.	.	.	B	B	BI
246.60	B	.	.	.	B	B	BI
246.40	.	.	.	.	.	.	I
246.20	.	.	.	.	.	.	I
246.00	.	.	.	.	.	.	I
245.80	.	.	.	.	.	.	I
245.60	.	.	.	.	.	.	I
245.40	.	.	.	.	.	.	I
245.20	.	.	.	.	.	.	I
245.00	.	.	.	.	.	.	I
244.80	.	.	.	.	.	.	I
244.60	.	.	.	.	.	.	I
244.40	.	.	.	.	.	.	IN
244.20	.	.	.	.	.	.	IMN
244.00	.	.	.	.	.	.	IMN
243.80	.	.	.	.	.	.	ILMN
243.60	.	.	.	.	.	.	ILMNPQ
243.40	.	.	.	.	.	.	IJLMNP
243.20	.	.	.	.	.	.	IJKLMNP
243.00	.	.	.	.	.	.	IJKLMNP
242.80	.	.	.	.	.	.	IJKLMNP
242.60	.	.	.	.	.	.	IJKLMNP
242.40	.	.	.	.	.	.	IJKLMNP
242.20	.	.	.	.	.	.	IJKLMP
242.00	.	.	.	.	.	.	IJKLMP
241.80	.	.	.	.	.	.	IKL
241.60	.	.	.	.	.	.	IKL
241.40	.	.	.	.	.	.	K
241.20	.	.	.	.	.	.	K
241.00	.	.	.	.	.	.	K
240.80	.	.	.	.	.	.	.
	B-E Auctions			B-E	B-H	B-P

Long Liquidation Breaks   The obverse side of a short covering rally is the long liquidation break. The market forces that cause long liquidation are the opposite of those that trigger short covering. Due to locals who have gotten too long (bought too much) or a large number of other timeframe participants exiting their long positions after an extended up trend, the quick sale drives price swiftly downward. Again, this selling break is primarily caused by the liquidation of old long positions, not placing of new shorts. Thus, the liquidating break generally lasts as long as there are longs to cover (unless the selling break brings new business into the market and exhibits follow-through). Once the "sale" is over, the market begins to correct itself. The resulting pattern often takes the shape of a "b" (the inverse of the short covering "P" formation). Figure 4–39 illustrates a long liquidation break.

In the S&P market on this day, the market opened and drove sharply lower through C period. As is characteristic of a long liquidation break, subsequent time periods showed a lack of seller continuation and a transition to one-timeframe buying (in this case, through H period). This particular example is not nearly as perfect as the short covering scenario highlighted on the preceding pages—and few are. Notice that in I period the S&P auctioned down near the C period lows once again. However, the seller's inability to auction *below* the C period lows reaffirmed the lack of seller follow-through and the continued buyer strength. Once the I period auction failed to attract new selling, buyers reemerged and "completed" the Profile.

The liquidation occurring on this day is a vivid illustration of the importance of visualization and pattern recognition. If you become too involved in the minute-to minute price movements, it is easy to fall victim to tunnel vision. The ability to visualize promotes the objectivity that is so necessary for developing a holistic view of the marketplace.

Summary of Short Covering and Long Liquidation   A Profile beginning to develop the shape of a "P" or a "b" does not infer that short covering or long liquidation is occurring. Remember, all facts are surrounded by other circumstances. Properly evaluating short covering or long liquidation patterns requires that the trader make careful note of the underlying conditions prevailing in the market and the requisite characteristics that signify each pattern. The main considerations are: (1) the recent market direction compared to the formation, (2) the open—near the low for a short covering and near the high for long liquidation, (3) the subsequent non-continuation after a drive away from the open, and (4) gradually retracing auctions as the short-term buying or selling releases temporary pressure.

Figure 4–39 Day timeframe long liquidation occurring in the March S&P 500, February 2, 1988.

258.00	.	.	.	.	.	.	.	.	.	.	.
257.80	.	.	.	.	.	.	.	.	.	.	.
257.60	.	.	.	.	.	.	.	.	.	.	.
257.40	.	.	.	.	.	.	.	.	.	.	.
257.20	.	.	.	.	.	.	.	.	.	.	L
257.00	.	.	.	.	.	.	.	.	.	.	LN
256.80	.	.	.	.	.	.	.	.	.	.	KLN
256.60	.	.	.	.	.	.	.	.	.	.	KLN
256.40	.	.	.	.	.	.	.	.	.	.	KLN
256.20	O	.	.	.	.	.	.	.	.	O	KLNP
256.00	B	.	.	.	.	.	.	.	.	B	KLMNP
255.80	B	.	.	.	.	.	.	.	.	B	KLMNPQ
255.60	B	.	.	.	.	.	.	.	.	B	KLMNP
255.40	B	.	.	.	.	.	.	.	.	B	KLMN
255.20	B	.	.	.	.	.	.	.	.	B	KLMN
255.00	B	C	.	.	.	G	.	.	.	BCG	BCGKM
254.80	B	C	.	.	.	G	H	.	J	BCGHJ	BCGHJKM
254.60	B	C	.	.	F	G	H	.	J	BCFGHJ	BCDFGHJ
254.40	B	C	.	.	F	G	H	I	J	BCFGHIJ	BCDFGHI
254.20	B	C	.	.	F	.	H	I	J	BCFHIJ	BCFHIJ
254.00	B	C	.	E	F	.	H	I	J	BCEFHIJ	BCEFHIJ
253.80	B	C	.	E	F	.	.	I	J	BCEFIJ	BCEFIJ
253.60	.	C	D	E	F	.	.	I	J	CDEFIJ	CDEFIJ
253.40	.	C	D	E	.	.	.	I	J	CDEIJ	CDEIJ
253.20	.	C	D	E	.	.	.	I	.	CDEI	CDEI
253.00	.	C	D	.	.	.	.	.	.	CD	CD
252.80	.	C	.	.	.	.	.	.	.	C	C
252.60	.	.	.	.	.	.	.	.	.	.	.
252.40	.	.	.	.	.	.	.	.	.	.	.
252.20	.	.	.	.	.	.	.	.	.	.	.
252.00	.	.	.	.	.	.	.	.	.	.	.
	B-J Auctions									B-J	B-P

Ledges   A ledge is a rather strange, awkward looking formation. In effect, ledges resemble one half of a normal distribution—as though someone chopped the Profile in two. Ledges form when a market repeatedly attracts the responsive participant in its attempt to auction in a given direction. Consequently, the market stalls again and again at one particular price level.

The half-completed structure of a ledge tends to make a trader feel uneasy. It seems as though something is bound to happen, that the day's Profile is still evolving. Logically and intuitively, the market is almost *expected* to spill over the ledge and fill in the day's Profile. However, if it does not and the ledge holds, the market may move significantly in the opposite direction. The key to successfully trading a ledge lies in monitoring the activity around the ledge for clues regarding which scenario will come to pass.

A ledge is often the result of short covering or long liquidation. The market moves in one direction with short-term conviction, then suddenly stalls. There is no follow-through to sustain the auction. The market auctions up, for example, and stalls once the participants who were long have covered their positions. As time goes on, one of two events can occur: (1) the lack of continuation to the upside gives sellers confidence to auction price below the ledge; or (2) the ledge offers support, and buyers enter to resume the up trend. A typical ledge pattern is shown in Figure 4–40.

The dynamics governing a day timeframe ledge are similar to those underlying a longer-term break-out from a balanced area. Several days of overlapping value generally indicate that a market is in balance. A "break-out" in either direction is a sign that the market is coming out of balance, and trades should be placed in the direction of the break-out. Similarly, a ledge is an indication of day timeframe balance, and a break-out from the ledge indicates a departure from balance. In terms of trading applications, if price auctions more than a few ticks "off the ledge," trades should be placed in the direction of the break-out (unless there are extraneous market conditions present—news events, etc.). In Figure 4–40, for example, shorts should have been placed at 4472 when gold dropped off the 4476 ledge in H period.

Summary   The three-day timeframe patterns introduced here are but a small fraction of the total number of patterns that exist in the marketplace. The different opening types each forms its own identifiable pattern. As the market's half-hour auctions unfold, the patterns characteristic of the different day types begin to emerge. Almost every aspect of the market's auction process can be categorized as some sort of pattern,

Figure 4–40 A ledge pattern in June Gold, May 3, 1988.

	.	.
4490	.	.
4488	.	.
4486	C	C
4484	ZBC	ZBC
4482	ZBCD	ZBCD
4480	YZABCDEFG	YZABCDEFG
4478	YZABDEFG	YZABDEFGH
4476	YADEFG	YADEFGH
4474	Y	YH
4472	Y	YH
4470	Y	YHI
4468	Y	YHI
4466	O	OHIJ
4464	Y	YIJ
4462	.	IJ
4460	.	JK
4458	.	JK
4456	.	JK
4454	.	JK
4452	.	K
4450	.	KL
4448	.	.
4446	.	.
	Y-G	Y-K

although not all of them are as specific as short covering, long liquidation, and ledge formations.

The importance of pattern recognition is not in the act of labeling different market structures. Rather, pattern recognition is essential for understanding current market activity, and more important, learning to visualize future market development.

The Liquidity Data Bank

Up to this point, we have discussed market structure solely in terms of TPOs. TPOs are used to organize day timeframe structure according to time, so that we can estimate the relative amount of business being transacted at each price. The Liquidity Data Bank (LDB), on the other hand, provides the *actual* volume of trade occurring at each price and is available midday and a few hours after the market close. In addition, the LDB discloses what type of trader participated in that volume: (1) local floor traders, (2) commercial clearing members, (3) members filling orders for other members or (4) members filling orders for the public or any other type of customer. These two pieces of information, price/volume and percentage participation, not only verify today's estimates, but also provide the concrete information so necessary to maintaining an objective view of the present tense.

In this section, we will first study the anatomy of the Liquidity Data Bank report, dissecting and examining its major parts. We then follow with a discussion of the general uses of the LDB. Finally, we close with a detailed analysis of commercial activity, one of the significant forces behind market behavior.

The Anatomy of the LDB   Figure 4–41 illustrates the volume summary report for Treasury bonds on April 28, 1989. The encircled numbers correspond to the following definitions:

1. *Trade Price*—The prices traded throughout the day.
2. *Volume*—The individual volume occurring at each price.
3. *% Vol*—Individual price volume expressed as a percentage of the day's volume.
4. *% Cti*—"Customer Trade Indicators." Each Cti number indicates the percentage of volume (at each price) that was conducted by the different categories of market participants. Cti1 represents local floor participation; Cti2 is commercial clearing members; Cti3 represents members filling orders through other

members; and Cti4 signifies members filling orders for the public or any other type of outside customer.

5. *The Profile Structure*—The Market Profile graphic for the day.

6. *Value Area*—The range in which 70 percent of the day's volume occured.

7. *Value Area Participation*—The average percentage of participation within the value area for each Cti representative.

8. *Range Participation*—The average percentage of participation within the day's entire range by each Cti representative.

9. *Total Volume*—The total transactional volume, or number of actual contracts bought and sold during the day's trading.

General Uses of the LDB The Market Profile graphic, by itself, organizes market-generated information into a format that is extremely useful for determining which way the market is trying to go. Often this determination is relatively straightforward—for instance, on days when the market opens on an extreme and trades in one direction for the entire day, or when an obvious trend is underway. On many other occasions, however, the market will auction both above and below the open, offering few clear signs of directional conviction. In terms of trade facilitation and attempted direction, these days are much more difficult to evaluate.

The LDB often provides valuable information on days that do not offer signs of clear conviction. In the following, we will examine a variety of LDB facts and figures that, when evaluated together, can help reveal the underlying control (or lack of control) that exists in the market. All derived or enhanced through the LDB report, these measures are listed below in the order that they are discussed:

1. Total Volume
2. The Value Area
3. Dispersion of Volume
4. Cti Figures
5. Acceptance of Value Outside the Value Area
6. High-Volume Concentrations
7. Top-5 versus Bottom-5 Tick Analysis
8. Trend Tests

1. Total Volume Two LDB measurements should not only be monitored daily, but also kept on a running record. They are *volume* and the *value* area. Volume is the truest and most reliable indicator of the market's ability to facilitate trade. Even in a trending market, if volume is decreasing, then the likelihood that the trend will continue much longer is in question. *A market that is not facilitating trade will not survive for long.*

All markets seek to trade at price levels that maximize volume. If a market is not facilitating trade at a given price level, it will move to a new level that will better facilitate trade. Thus, if price movement is relatively static and volume continues to decline, the chances are great that the market will break-out of that region in search of new activity. Evaluating the daily progression of total contract volume is one way to begin to detect early signs of nonfacilitation and potential change. The implications of volume levels in relation to day-to-day structure play a pivotal role in longer-term market analysis. This is covered in detail in Section Two of this chapter, Long-Term Trading.

2. The Value Area   The value area, probably the most widely used piece of information contained in the LDB report, represents the area where 70 percent of the day's trade occured. The LDB calculates the value area using volume as opposed to TPOs. (For a complete discussion of value area calculation, see Appendix 1.)

In the day timeframe, the value area is an important reference point by which to compare developing market activity. As discussed earlier, the opening's relationship to the previous day's value area is an early indication of the level of market balance. In addition, the migration of the value area and its accompanying width provide basic clues regarding overall market direction and the underlying strength of the other timeframe buyer or seller. Along with volume, these concepts will be developed further in Section Two.

3. Dispersion of Volume   Dispersion of volume analysis is conducted to arrive at an accurate depiction of whether the other timeframe buyer or seller is exerting the greatest influence in the value area. In other words, who is winning the battle for value area control and to what extent. Dispersion of volume measures the distribution of volume within the value area occurring above and below the high-volume price. We illustrate below how to calculate the dispersion of volume for April 28, 1989.

Methodology   Using Figure 4–41 as reference, the following steps describe how to calculate dispersion of volume within the value area:

1. Find the high-volume price (within the value area): 90–06.
2. Sum all of the "% Vol" figures above the high-volume price (within the value area).

3. Do the same for the volumes below the high-volume price.

4. Divide the high volume price and add it to both sides.

Figure 4–41 shows that 34 percent of the volume took place above the high-volume price (90–06), while 38.5 percent occured below it. This ratio indicates that the bond market was relatively balanced between buyers and sellers within the value area, with the buyer showing slightly greater strength. When one side of the value area contains substantially higher volume, the imbalance usually carries over into the following day.

Dispersion of volume in favor of the other timeframe buyer (when the greatest volume occurs below the high-volume price) indicates that participants are more willing to buy and hold below value than sell and hold above value. Conversely, dispersion of volume in favor of sellers suggests that a greater number of sellers are willing sell and stay short. Readers wishing to refresh their minds on value area dynamics should refer back to "The TPO Count," in Chapter 3.

Like the TPO count, dispersion of volume analysis is useful only for days exhibiting two-timeframe, rotational trade and relative balance. A Trend day, on the other hand, exhibits clear other timeframe control. The overpowering dynamics of Trend situations not only negate the need for a subtle indicator such as dispersion of volume, but also distort the dispersion calculation, making it misleading.

Total percentage volume above high-volume price	*Total percentage volume below high-volume price*
6.9[*]	
10.1	6.9[*]
7.7	11.8
3.1	9.1
3.4	7.4
+ 2.8	+ 3.3
34.0%	38.5%

[*] High-volume percentage divided by two and added to each side.

Figure 4–41 Anatomy of the Liquidity Data Bank (LDB), June Treasury Bonds, April 28, 1989.

Volume Summary

Price	Volume	%Vol	%Cti1	%Cti2	%Cti3	%Cti4	Brackets
9017	590	0.2	48.1	17.6	1.7	32.5	$
9016	6554	1.9	57.5	13.9	0.9	27.8	$
9015	12398	3.6	55.5	8.5	8.8	27.2	Z$
9014	22440	6.6	62.4	11.7	7.3	18.6	Z$A
9013	27314	8.0	62.8	14.5	7.7	15.1	Z$A
9012	14738	4.3	61.1	11.8	4.2	22.9	Z$A
9011	9478	2.8	58.6	15.0	4.1	22.3	Z$A
9010	11494	3.4	55.4	8.0	5.0	31.7	Z$A
9009	10714	3.1	55.1	11.1	3.8	30.1	ZAB
9008	26336	7.7	63.2	10.6	6.0	20.2	ABC
9007	34576	10.1	58.1	12.6	5.2	24.1	ABCEFGL
9006	46872	13.7	56.6	14.8	4.2	24.3	ABCEFGHIJLM
9005	40244	11.8	56.6	16.0	7.0	20.4	ACDEFGHIJKLM
9004	31050	9.1	52.1	12.2	9.0	26.7	CDEFGIJKL
9003	25124	7.4	57.1	16.1	5.6	21.2	CDEJK
9002	11356	3.3	46.1	15.3	7.6	31.0	CDK
9001	8020	2.3	55.6	15.3	4.3	24.8	D
9000	2434	0.7	51.4	12.7	3.1	32.8	D
	247244	72.4	56.5	13.6	5.9	24.0	ABCDEFGHIJKLMZ$

70% 9011
V-A 9002

		%CTI1	%CTI2	%CTI3	%CTI4
Volume for T-BOND (CBOT) DAY JUN 89	341732	57.5	13.3	6.0	23.2
Volume for all T-BOND (CBOT) DAY	358706	57.6	13.1	5.9	23.4

4. Cti Figures   Understanding which participants are in control of the market and to what extent they are influencing price is one of the keys to successful trading. Cti figures help identify the who, what and where of other timeframe activity. In Treasury bonds, for instance, Cti1 (locals) usually averages around 55 to 60 percent. An unusually high Cti1 indicates that the local is primarily in control. Such days are often termed a "locals' market." Significant movement in price would be unlikely because of the limited influence of the other timeframe.

On the other hand, when the Cti1 figure is unusually low and/or the Cti2, Cti3, or Cti4 percentages are unusually high, outside participants are showing greater interest. Consequently, the potential for a significant movement in price is greater. Using Cti codes to identify other timeframe activity is illustrated in the following discussion and later in the section entitled "Evaluating Commercial Activity."

5. Acceptance of Value Outside the Value Area   Evaluating the acceptance (or rejection) of value outside the value area can shed important light on the direction of trade facilitation. For example, occasionally a market will break-out of a narrow trading range late in the day. If the break-out comes too late, the market may not have enough time to form value at new levels or generate sufficient volume to significantly change the calculation of the value area. Figure 4–42 shows how a "value inside versus value outside" comparison can yield information not necessarily identifiable from the bare Profile graphic.

Prior to L period on May 22, the only evidence of the buyer was a six tick initiative buying tail. Otherwise, the Profile structure showed unusually narrow value build-up and strong selling TPOs (49/33 at the end of K period). However, a rally in L period sparked the first range extension of the day and closed the bond market on its highs. Despite the strong close, the validity of the late rally was suspect due to the narrow value, selling TPOs and the fact that the range extension occured too late in the day to be confirmed by value (double TPO prints).

The LDB report painted a different picture. As we noted earlier, the best indication of trade facilitation is volume. Upon examining the volumes around the L period range extension on May 22, the "% of total" figures occurring in the 89–07 to 89–17 range do not show particularly large volumes. Thus, at first glance the L period rally did not appear too well accepted. One must keep in mind, however, that the L period move occured practically on the close. In addition, note the unusually high Cti2 percentages (commercial activity) at the upper extreme of the range. Had this activity been selling, Treasury bonds would not have closed on the highs. Thus, the significantly larger Cti2 figures were

Figure 4–42 Acceptance of value outside of the value area. June Treasury Bonds, May 22, 1987.

** NOTE **   VOLUME FIGURES SHOWN ARE ACTUAL NUMBER OF CONTRACTS MULTIPLIED BY 2

Contract	Trade Price	Volume	% Of Total	Cti1%	Cti2%	Half Hour BracketTimes At Which Prices Occurred
	89 17/32	1434	0.5	30.1	15.3	M
	89 16/32	2014	0.6	33.0	32.3	LM
JUN 87	89 15/32	1004	0.3	43.2	6.5	LM
	89 14/32	520	0.2	9.8	46.0	LM
	89 13/32	1014	0.3	20.0	25.8	LM
	89 12/32	2086	0.7	34.3	31.0	LM
	89 11/32	1376	0.4	44.5	10.5	LM
	89 10/32	2374	0.7	34.2	20.2	L
	89 9/32	3126	1.0	41.4	14.5	L
	89 8/32	1568	0.5	47.3	11.5	L
	89 7/32	2000	0.6	41.8	13.9	L
	89 6/32	2282	0.7	42.5	15.2	BL
	89 5/32	7730	2.4	41.0	17.9	BL
	89 4/32	6234	2.0	48.6	8.6	BL
	89 3/32	4264	1.3	48.5	8.6	BL
	89 2/32	6392	2.0	49.0	14.7	BCL
	89 1/32	8366	2.6	56.3	15.9	BCL
	89	11702	3.7	52.5	15.4	BCKL
	88 31/32	7690	2.4	53.9	18.0	BCKL
	88 30/32	8106	2.5	45.4	17.8	BCJKL
	88 29/32	10570	3.3	51.5	9.5	BCFJKL
	88 28/32	12086	3.8	48.2	22.7	BCDFJKL
	88 27/32	14414	4.5	51.7	13.5	BCDFIJK
	88 26/32	18702	5.9	51.5	14.7	BCDEFIJK
	88 25/32	16082	5.1	50.7	10.4	ABCDEFIJK
	88 24/32	22732	7.1	49.2	10.7	ABCDEFGHIJ
	88 23/32	21144	6.6	53.3	8.9	ABDEFGHIJ
	88 22/32	21126	6.6	52.1	10.8	ABDEGHIJ
	88 21/32	15282	4.8	53.3	13.8	ABDEGH
	88 20/32	15674	4.9	54.3	12.4	ABGH
	88 19/32	19424	6.1	58.4	7.0	ABG
	88 18/32	13022	4.1	54.5	6.4	ABG
	88 17/32	7882	2.5	55.1	6.9	A
	88 16/32	2586	0.8	44.3	8.7	A
	88 15/32	2392	0.8	43.0	12.0	A
	88 14/32	2544	0.8	59.2	8.3	A
	88 13/32	1676	0.5	65.5	3.3	A
	88 12/32	122	0.0	82.8	0.0	A
	88 3/32	364	0.1	39.8	3.0	W
	88 2/32	11574	3.6	36.0	24.0	UVWY
	88 1/32	2614	0.8	45.6	13.8	SUVWY
	88	2834	0.9	38.8	15.8	STUVWY
	87 31/32	1738	0.5	44.5	9.2	STUY
	87 30/32	238	0.1	70.6	1.7	ST
JUN 87	87 29/32	162	0.1	22.8	0.0	S

70% RANGE 88 18/32
OF DAILY TO   227756   71.6   52.3   12.1   BCKL
VOLUME 89

	% OF TOTAL	
	CTI1	CTI2
Total Volume For JUN 87 U S BONDS -- 318,266	50.2	12.9
Total Volume For U S BONDS -- 350,548	50.0	12.6
Total Spread Volume For JUN 87 U S BONDS -- 8,576	45.7	28.1

clearly caused by buying. This market needed to auction higher to facilitate trade.

Traders who had access to the volume information and interpreted it correctly should have prepared themselves to take advantage of potential opportunities to buy, perhaps in the London market or on the open of the next day. Treasury bonds opened one full point higher during the following trading session and traded two points higher by the end of the day.

6. High Volume Concentrations   High-volume concentrations identify potential areas of acceptance by the marketplace. If price is accepted at a particular level, then the market will probably spend time trading there. Thus, past high-volume areas should be viewed as potential support/resistance points and may offer a period of limited risk for trade entry and exit. Because high- and low-volume areas have such broad applications to trading, we save their discussion for a later section (see "High- and Low-Volume Areas," following "The Liquidity Data Bank").

7. Top Five versus Bottom Five   Another LDB barometer useful for gauging the market's directional inclinations is to add the five "% of Total" volumes occurring at the top of the range and compare them to the sum of the five "% of Total" volumes at the bottom of the range. The extreme exhibiting the greater total volume generally indicates that the market was doing a better job of facilitating trade in that direction. In Figure 4–43, volume in the top five ticks far outweighed volume in the bottom five ticks, suggesting that the market was "doing a better job" of auctioning higher. Treasury bonds opened higher on the following day, confirming this opinion.

The decision to use five ticks in the calculation rather than three or seven is entirely subjective. As the day's range fluctuates, this number should be adjusted accordingly (the wider the range, the greater the number of ticks included in the count).

8. Trend Tests   There are several LDB tests that can be employed to evaluate a market's potential to trend. Two of these, "Average High Volume" and "Opening-Range Volume" are described below and illustrated in Figure 4–44.

Average High Volume   The first trend test is to simply identify the five highest "% of Total" volume figures, add them together and then calculate their average. The larger the average volume figure, the lower the

Figure 4-43 Top-5 vs. bottom-5 volume analysis. September Treasury Bonds, June 22, 1987. Data courtesy of CISCO.

** NOTE ** VOLUME FIGURES SHOWN ARE ACTUAL NUMBER OF CONTRACTS MULTIPLIED BY 2

Contract	Trade Price	Volume	% Of Total	Cti1%	Cti2%	Half Hour Bracket Times At Which Prices Occurred	
	93 16/32	290	0.1	51.7	0.0	HJ	
	93 15/32	9436	2.7	48.8	17.1	HJ	Top-5
	93 14/32	11966	3.4	56.3	14.0	DEGHIJ	Total = 20.4%
	93 13/32	20302	5.8	55.9	10.6	DEFGHIJ	
	93 12/32	29568	8.4	55.9	11.2	DEFGHIJK	
	93 11/32	23304	6.6	56.9	10.8	DEFGHIJK	
	93 10/32	33006	9.4	55.2	12.1	ADEFGHIJKL	
	93 9/32	33650	9.6	57.0	10.4	ABCDEFGIJKL	
	93 8/32	28900	8.2	57.4	10.4	ABCDFGIJKL	
	93 7/32	44938	12.8	55.5	8.9	ABCDFGJKL	
	93 6/32	44926	12.8	55.4	10.4	ABCFJL	
	93 5/32	28792	8.2	56.3	10.6	ABCFJL	
	93 4/32	14076	4.0	55.3	13.5	ABCJL	
	93 3/32	10398	3.0	54.1	12.4	ABCL	
	93 2/32	8222	2.3	55.2	7.9	BCL	
	93 1/32	5222	1.5	61.2	15.0	BL	Bottom-5
	93	4504	1.3	52.3	11.9	BL	Total = 8.2%
	92 31/32	250	0.1	44.8	16.0	B	
SEP 87		267084	75.9	56.1	10.5	DEFGHIJK	

70% RANGE 93 5/32 TO 93 12/32
OF DAILY VOLUME

			% OF TOTAL	
			CTI1	CTI2
Total Volume For SEP 87 U S BONDS	---	351,750	55.8	11.0
Total Volume For U S BONDS	---	354,684	55.9	10.9
Total Spread Volume For SEP 87 U S BONDS	---	1,316	53.0	18.3

probability that a trend is underway. In Figure 4–44, the five highest volumes are denoted by asterisks (*).

Opening Range Volume   An alternative is to sum the "% of Total" volumes occurring in the opening range. The higher the resulting figure, the less likely the potential for a trend.

Both of these tests are of little value unless a running record of each is maintained. It is imperative that you develop an understanding for what is considered an average "opening-range volume" or "high volume average." Without some benchmark by which to evaluate these figures, they can be misleading.

Summary   The preceding discussion highlights just a few key areas of the Liquidity Data Bank, as well as a sampling of the methods by which to approach and use the wealth of information provided by this report. There are literally countless ways by which to use the LDB. In the section that follows, we take a detailed look at how to evaluate and use the Cti2 (commercial) portion of the report. For information on additional analyses of the LDB, readers should consult the *CBOT Market Profile Manual 1*. It is referenced in Appendix 2.

Evaluating Commercial Activity   Of all the market's participants, the commercial groups provide perhaps the best indication of the day timeframe importance of specific price regions. This is largely because commercial clearing members use the marketplace for business purposes and not for speculation (although some do speculate, as we shall see later). Hence, they generally respond to price fluctuations on the basis of what they perceive to be developing value.

Because commercial activity is isolated in the CBOT Liquidity Data Bank report, commercial responses to changes in price can be observed and evaluated. An understanding of what business the commercial is in, and therefore, how they are likely to respond to changes in price, helps the trader identify significant day and longer timeframe price levels. In this discussion, we will closely examine the commercial participant and the methods of measuring commercial activity.

A Definition   A "commercial clearing member" is another timeframe participant with commercial interests in the futures markets. Examples include grain merchants, livestock producers, savings and loans, and so forth. Dealing in futures is often part of their everyday business. There-fore, commercials tend to do *some* futures business during every trading session in order to fulfill their inventory requirements. Of all market par-

Figure 4–44 Trend tests. September Treasury Bonds, June 22, 1987.

** NOTE ** VOLUME FIGURES SHOWN ARE ACTUAL NUMBER OF CONTRACTS MULTIPLIED BY 2

Contract	Trade Price	Volume	% Of Total	Cti1%	Cti2%	Half Hour Bracket Times At Which Prices Occurred
	93 16/32	290	0.1	51.7	0.0	HJ
	93 15/32	9436	2.7	48.8	17.1	HJ
Average	93 14/32	11966	3.4	56.3	14.0	DEGHIJ
High	93 13/32	20302	5.8	55.9	10.6	DEFGHIJ
Volume =	93 12/32	29568	8.4 *	55.9	11.2	DEFGHIJK
10.6%	93 11/32	23304	6.6	56.9	10.8	DEFGHIJK
	93 10/32	33006	9.4 *	55.2	12.1	ADEFGHIJKL
	93 9/32	33650	9.6 8	57.0	10.4	ABCDEFGIJKL
	93 8/32	28900	8.2	57.4	10.4	ABCDFGIJKL
	93 7/32	44938	12.8 *	55.5	8.9	ABCDFGJKL
Opening	93 6/32	44926	12.8 *	55.4	10.4	ABCFJL
Range	93 5/32	28792	8.2	56.3	10.6	ABCFJL
Volume =	93 4/32	14076	4.0	55.3	13.5	ABCJL
28.0%	93 3/32	10398	3.0	54.1	12.4	ABCL
	93 2/32	8222	2.3	55.2	7.9	BCL
	93 1/32	5222	1.5	61.2	15.0	BL
	93	4504	1.3	52.3	11.9	BL
SEP 87	92 31/32	250	0.1	44.8	16.0	B
70% RANGE OF DAILY VOLUME	93 5/32 TO 93 12/32	267084	75.9	56.1	10.5	DEFGHIJK

		% OF TOTAL	
		CTI1	CTI2
Total Volume For SEP 87 U S BONDS	351,750	55.8	11.0
Total Volume For U S BONDS	354,684	55.9	10.9
Total Spread Volume For SEP 87 U S BONDS	1,316	53.0	18.3

ticipants, the commercial clearing members react to price fluctuations in the "truest" sense.

Occasionally, commercial participants will enter trades beyond their basic inventory needs if they perceive that an opportunity exists to buy below value or sell above value. And, due to the substantial size of most commercials, their activity can have a large effect on price movement and market direction. Monitoring commercial activity through the LDB often reveals other timeframe conviction and imbalance before the market reacts to evolving conditions.

Commercial Logic   The significance of commercial activity lies not so much in identifying price levels at which the commercial participant is active, but rather in recognizing how the commercial participant is behaving. In other words, are the commercials behaving as *expected* or are their responses *unexpected?* Or are they interested at all? Recognizing and identifying these types of responses is the key to using commercial understanding effectively.

Expected Response   Because commercials do at least some business every day, one would logically expect them to respond to price away from value. In other words, the expected commercial activity is to enter responsively near the day's extremes. As we mentioned before, the commercial participants may even increase their business beyond inventory requirements if price moves substantially away from established value.

Commercial entry near the day's extremes often serves to "buffer" day timeframe price movement, providing support to falling prices and resistance to rising prices. Examine the LDB report shown in Figure 4–45. Briefly, the percentage of total volume represented by commercial activity appears in the column labeled "Cti2%." These figures, shown for each price, clearly identify areas of significant commercial participation. Note the higher percentages of commercial activity occurring on the extremes, relative to those occurring in the value area. Although not dramatically above average (for Treasury bonds, 12–14 percent was a good "average" at the time of this example), the 16.3 Cti2% figure on the 89–23 high indicates potential aggressive commercial selling. Conversely, the Cti2% readings of 17.7, 18.9, and 17.9 at 88–16, 88–21, and 88–23 on the lower extreme reflect the entry of aggressive commercial buyers. Note also from Figure 4–45 that trade returned to the center of the developing value, illustrating the day timeframe, commercial buffering effect. Such *expected* activity is most often seen during more balanced, trading conditions, as typified by Neutral, Normal and Normal Variation days.

Figure 4–45 Expected commercial activity. March Treasury Bonds, January 5, 1988.

Volume Summary

Price	Volume	%Vol	%Cti1	%Cti2	%Cti3	%Cti4	Brackets
8923	734	0.1	52.6	16.3	0.0	0.0	B
8922	1620	0.3	50.5	10.8	0.0	0.0	B
8921	1868	0.3	52.6	1.4	0.0	0.0	B
8920	5066	0.9	55.4	12.0	0.0	0.0	B
8919	13662	2.5	56.2	9.5	0.0	0.0	B
8918	23892	4.4	60.2	10.4	0.0	0.0	B
8917	24148	4.4	65.1	11.6	0.0	0.0	B
8916	8454	1.5	56.1	14.6	0.0	0.0	B
8915	1518	0.3	62.1	12.3	0.0	0.0	BC
8914	7766	1.4	55.3	10.5	0.0	0.0	BC
8913	7544	1.4	58.6	14.1	0.0	0.0	ABC
8912	15898	2.9	52.3	12.5	0.0	0.0	ABC
8911	14750	2.7	63.1	13.3	0.0	0.0	ABC
8910	13066	2.4	56.5	9.2	0.0	0.0	AC
8909	14856	2.7	60.8	12.3	0.0	0.0	ACD
8908	19496	3.6	58.8	15.5	0.0	0.0	ACDEF
8907	23246	4.2	62.4	8.5	0.0	0.0	ACDEF
8906	23412	4.3	58.9	12.4	0.0	0.0	ACDEF
8905	16084	2.9	58.4	7.8	0.0	0.0	ACDEF
8904	21248	3.9	60.9	10.7	0.0	0.0	UACDEFI
8903	23506	4.3	57.6	13.1	0.0	0.0	UVADEFIJK
8902	36464	6.7	55.4	14.7	0.0	0.0	UVADEFIJK
8901	28312	5.2	62.1	10.7	0.0	0.0	UVWYADEFIJKL
8900	44140	8.1	56.6	12.3	0.0	0.0	UVWYADEFIJKL
8831	36290	6.6	57.8	12.4	0.0	0.0	UVWWADEFIJKLM
8830	23714	4.3	53.0	14.1	0.0	0.0	TUVWDFIJKLM
8829	8846	1.6	57.9	13.7	0.0	0.0	TUWFIJKL
8828	8760	1.6	51.9	14.5	0.0	0.0	TUFGHI
8827	11194	2.0	52.4	13.4	0.0	0.0	TFGHI
8826	17456	3.2	57.0	12.9	0.0	0.0	STFGHI
8825	15004	2.7	60.2	11.3	0.0	0.0	STFGH
8824	13656	2.5	56.0	12.5	0.0	0.0	STFGH
8823	10880	2.0	55.9	17.9	0.0	0.0	SFGH
8822	2372	0.4	56.4	12.4	0.0	0.0	SFG
8821	562	0.1	55.3	18.9	0.0	0.0	SG
8820	1400	0.3	46.9	14.1	0.0	0.0	QS
8819	906	0.2	58.8	16.0	0.0	0.0	QRS
8818	2010	0.4	51.7	15.3	0.0	0.0	QRS
8817	1698	0.3	48.9	16.3	0.0	0.0	QRS
8816	1382	0.3	50.8	17.7	0.0	0.0	QRS
8815	678	0.1	65.8	13.7	0.0	0.0	QR
8814	228	0.0	27.2	15.4	0.0	0.0	Q
8813	2	0.0	50.0	0.0	0.0	0.0	Q
70% V-A	400738	73.2	57.8	12.3	0.0	0.0	STUVWYABCDEFGHIJKLM

			%CTI1	%CTI2	%CTI3	%CTI4
Volume for T-BOND (CBOT) D-E MAR 88	547788		57.9	12.3	0.0	0.0
Volume for all T-BOND (CBOT) D-E	558562		57.4	12.1	0.0	0.0

Unexpected Response   A significant change in market conditions may elicit an *unexpected* response from the commercial participant. For instance, lower prices may actually attract new commercial *selling*, rather than opposing buying. The unexpected response may mean that the commercial's perception of value has changed.

Consider the plight of the grocer who hears news of a potential bumper coffee crop in Brazil. To quickly liquidate his now overvalued inventory, he marks down price and runs a "coffee extravaganza." However, to the average consumer, value is probably still associated with the previous price of coffee. Selling below value is unexpected activity to the shopper.

When the commercial participant begins to act out of his norm (unexpectedly), the trader is alerted that conditions may have changed. Figure 4–46 provides an example of an unexpected commercial response occurring in the Treasury bond market. On December 15, trade during A through C periods was basically two-timeframe, given the overlapping half-hour auctions and that bonds had easily traded back and forth through the open. However, a price probe up in D period, which would normally be expected to attract responsive sellers, elicited an unexpected response—more buying. Note the 26.6 Cti2% reading at 84–22. Unexpected buying activity continued throughout the entire day and into the close. The Cti2% readings in Figure 4–46 reveal higher-than-normal commercial participation appearing sporadically throughout the day's range (84–22, 85–00 and 85–22). In fact, commercial presence increased nearly every time the range was extended.

Note also the high levels of commercial activity taking place at or near the close. Since aggressive commercial selling would probably have returned price lower, this activity was most likely buying. Concentrated commercial buying on the close suggests that the market may still need to trade higher before the commercial is willing to sell.

When commercial groups act unexpectedly, they are usually speculating on price movement. The commercial participants are no longer acting as a buffer in the day timeframe but are instead adding fuel to longer term price movement.

No Response   Occasionally, price probes away from value generate no commercial response whatsoever. And, in rare instances, the commercial may show little or no interest in any price offered on a given day. These two scenarios have different implications for market activity.

First, if the LDB shows that the commercial did not respond to price probes near the extremes, then it is likely that price did not auction far enough on that day to attract the commercial participant. For instance, a lack of commercial activity on the lower extreme may indicate an unwill-

Figure 4–46 Unexpected commercial activity. March Treasury Bonds, December 15, 1987.

Price	%Cti2	Brackets
8524	17.7	LM
8523	11.8	LM
8522	25.1	LM
8521	18.3	LM
8520	13.4	L
8519	19.0	L
8518	13.9	L
8517	12.4	L
8516	13.2	KL
8515	11.8	KL
8514	19.7	KL
8513	19.3	FKL
8512	19.9	FHK
8511	14.1	FHK
8510	14.8	FHK
8509	12.8	FGHK
8508	15.0	FGHIK
8507	16.3	FGHIJK
8506	14.1	FGIJ
8505	15.2	FGIJ
8504	10.7	FGIJ
8502	12.1	F
8501	17.2	F
8500	23.3	F
8431	8.2	F
8430	15.8	EF
8429	10.2	EF
8428	13.0	DEF
8427	10.7	DEF
8426	11.2	DE
8425	19.5	D
8424	9.9	D
8423	8.6	D
8422	26.6	CD
8421	19.5	ACD
8420	12.2	ACD
8419	12.3	AC
8418	14.6	ABC
8417	18.0	ABC
8416	14.9	ABC
8415	12.7	B
8414	12.8	B
8413	7.3	B
8412	24.1	B

Average CTi2% = 14.1

ingness to buy. The market will probably have to auction lower to facilitate trade with the commercial buyer. Conversely, lack of Cti2 activity on the upper extreme suggests that higher prices are needed to attract commercial selling.

Second, on rare occasions the total Cti2% is significantly below average. That is, prices offered throughout the day spark little or no commercial interest. When such a no-response day develops, there is a good probability that the market will seek new price levels. Remember, the market's primary purpose is to facilitate trade—*with all participants.* If current prices are not bringing in commercial activity, then the market will most likely auction higher or lower in search of balanced trade.

Figure 4–47 provides a good example of a no-response day in Treasury bonds. The average, overall commercial activity (11.7 percent, circled in the lower right hand corner of Figure 4–47) occurring on October 1, 1987 was significantly lower than the average of the prior ten days (14.6 percent). The low Cti% figure suggests that prices offered on that day generated little commercial interest. Hence, the market had to probe to new price levels to generate activity (at least with the commercial).

On the following day, Treasury bonds built extremely wide, overlapping value amid a Multiple Distribution Buying Trend day. October 1 and 2 are shown together later in Figure 4–50.

Identifying the Significance of Price   Performing four relatively simple calculations each day helps a trader maintain an ongoing, objective assessment of overall commercial presence. The calculations stem from the basic need to be aware of how the commercial is behaving above value, within value and below value. The daily measurements consist of four parts:

1. The average daily Cti2%.
2. Average Cti2% above the value area.
3. Average Cti2% within the value area.
4. Average Cti2% below the value area.

Through an ongoing assessment of commercial participation on either side of value, traders can identify which price levels are successfully attracting the commercial participant and which are not. The LDB report, shown in Figure 4–48, provides examples of how the four Cti2% calculations are performed.

Figure 4-47 No commercial response. December Treasury Bonds, October 1, 1987.

Volume Summary

Price	Volume	%Vol	%Cti1	%Cti2	%Cti3	%Cti4	Brackets
8208	430	0.1	16.0	6.0	0.0	0.0	Y
8207	1220	0.3	26.5	15.7	0.0	0.0	Y
8206	2016	0.4	46.8	5.9	0.0	0.0	Y
8205	5600	1.2	38.4	5.6	0.0	0.0	WY
8204	4420	0.9	47.8	9.8	0.0	0.0	VWY
8203	3952	0.8	47.6	12.5	0.0	0.0	VW
8202	1584	0.3	31.3	7.4	0.0	0.0	TUVW
8201	2884	0.6	50.2	9.6	0.0	0.0	STUV
8200	5590	1.2	47.3	6.3	0.0	0.0	STUV
8131	3666	0.8	43.1	6.4	0.0	0.0	STUD
8130	7728	1.6	53.1	12.7	0.0	0.0	STD
8129	9478	2.0	55.0	15.5	0.0	0.0	STDH
8128	14382	3.0	57.6	10.2	0.0	0.0	STDHI
8127	19670	4.1	50.2	9.5	0.0	0.0	SADEHIL
8126	35818	7.5	56.8	10.4	0.0	0.0	SADEFHIJL
8125	56040	11.8	56.8	11.4	0.0	0.0	ADEFGHIJLM
8124	49576	10.4	58.3	12.0	0.0	0.0	ABDEFGHIJLM
8123	40358	8.5	59.7	11.2	0.0	0.0	ABDFGHJLM
8122	45790	9.6	59.9	14.3	0.0	0.0	ABCDFGHJKL
8121	43708	9.2	58.8	11.5	0.0	0.0	ABCDFGHJKL
8120	36692	7.7	58.0	13.9	0.0	0.0	BCGHJKL
8119	37872	8.0	62.6	11.8	0.0	0.0	BCJKL
8118	26876	5.6	55.2	13.6	0.0	0.0	BCJKL
8117	12242	2.6	58.2	8.6	0.0	0.0	BKL
8116	7488	1.6	47.0	6.1	0.0	0.0	KL
8115	690	0.1	48.7	1.7	0.0	0.0	K

	Price	Volume	%Vol	%Cti1	%Cti2	%Cti3	%Cti4	Brackets
70%	8126	345854	72.7	58.8	12.1	0.0	0.0	SABCDEFGHIJKLM
V-A	8119							

	CTI1	CTI2
% OF TOTAL	57.7	11.7

TOTAL VOLUME FOR U S BONDS 441,298

Figure 4–48 Cti2% calculations. June Treasury Bonds, April 25, 1989.

Volume Summary

* (2) Cti2% Above Value

Price	Volume	%Vol	%Cti1	%Cti2	%Cti3	%Cti4	Brackets	
							Brackets	
8925	444	0.1	50.9	5.0 *	1.8	42.3	B	
8924	5422	1.8	51.5	15.4 *	2.7	30.5	$ABCF	Cti2 = 12.9%
8923	28930	9.3	60.9	12.6 *	4.3	22.3	$ABCDEFG	
8922	59858	19.3	59.3	15.4	4.7	20.6	$ABCDEFGLM	
8921	49396	16.0	59.0	16.2	3.5	21.3	$ABCDEFGLM	Cti2 = 16.0%
8920	41950	13.6	60.6	17.5	4.3	17.6	$ABDEGL	
8919	34980	11.3	60.4	14.7	3.6	21.3	$AGHL	
8918	31456	10.2	56.8	16.4	4.6	22.3	$AGHIJKL	
8917	20626	6.7	62.7	16.3	4.6	16.3	$GHIJKL	
8916	16654	5.4	60.2	21.5	4.4	13.8	$JK	
8915	4242	1.4	51.2	18.7	1.4	28.7	$JK	
8914	2976	1.0	46.5	14.4	0.9	38.1	Z$K	Cti2 = 18.7%
8913	8422	2.7	56.0	23.0	6.6	14.3	Z$	
8912	2380	0.8	61.7	19.5	3.2	15.5	Z$	
8911	894	0.3	58.3	7.2	3.5	31.1	Z$	
8910	230	0.1	52.2	19.6	0.0	28.3	$	
8909	418	0.1	47.4	4.3	2.4	45.9	$	
8908	302	0.1	46.7	0.0	0.0	53.3	$	
70% 8922	217640	70.3	59.3	16.0	4.2	20.5	ABCDEFGHIJKLM$	
V-A 8918								

		%CTI1	%CTI2	%CTI3	%CTI4
		(3)			
Volume for T-BOND (CBOT) DAY JUN 89	309580	59.2	16.2	4.2	20.4
Volume for all T-BOND (CBOT) DAY	318764	59.3	15.8	4.3	20.5

(1) Avg. Daily
Cti2 = 16.2%

1. Average Daily Cti2% (Total)   The average Cti2% for the entire day (16.2%) is provided by the LDB, shown across from the section of the LDB report entitled "Volume for T-Bond (CBOT) Day" (see Point 1 in Figure 4–48). This figure represents the percentage of the day's entire volume attributed to commercial clearing members.

2. Average Cti2% above the Value Area   Measuring the average Cti2% above value is a somewhat detailed process. For each price above value, multiply the Cti2% by the total volume traded at that price. The resulting figure is the number of contracts attributable to commercial activity at that price. Examine Point 2 in Figure 4–48 for illustration. At 89–23, volume totaled 28,930 contracts. The Cti2% for 89–23 is 12.6%, which equates to 3,645 contracts attributed to the commercials. This process is repeated for each price above value. Finally, total Cti2 volume above value is divided by total volume above value to arrive at the average Cti2% above value. The entire process is detailed on the following page.

3. Average Cti2% Within the Value Area   This figure is also provided by the LDB report. See Point 3 in Figure 4–48.

4. Average Cti2% Below the Value Area   The average Cti2% below the value area is derived in the same manner as the average Cti2% above value discussed in number 2 above.

Price	Total Volume	Cti2%	Cti2% Volume
89–25	444	5.0	22
89–24	5,422	15.4	835
89–23	28,930	12.6	3,645
Total	34,796		4,502

Total Volume Above Value: 34,796
Total Commercial Volume Above Value: 4,502
Average Cti2% = 4,502/34,796 = 12.9%

The Cti2% total above, within, and below value calculations help to isolate areas of commercial participation that differ significantly from the norm. When an imbalance develops, the trader is alerted to the fact that the market may have to move in search of commercial activity. For illustration, let us briefly consider an example in the Treasury bond market. Figure 4–49 shows that on April 25, the LDB report for bonds exhibited a clear commercial imbalance. The Cti2% below value was 18.7%, the Cti2% within value averaged 16.0%, while the Cti2% above value measured 12.9%. Commercial sellers were simply not as active on the day's highs, indicating that the bond market still needed to go higher to cut off the commercial buying and attract commercial selling. On the following day, Treasury bonds auctioned considerably higher and eventually attracted the commercial sellers.

We stress once again the importance of maintaining a continuous record of these figures. Knowing the commercial percentage for an isolated day reveals little about the underlying make-up of the market. Obviously, if we are to make judgments, we need some "ball-park" figure to use for comparison. Two possibilities are an average for the current auction (swing or longer term), or a moving average that corresponds to your trading timeframe.

Being able to recognize the subtle changes in commercial behavior helps traders identify when market conditions may be changing—before structure has provided confirmation, and, more important, before the opportunity is out of reach.

Cti2% in Action To demonstrate the benefits of Cti2% analysis, a summary of 10 days of market activity is provided in the following paragraphs. From a longer-term perspective, commercial activity proves most useful when it differs greatly from the norm. We stress, however, that while commercial activity is an important influence and merits monitoring, it is just one of many pieces of information. December Treasury Bond activity over September 28 through October 9, 1987 period provides reference for the following discussion (see Figure 4–50).

September 28 Commercial behavior on September 28 is significant in two areas: aggressive selling on the upper extreme and a general lack of commercial buying on the lower. The heavy commercial selling (30.2% at 82–28) on the high suggests that the commercials perceived price to be significantly above value at these levels. Reduced response on the lower extreme, however, indicates price did not move low enough in the day timeframe to incite aggressive commercial buying. The market may need to auction lower to spark commercial buying interest.

September 29 Sellers managed to establish lower value on this day. The Cti2% readings indicate continued commercial selling, as illustrated by the unusually high Cti2% figures at 82–09 (29.4%) and, to a lesser extent, on the day's close. This market still needs to move lower.

Figure 4–49   Commercial imbalance. June Treasury Bonds, April 25-26, 1989.

Volume Summary

		April 25		April 26	
Price	%CTi2	Profile	%Cti2	Profile	
9008		.	0.0	$	
9007		.	3.8	$	
9006		.	23.3	$	
9005		.	19.4	$	
9004		.	10.4	$	
9003		.	8.4	$	
9002		.	18.0	Z$	
9001		.	9.9	Z$	
9000		.	13.6	Z$	
8931		.	14.0	Z$	
8930		.	11.6	Z$	
8929		.	17.0	Z$	
8928		.	11.8	Z$	
8927		.	8.9	Z$	
8926		.	12.5	$DEF	
8925	12.9%	5.0	B	14.5	$DEFG
8924		15.4	$ABCF	18.5	$ABDEFG
8923		12.6	$ABCDEFG	15.4	$ABCDEFG
8922		15.4	$ABCDEFGLM	14.2	$ABCDGL
8921		16.2	$ABCDEFGLM	14.7	$ABCGHKLM
8920	16.0%	17.5	$ABDEGL	14.0	$ABCHIJKLM
8919		14.7	$AGHL	16.0	$AHIJK
8918		16.4	$AGHIJKL	9.9	AHIJ
8917		16.3	$GHIJKL	6.3	I
8916		21.5	$IJK	0.3	I
8915		18.7	$JK	.	
8914		14.4	Z$K	.	
8913	18.7%	23.0	Z$	.	
8912		19.5	Z$	.	
8911		7.2	Z$	.	
8910		19.6	$	.	
8909		4.3	$	.	
8908		0.0	$	.	

Figure 4–50   Cti2% in action. December Treasury Bonds, September 28-October 9, 1987.

Price	September 28	September 29	September 30	October 1	October 2
83 30 /32	.	.	.	.	.
82 31 /32	.	.	.	.	.
82 30 /32	.	.	.	.	.
82 29 /32	.	.	.	.	.
82 28 /32	30.2 B	.	.	.	.
82 27 /32	15.7 AB	.	.	.	.
82 26 /32	13.2 AB	.	.	.	.
82 25 /32	13.3 OB	.	.	.	.
82 24 /32	13.5 ABK	.			1.9 L
82 23 /32	14.5 ABK				15.4 L
82 22 /32	12.2 ABIK	1.7 O			17.7 L
82 21 /32	15.8 ABCIK	3.6 A			12.2 ILM
82 20 /32	9.5 BCIJKL	14.9 A			16.9 IL
82 19 /32	15.7 BCIJKL	4.8 A			8.1 IL
82 18 /32	13.8 CIJKL	8.1 A			13.6 IKL
82 17 /32	15.3 CHIJKL	9.8 A			12.9 IKL
82 16 /32	12.8 CHIJKLM	11.2 A			10.5 IKL
82 15 /32	15.1 CDGHIL	7.9 A			17.3 IKL
82 14 /32	10.5 CDGHL	14.5 A			14.3 IJKL
82 13 /32	11.2 CDGH	6.0 A			19.9 IJKL
82 12 /32	13.7 CDFG	13.7 A			13.8 IJKL
82 11 /32	15.1 CDFG	6.0 A			11.5 IJKL
82 10 /32	13.7 DEF	14.5 A			12.4 IJKL
82 9 /32	16.5 DEF	29.4 A			8.7 IJK
82 8 /32	16.2 DEF	16.7 ACFGH			14.6 IJK
82 7 /32	10.2 DEF	11.9 ABCFGHK			8.3 IJK
82 6 /32	14.9 DEF	11.6 ABCFGHK			18.1 IJK
82 5 /32	10.9 DEF	13.6 ABCFGHIJK			7.0 IJK
82 4 /32	7.3 D	15.1 ABCDFGHIJK			12.2 IJK
82 3 /32	.	14.4 ABCDFGHIJK			19.1 IK
82 2 /32	Avg. Cti2%= 13.6	16.7 ABCDEFGHIJK			6.4 IK
82 1 /32	.	13.5 ABCDEFGHIJK			15.3 IK
82 0 /32	.	15.0 ABDEGHIJKL			7.1 I
81 31 /32	.	15.0 ABDEHIJKL		1.1 D	8.9 I
81 30 /32	.	12.1 BDEHKL		4.2 D	20.7 I
81 29 /32	.	14.7 BDEL		15.3 ADH	12.1 I
81 28 /32	.	16.7 BDEL		10.4 ADHI	18.5 I
81 27 /32	.	18.0 BDEL		9.5 ADEHIL	8.0 I
81 26 /32	.	13.2 BEL		10.5 ADEFHIJL	10.3 I
81 25 /32	.	9.9 BEL		11.4 ODEFGHIJL	5.3 I
81 24 /32	.	15.7 BL	3.3 HL	12.0 ABDEFGHIJLM	16.5 I
81 23 /32	.	14.4 BL	20.7 AHL	11.2 ABDFGHIJL	11.0 I
81 22 /32	.	16.0 BLM	14.4 AGHILM	14.3 ABCDFGHIJKL	6.6 I
81 21 /32	.	14.7 BL	13.6 AFGHIL	11.5 ABCDFGHIJKL	11.4 I
81 20 /32	.	7.2 L	17.8 ABFGHIL	13.9 BCGHIJKL	13.2 I
81 19 /32	.		14.8 ABFGHIL	11.8 BCJKL	15.1 HI
81 18 /32	.	Avg. Cti2%= 14.1	15.8 ABEFGIL	13.6 BCJKL	8.7 JI
81 17 /32	.	.	13.1 ABCEFGIL	8.6 BKL	28.9 HI
81 16 /32	.		13.7 ABCDEFGIJL	6.1 KL	13.9 H
81 15 /32	.		13.5 OBCDEUKL	1.7 K	10.0 H
81 14 /32	.		11.1 ABCDEUKL		22.2 H
81 13 /32	.		10.3 ABCDEUKL	Avg. Cti2%= 11.8	10.6 H
81 12 /32	.		14.4 ABCDEUKL		13.3 AGH
81 11 /32	.		11.8 ABCDJK		14.0 AGH
81 10 /32	.		17.9 ADJK		12.2 OGH
81 9 /32	.		12.3 AJK		9.9 AGH
81 8 /32	.		7.5 AK		9.0 AG
81 7 /32	.		1.7 K		14.4 AEG
81 6 /32	.				14.4 ADEFG
81 5 /32	.		Avg. Cti2%= 13.8		13.9 ABCDEFG
81 4 /32	.				12.5 ABCDEF
81 3 /32	.				9.6 ABCDEF
81 2 /32	.				11.7 ABCF
81 1 /32	.				12.9 ABC
81 0 /32	.				10.1 ABC
80 31 /32	.				6.2 A
80 30 /32	.				9.7 A
80 29 /32	.				10.5 A
80 28 /32	.				18.6 A
80 27 /32	.	.	.	.	.
80 26 /32	.	.	.	.	Avg. Cti2%= 12.4
80 25 /32	.	.	.	.	.
80 24 /32	.	.	.	.	.
80 23 /32	.	.	.	.	.
80 22 /32	.	.	.	.	.
80 21 /32	.	.	.	.	.
80 20 /32	.	.	.	.	.
80 19 /32	.	.	.	.	.
80 18 /32	.	.	.	.	.
80 17 /32	.	.	.	.	.
80 16 /32	.	.	.	.	.
80 15 /32	.	.	.	.	.
80 14 /32	.	.	.	.	.
80 13 /32	.	.	.	.	.
80 12/32	.	.	.	.	.
80 11/32	.	.	.	.	.
80 10/32	.	.	.	.	.
80 8/32	.	.	.	.	.
80 7/32	.	.	.	.	.
80 6/32	.	.	.	.	.
80 5/32	.	.	.	.	.
80 4/32	.	.	.	.	.
80 3/32	.	.	.	.	.
80 2/32	.	.	.	.	.
80 1/32	.	.	.	.	.
80 0/32	.	.	.	.	.
79 31/32	.	.	.	.	.
79 30/32	.	.	.	.	.
79 29/32	.	.	.	.	.

Figure 4–50
Continued

Price	October 5	October 6	October 7	October 8	October 9
83 0 /32					
82 31 /32					
82 30 /32					
82 29 /32					
82 28 /32					
82 27 /32					
82 26 /32					
82 25 /32					
82 24 /32					
82 23 /32					
82 22 /32					
82 21 /32					
82 20 /32					
82 19 /32			9.9 H		
82 18 /32			9.7 H		
82 17 /32			12.2 H		
82 16 /32	0.0 B		8.6 H		
82 15 /32	7.2 B		8.7 H		
82 14 /32	9.2 AB		17.0 H		
82 13 /32	11.4 AB		12.7 DGHIJ		
82 12 /32	13.4 AB		12.7 DGHIJ		
82 11 /32	7.5 ABDIJ		8.8 DEGHIJ		
82 10 /32	12.2 ABDIJ		15.2 DEFGHIJ		
82 9 /32	14.2 ABCDELJ		14.5 DEFGIJ		
82 8 /32	15.3 OBCDEHIJ		15.8 DEFGIJ		
82 7 /32	13.6 ABCDEHIJKL		14.6 DEFIJ		
82 6 /32	12.9 ACDEGHIJKL		10.3 DEFIJK		
82 5 /32	14.4 CDEFGHIJKL		12.7 DIK		
82 4 /32	14.3 CEFGHIJKL		13.7 DK		
82 3 /32	14.3 CEFGHIJKL		17.7 DK		
82 2 /32	12.4 CEFGHIJKL		8.8 DK		
82 1 /32	10.7 CEFGHIJKL		11.3 DK		
82 0 /32	8.1 FGL		12.3 DK		
81 31 /32	6.5 FL		14.7 DK		
81 30 /32	12.6 FL		13.9 DK		
81 29 /32	12.1 FL		14.2 DK		
81 28 /32	9.5 FL		13.2 CDKL		
81 27 /32	10.3 FL		9.1 CDKL		
81 26 /32	13.1 L		14.5 CDL		
81 25 /32	7.0 L		14.8 BCDL		
81 24 /32	25.5 L	1.5 L	14.4 BCDL	29.6 D	
81 23 /32	6.1 LM	9.9 L	15.3 BCDL	16.3 AD	
81 22 /32	10.5 L	3.7 L	11.0 ABCL	11.5 ABCD	
81 21 /32	15.6 L	7.4 GHL	11.2 ABL	15.0 ABCD	
81 20 /32	9.0 L	10.1 FGHLM	15.1 ABLM	12.5 ABCD	
81 19 /32	Avg. C@2% = 12.7	13.3 FGHIJL	11.0 ABL	8.9 ABCD	
81 18 /32		9.6 CFGHIJL	12.4 ABL	12.4 ABCD	
81 17 /32		10.9 CDEFGHIJL	5.1 ABL	14.2 ABCD	
81 16 /32		11.4 ACDEFIJL	9.1 O	11.3 OBCDEF	
81 15 /32		13.8 ABCDEFIJL	10.0 A	11.5 ABDEFG	
81 14 /32		12.2 ABCDEFIJL	7.5 A	12.6 ABDEFG	
81 13 /32		11.8 ABCDEJKL	3.3 A	13.7 ABDEFG	
81 12 /32		11.8 ABDKL		14.2 ABDEFG	
81 11 /32		15.2 ABDKL	Avg. C@2%= 12.8	17.5 ABDEFG	
81 10 /32		14.8 OBK		9.3 EFG	
81 9 /32		10.6 ABK		13.0 EFG	
81 8 /32		9.1 ABK		11.9 G	
81 7 /32		0.0 A		12.8 G	
81 6 /32					
81 5 /32		Avg. C@2%= 12.0		15.9 GH	
81 4 /32				12.5 GHJK	
81 3 /32				10.5 GHJK	
81 2 /32				12.3 GHJK	
81 1 /32				14.5 GHJK	
81 0 /32				11.9 GHJK	
80 31 /32				13.3 HJK	
80 30 /32				11.4 HJK	
80 29 /32				16.9 HJK	
80 28 /32				15.3 HJKL	9.2 DE
80 27 /32				11.5 HIKL	10.4 DE
80 26 /32				15.5 HIKL	13.7 DE
80 25 /32				13.6 HIKL	13.9 DE
80 24 /32				13.2 HIKL	12.5 DEF
80 23 /32				9.6 HIKLM	12.4 ACDEFH
80 22 /32				11.1 HIL	9.9 ACDEFH
80 21 /32				7.9 L	14.2 ACEFH
80 20 /32				Avg. C@2%= 13.2	13.6 OCEFGH
80 19 /32					13.1 ACFGHI
80 18 /32					11.2 ACFGI
80 17 /32					15.9 ABCGI
80 16 /32					13.1 ABCI
80 15 /32					14.7 ABI
80 14 /32					14.3 ABI
80 13 /32					18.6 BIJ
80 12/32					14.0 BIJL
80 11/32					18.5 IJL
80 10/32					14.4 IJL
80 8/32					11.7 JKL
80 7/32					14.5 JKL
80 6/32					17.3 JKL
80 5/32					16.7 JKL
80 4/32					14.0 JKL
80 3/32					14.8 JKLM
80 2/32					16.7 KL
80 1/32					7.8 KL
80 0/32					28.3 L
79 31/32					
79 30/32					
79 29/32					Avg. C@2%= 14.0

September 30   At first glance, the high percentage commercial participation (20.7%) at 81–23, coupled with a close on the high leads one to believe that commercials were buying on the close. However, if commercials were there in strength, they were by no means convincing. Buyers managed just one tick of buying range extension and never challenged the previous day's value area.

Except for the close on the upper extreme, commercial activity on this day appears to be of the "expected" type, that is, responding in opposition as price probes away from value. Note the above average participation near the extremes.

October 1   At 11.8%, overall commercial activity was well below average on this day. The commercial participant showed virtually no interest in all areas of the Profile. This suggests that the market needs to auction elsewhere to better facilitate trade with the commercial groups. October 2 shows it did.

October 2   This day developed Buying Trend day structure. Aggressive buying can be seen at the day's low (18.6%), 81–14 (22.2%), 81–17 (28.9%), 81–30 (2.7%) and at 82–03 (19.1%). The strong close and relatively high commercial participation on the day's high suggest that this final activity was likely buying. After such a dramatic move to the upside, however, the market may need to come into balance before seeking to auction higher.

October 5   October 5 is a prime illustration of a late "unexpected" response. Note the high Cti2% occurring at 81–24 (25.5%). The fact that Treasury bonds closed below 81–24 suggests that this activity is selling. Structural evidence of other timeframe activity (the B period selling tail and ensuing selling range extension) adds support to the conclusion that the Bond market should continue to auction lower.

October 6   Unusually low overall commercial participation (12.0%) relative to the average (14.6%) suggests that present levels are not facilitating trade with the commercials. Price will likely probe away from current levels in search of trade.

October 7   This day developed into a Buying Trend day that resulted in an Auction Failure late in the day. An attempt to auction above the October 5 highs and test the upper extreme of the 2nd did not attract new buying. The responsive seller entered (as did commercials at 82–14) and quickly retraced the range.

October 8   The commercials were heavy sellers on the day's high (29.6%). Above average Cti2% in the lower distribution and a close near the low indicates that commercial activity in this region was predominantly selling. Moreover, the lack of aggressive commercial entry on the lows suggests that this market did not move low enough to encourage commercial buying.

October 9   Lower value developed on October 9. The above average commercial participation in the lower half of the range, combined with a close on the low indicates that aggressive commercial selling persisted through the day's end. Treasury bonds traded a full point lower on the following day.

LDB Summary   If we were to offer just two pieces of advice for those using the Liquidity Data Bank information, they would be:

1.   Do not base your evaluation on one calculation or aspect of the LDB. Look at all of the information before formulating decisions (avoid tunnel vision).

2.   The LDB requires some analytical effort to read and understand it. Do not be intimidated by the wealth of numbers. The power of the LDB is not so much in the numbers themselves but in your ability to discern in these numbers the interplay of factors affecting market behavior and interpret them logically, not analytically.

High- and Low-Volume Areas

To conclude our discussion of Day Timeframe Trading, we will examine high- and low-volume areas and their use in identifying changes in market sentiment. Market change is accompanied by both risk and opportunity. The key to securing optimal trade location is the ability to identify market change as it is developing, before the change is confirmed by structure. By monitoring significant volume-generated reference points, a trader can anticipate market behavior and maximize trade location in the early stages of change.

High-Volume Areas   High-volume concentrations develop when the market spends a relatively large amount of time trading within a narrow range of prices. Both the buyer and seller are active, forming a short-term balance region in which price slows to accommodate two-sided trade. In other words, the market perceives that area to be fair, and volume builds over a period of time.

In the shorter timeframes, high-volume areas represent the market's most recent perception of value and, therefore, have a tendency to *attract* price. Naturally, all markets eventually undergo change and leave the high-volume area in search of new value. Should the market subsequently return to those price levels, the high volume region should once again attract (slow) price.

We caution that the market's memory is primarily short term. The longer price remains away from a specific region of acceptance, the less significance the high volume will have on the market as it reenters that region. However, with regard to day and swing traders, an area of previously established high volume should slow price movement long enough to provide sufficient time to enter or exit a trade.

For example, suppose the swing auction in Treasury bonds is up, but the market probes downward into an area of previous high volume. The slowing of price should provide time to enter a responsive long and then monitor it for the reemergence of the buyer. Similarly, when seeking to exit an existing long, a trader can be relatively sure that when a market moves up into a high-volume area, price will slow enough to allow time to liquidate the long position.

Identifying High-Volume Levels Depending on the data vendor, day timeframe traders have three potential sources for high-volume price information:

1. The Liquidity Data Bank (LDB)   Shown in Figure 4–51, the LDB displays individual price volume information (as discussed earlier). With respect to isolating areas of high volume, the most significant figure is found in the "%Vol" column. These figures represent the percentage of total volume occurring at each price traded during the day. In Figure 4–51, the area marked near the center of the range—89–05 through 89–08—represents the four prices showing the greatest volume during trade on the 25th. In other words, 9.7 percent of the day's trade took place at 89–08, while 10.4 percent occured at 89–07, and so forth. These four prices add up to 40.3 percent of the day's trade and represent an area where the following trading session's auction rotations should slow, allowing time to position or exit a trade (if an opportunity is presented at all).

2. The Market Profile Graphic   For those markets without the benefit of LDB information, the Market Profile graphic provides solid structural clues regarding the day's high-volume levels. In the absence of real volume

Figure 4–51 High-volume areas.   December Treasury Bonds, October, 25, 1988.

Volume Summary

Price	Volume		%Vol	%Cti1	%Cti2	%Cti3	%Cti4	Brackets
8916	358		0.1	47.5	15.4	9.2	27.9	A
8915	6588		1.6	61.7	9.1	3.4	25.7	A
8914	9048		2.2	58.7	9.2	4.6	27.6	ABC
8913	19398		4.8	56.8	11.3	11.4	20.4	ABC
8912	35200		8.7	59.5	11.0	11.8	17.7	ABCL
8911	17470		4.3	57.7	10.3	6.3	25.7	ABCKL
8910	21494		5.3	55.9	13.4	7.9	22.9	CKL
8909	17212		4.3	61.1	8.3	3.8	26.8	CJKLM
8908	39224	*	9.7	56.0	15.7	3.8	24.6	CDJKLM
8907	41934	*	10.4	58.7	14.6	3.3	23.4	CDJKLM
8906	42232	*	10.4	59.0	10.2	8.1	22.7	CDEGHJKL
8905	39852	*	9.8	58.3	13.2	8.8	19.7	CDEGHIJ
8904	28830		7.1	54.7	15.1	3.9	26.3	CEFGHIJ
8903	21572		5.3	59.2	14.7	4.9	21.2	EFGHI
8902	19286		4.8	63.2	10.4	3.6	22.8	EFHI
8901	25774		6.4	58.3	10.8	6.4	24.5	EF
8900	14448		3.6	58.5	15.2	6.6	19.7	EF
8831	4712		1.2	60.0	8.1	2.9	29.0	F
70%	8909 290364		71.8	58.4	13.0	5.5	23.2	CDEFGHIJKLM
V-A	8900							

		%CTI1	%CTI2	%CTI3	%CTI4
Volume for U S BONDS DAY DEC 88	404632	58.3	12.5	6.4	22.9
Volume for all U S BONDS DAY	414442	57.7	12.5	6.7	23.1

figures, the second best measure of high-volume concentrations are the high TPO prices surrounding the point of control. The thick, middle portion of the Profile usually closely parallels the LDB high-volume prices. Price should slow as it enters the "fat" region of the previous trading session's Profile.

3. Tick Volume   Tick volume is available through several quote services, some of which now provide a tick-volume graphic representing the relative "tick" volume for each price traded as the day's structure evolves. Readers should note that tick volume measures the number of trades that take place, it does not reflect the actual contract volume in each trade. Thus, one tick may equal two contracts or 2,000 contracts—quite a difference from a trading logic standpoint. Moreover, on low volume days (like holidays) tick volume can register quite high because of heavy local activity, while in reality, actual volume is low. Still, high tick-volume prices generally coincide closely with the high TPO prices and, therefore, may be a useful estimate of the high volume prices (Figure 4–52). When using tick volume, traders simply need to be more aware of the underlying liquidity of the market in which they are trading.

High-Volume Examples

Example 1: Up Auction; Probe Down Into High-Volume Area   During late October, Treasury bonds were in the midst of a longer-term buying auction. As is demonstrated by Figure 4–53, October 25 recorded high-volume prices in the 89–05 to 89–08 region. After a higher opening on the 26th, responsive sellers attempted to auction price lower during A and B periods. The selling auctions eventually slowed near the area of the highest volume concentrations of the previous day. Buyers then entered the market and returned price above the 25th's value area.

Given that the longer-term direction was up and that the bond market had opened higher, traders looking for a good location to place a long could expect price to slow if it auctioned down near the high-volume area of the the 25th. If the buying auction was exceptionally strong, however, price would not have returned to the high-volume area at all. It is important to stress that traders should not expect the market to stop precisely at the high-volume levels—remember, high volume *attracts* price, but it is not a rigid floor or ceiling. It is logical for the market to trade *around* a high-volume area. Thus, the market could just as easily find support or resistance before the high-volume region as beyond it. The key to taking advantage of high volume is: (1) do not try to be perfect—first execute the trade; and then (2) place your confidence in the slowing properties of volume. If price had subsequently been accepted

**Figure 4–52   Tick volume Profile in June Treasury Bonds, May 30, 1989. Data
courtesy of Commodity Quote Graphics.**

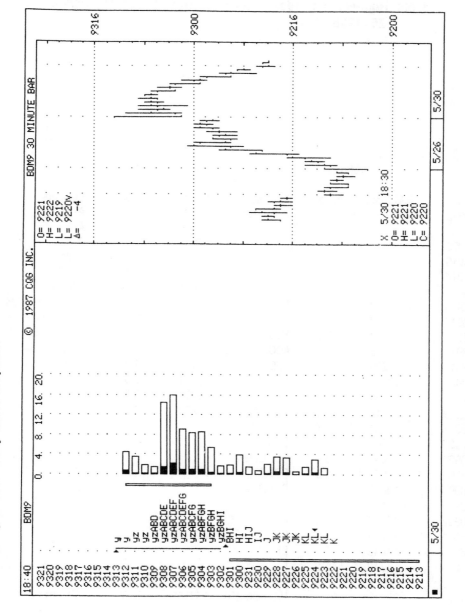

Figure 4–53   High-volume areas. December Treasury Bonds, October 25 and 26, 1988.

	October 25, 1988			October 26, 1988		
Price	Volume	%Vol	Brackets	Volume	%Vol	Brackets
8922	.	.	.	1734	0.5	A
8921	.	.	.	9512	2.7	A
8920	.	.	.	5760	1.7	A
8919	.	.	.	15274	4.4	AHK
8918	.	.	.	32180	9.2	AHIK
8917	.	.	.	32782	9.4	ABHIKLM
8916	358	0.1	A	39916	11.4	ABDFGHIJKLM
8915	6588	1.6	A	69704	20.0	ABCDEFGHIJKLM
8914	9048	2.2	ABC	64580	18.5	ABCDEFGHIJL
8913	19398	4.8	ABC	40570	11.6	ABCDEFGJ
8912	35200	8.7	ABCL	14502	4.2	BCE
8911	17470	4.3	ABCKL	10026	2.9	BC
8910	21494	5.3	CKL	12088	3.5	BC
8909	17212	4.3	CJKLM	272	0.1	B
8908	39224 *	9.7	CDJKLM	.	.	.
8907	41934 *	10.4	CDJKLM	.	.	.
8906	42232 *	10.4	CDEGHJKL	.	.	.
8905	39852 *	9.8	CDEGHIJ	.	.	.
8904	28830	7.1	CEFGHIJ	.	.	.
8903	21572	5.3	EFGHI	.	.	.
8902	19286	4.8	EFHI	.	.	.
8901	25774	6.4	EF	.	.	.
8900	14448	3.6	EF	.	.	.
8831	4712	1.2	F	.	.	.
VA	290364	71.8	VA 8900-8909	247552	71.0	VA 8913-8917

Figure 4–54   High-volume areas. December Treasury Bonds, September 14 and 15, 1988.

September 14, 1988   September 15, 1988

Price	Volume		%Vol	Brackets	Volume	%Vol	Brackets
8909	410		0.1	A	.	.	.
8908	4506		0.8	A	.	.	.
8907	7150		1.3	A	.	.	.
8906	2932		0.5	A	.	.	.
8905	1202		0.2	A	.	.	.
8904	1368		0.2	A	.	.	.
8903	916		0.2	A	.	.	.
8902	4440		0.8	A	.	.	.
8901	14450		2.5	A	.	.	.
8831	9554		1.7	A	.	.	.
8830	13804		2.4	A	.	.	.
8829	11240		2.0	AB	.	.	.
8828	11276		2.0	ABC	.	.	.
8827	13176		2.3	ABC	.	.	.
8826	28366		5.0	ABCF	72	0.0	C
8825	53476	*	9.4	ABCFGI	4540	1.0	BC
8824	44194	*	7.8	ABCFGHIJ	15212	3.2	ABC
8823	36506	*	6.4	ABCDEFGHIJK	14932	3.1	ABC
8822	55690	*	9.8	ABCDEFGHIJK	30170	6.3	ABCDEF
8821	6496	*	11.4	ABCDEFHIJK	42492	8.9	ABCDEF
8820	50842	*	8.9	ABCDEFHIJK	57832	12.1	ABCDEFG
8819	35982		6.3	ABCDEFIKLM	32976	6.9	ABCDEFG
8818	35898		6.3	DEFKLM	34598	7.3	ABCDFG
8817	19336		3.4	DEKL	22588	4.7	ACDFGH
8816	10964		1.9	DKL	15084	3.2	CDGH
8815	7878		1.4	KL	4268	0.9	DH
8814	5824		1.0	KL	12250	2.6	H
8813	3434		0.6	K	14038	2.9	HI
8812	178		0.0	K	14090	3.0	HI
8811	.		.	.	18452	3.9	HIJKL
8810	.		.	.	42360	8.9	HIJKL
8809	.		.	.	26878	5.6	IJKLM
8808	.		.	.	31524	6.6	IJKLM
8807	.		.	.	22528	4.7	JKLM
8806	.		.	.	15062	3.2	JLM
8805	.		.	.	4382	0.9	L
VA	425254		74.8	VA 8817-8826	371342	78.0	VA 8810-8824

below the high-volume area, traders would have been alerted that market perceptions of value had changed. Long positions should have been exited immediately.

While October 26 did not evolve into a big day, it did show general continuation to the upside through higher value placement. Moreover, when the Treasury bond market attempted to auction lower in C period, price slowed and found support at the high-volume levels. Day traders could observe the downward testing to 89–10, place longs against that level, and rely on the slowing properties of volume should price probe lower.

Example 2: Down Auction; Probe Up Into High-Volume Area   Figure 4–54 shows Treasury bonds at the start of a potential short-term down auction. September 14 demonstrates a Normal Variation selling day, characterized by a strong responsive selling tail and late selling range extension in K period, resulting in a close in the lower half of the range. The unusually large selling tail alerted traders to potential buying excess on the high. Figure 4–54 shows the Profiles for September 14 and 15, along with the %Vol figures for both. The 14th's high-volume prices spanned from roughly 88–20 to 88–25, accounting for 53.7 percent of the day's volume. On September 15, bonds opened and auctioned within the area of the 14th's high-volume concentrations. The A, B, and C period rotations within this high-volume region demonstrated the "time" offered by high volume—time to enter or exit a trade. Traders may have chosen to use this particular opportunity in one of two ways, depending on their level of confidence in the start of the down auction:

1. No trade, until more information was furnished by the market. The morning's auction rotations within the previous day's high-volume areas indicated balance. Traders may have elected to enter shorts on a break-out of this balance, which occurred in H period.

2. Those with more faith in the strength of seller conviction may have used the time offered early in the morning to enter shorts with good trade location. When C period buying probe beyond the initial balance (A and B periods in Treasury bonds) met with rejection just above the high-volume area (a form of auction failure), traders recognizing the continued strength of the seller could have confidently entered short trades (or exited longs). On the other hand, had price auctioned higher, above 88–26 and into the *low volume price levels*, traders would have been alerted that conditions had changed. September 15 eventually developed Double Distribution Selling Trend structure,

generating overlapping to lower values in the direction of the short-term auction.

Low-Volume Areas   Low volume typically represents other timeframe directional conviction. Therefore, it is more likely to see low-volume areas occurring in unbalanced, trending markets. Low-volume prices are caused by the same forces that create excess and usually exhibit the same characteristics: gaps, single TPO prints, and tails (short and long term).

When the rejection demonstrated by a low-volume area develops, short-term strategy is to place trades using the area of price rejection for support or resistance. The low-volume area, like excess, should hold against future auction rotations. For example, single TPO prints separating a Double Distribution Selling Trend day indicate swift rejection of the initial distribution in search of a new, lower-value area. Shorts placed just below the single-print low-volume area should offer good day timeframe trade location. However, if price auctions back up through the single prints, then market sentiment has changed and shorts should be exited. When price auctions through an area of previous low volume, the other timeframe conviction that initially influenced price has changed. Traders should heed the market's warning and exit any opposing trades.

Imagine a low-volume area as a balloon. The surface of the balloon offers resistance to the probing of the tip of a pencil. Once the pencil pierces the balloon, however, there is nothing to stop its motion in the direction of the initial probe. If a price probe "penetrates" the extreme of a low volume region, then the subsequent price movement is often swift through the remainder of the low-volume area. However, like the balloon, the low-volume area "gives" before it breaks. Price must often trade substantially through the low-volume area before it no longer offers support or resistance.

Identifying Low-Volume Areas   The means to identify low-volume areas are similar to those previously covered in the high-volume discussion. The most significant measure is again found in the "%Vol" column of the LDB, followed by structural indicators, such as tails and single TPO prints, and tick volume. As an example of using real volume levels, let us examine the September 15 LDB, shown in Figure 4–55.

Two obvious low-volume price areas that came into play on this day span from 88–25 to 88–26, and from 88–12 to 88–16. The low volume at the upper extreme of the day's range represents rejection of the 88–26 high. The lower volumes in the center of the range suggest that aggressive other timeframe sellers drove price lower with conviction. These five prices add up to only 12.6 percent of the day's trade and represent a

Figure 4–55 Low-volume areas. December Treasury Bonds, September 15, 1988.

September 15, 1988

Price	Volume		%Vol	Brackets
8826	72	*	0.0	C
8825	4540	*	1.0	BC
8824	15212		3.2	OBC
8823	14932		3.1	ABC
8822	30170		6.3	ABCDEF
8821	42492		8.9	ABCDEF
8820	57832		12.1	ABCDEFG
8819	32976		6.9	ABCDEFG
8818	34598		7.3	ABCDFG
8817	22588		4.7	ACDFGH
8816	15084	*	3.2	CDGH
8815	4268	*	0.9	DH
8814	12250	*	2.6	H
8813	14038	*	2.9	HI
8812	14090	*	3.0	HI
8811	18452		3.9	HIJKL
8810	42360		8.9	HIJKL
8809	26878		5.6	IJKLM
8808	31524		6.6	IJKLM
8807	22528		4.7	JKLM
8806	15062		3.2	JLM
8805	4382		0.9	L
	371342		78.0	VA 8810-8824

region where future auction rotations will probably be rejected rather than slowed. This rejection can assume one of two forms: (1) a dramatic reversal if the low volume area holds, visually represented by a tail, or (2) swift continuation back through the low-volume area, commonly represented by single TPO prints.

Low-Volume Examples

Example 1: Low Volume as Resistance   At the time of this example, Treasury bonds had formed short term buying excess at 89–09 on September 14 (circled in Figure 4–56) and were starting a down auction. September 15 developed a late-forming Double Distribution Selling Trend day (Figure 4–57), confirming the buying excess. Figure 4–57 displays the Profiles for the 15th and 16th, and their accompanying price/volume figures. Again, the low-volume area from 88–12 to 88–16 on the 15th represents swift continuation and other timeframe seller conviction. This territory should offer resistance during subsequent buying attempts, at least over the short term.

Two scenarios may confront a trader looking to sell on the 16th. First, assuming an unchanged to lower opening, good trade location would be gained just below the 88–12 to 88–16 low-volume region. Ideally, price would test higher and be rejected, providing an opportunity to place shorts near the 16th's highs. If the market is extremely weak, however, price may never auction that high. This brings us to the second scenario, again assuming an unchanged to lower open. If Bonds show early selling via an Open-Drive type of opening, there will be no "ideal" opportunity for short placement. In such a high conviction situation, it is best to position shorts early and then monitor subsequent activity for continuation. Here, the low-volume area acts as a form of excess, giving credence to the developing down auction.

As Figure 4–57 illustrates, on September 16 bonds gapped open below the 15th's lows, indicating potential seller continuation. The lower opening proved to be too low, however, and responsive buyers entered the market to take advantage of price perceived to be below value. Subsequent time periods showed buyers struggling to auction price higher. Eventually, the buying attempts met with rejection at the 88–12 level— the bottom of the low volume area separating the two distributions from September 15. The failure to auction back into the low-volume region offered traders an excellent opportunity to place short positions.

Ultimately, day timeframe resistance was found just below the low-volume area and the single print from the previous day's selling Trend structure. As with anticipating price slowing near high-volume areas, it is equally important that traders avoid trying to achieve "perfect" trade

**Figure 4–56   Low-volume area. December Treasury Bond—excess. Data cour-
tesy of Commodity Quote Graphics.**

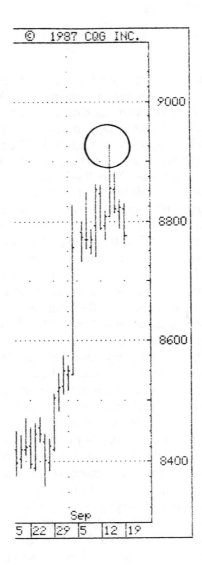

Figure 4–57 Low-volume areas. December Treasury Bonds, September 15 and 16, 1988.

September 15, 1988 — September 16, 1988

Price	Volume		%Vol	Brackets	Volume	%Vol	Brackets
8826	72	*	0.0	C	.	.	.
8825	4540	*	1.0	BC	.	.	.
8824	15212		3.2	OABC	.	.	.
8823	14932		3.1	ABC	.	.	.
8822	30170		6.3	ABCDEF	.	.	.
8821	42492		8.9	ABCDEF	.	.	.
8820	57832		12.1	ABCDEFG	.	.	.
8819	32976		6.9	ABCDEFG	.	.	.
8818	34598		7.3	ABCDFG	.	.	.
8817	22588		4.7	ACDFGH	.	.	.
8816	15084	*	3.2	CDGH	.	.	.
8815	4268	*	0.9	DH	.	.	.
8814	12250	*	2.6	H	.	.	.
8813	14038	*	2.9	HI	.	.	.
8812	14090	*	3.0	HI	2506	0.9	K
8811	18452		3.9	HIJKL	9538	3.5	K
8810	42360		8.9	HIJKL	15648	5.7	KL
8809	26878		5.6	IJKL	17472	6.4	FKLM
8808	31524		6.6	IJKLM	19612	7.2	FIJKLM
8807	22528		4.7	JKLM	25620	9.4	DEFGHIJL
8806	15062		3.2	JLM	37704	13.8	DEFGHIJL
8805	4382		0.9	L	21448	7.9	DEFGHIJL
8804	.		.	.	13574	5.0	DEFI
8803	.		.	.	2070	0.8	BDEF
8802	.		.	.	11162	4.1	ABCD
8801	.		.	.	28476	10.4	ABCD
8800	.		.	.	26722	9.8	ABC
8731	.		.	.	126284	9.6	OB
8730	.		.	.	12950	4.7	A
8729	.		.	.	2398	0.9	A
	371342		78.0	VA 8810-8824	192786	70.6	VA 8801-8810

...ne region of low volume. The keys to taking advantage of ...ne areas are: (1) keep accurate notes of where they are; (2) ...w in which direction you expect to see rejection and monitor for signs of that rejection; (3) place orders ahead of time at price levels representing good trade location to insure execution; and (4) abandon low-volume strategies if price builds acceptance beyond previous low-volume regions (a price probe pierces the "balloon").

Despite the obvious structural buying preference throughout the day's activity, September 16 resulted in lower values. This fact, along with the buyer's inability to auction price beyond the low-volume area from the 15th, suggested that other timeframe control remained in the hands of the seller.

Example 2: High and Low Volume Used Together   Activity on the following day, September 19, shows an integration of the logical workings of both high- and low-volume areas. In Figure 4–58, the Treasury bond market opened at 88–09 and found early rejection just below the 88–11 and 88–12 low-volume prices that formed the highs of September 16. Sellers easily auctioned through the 88–03 level, despite its low-volume percentage (0.8%), increasing confidence in short trades. The fact that price auctioned through 88–03 on the 19th confirmed that this area that had supported the previous afternoon's buying auctions was no longer valid.

From a Profile standpoint, note that activity on September 19 generated an initiative selling tail directly below the low-volume region of the 16th. In addition, the *high-volume levels* of the 16th (around 88–06 and 88–07) slowed price enough to allow traders time to place shorts with initiative selling activity.

Summary   The following is a brief listing of the salient concepts involved in understanding high- and low-volume areas:

1. Both high- and low-volume regions may be present on the same day if a transition takes place—if a market evolves from a balanced, two-timeframe market to one-timeframe trade, or vice versa.

2. Low volume represents rejection, but if the market should return to auction beyond the low-volume area and build value, then directional conviction has changed, and the region is no longer a valid reference point.

3. Both high- and low-volume areas represent support or resistance, but in vastly different ways.

4. Traders can expect to be able to place or exit trades within

Figure 4–58 Low-volume areas. December Treasury Bonds, September 16 and 19, 1988.

	September 16, 1988			September 19, 1988		
Price	Volume	%Vol	Brackets	Volume	%Vol	Brackets
8812	2506 *	0.9	.	.	.	.
8811	9538 *	3.5	.	.	.	.
8810	15648	5.7	KL	3388	0.9	A
8809	17472	6.4	FKLM	7842	2.2	O
8808	19612	7.2	FIJKLM	10970	3.0	A
8807	25620	9.4	DEFGHIJL	3318	0.9	AB
8806	37704	13.8	DEFGHIJL	4390	1.2	ABC
8805	21448	7.9	DEFGHIJL	12346	3.4	ABC
8804	13574	5.0	DEFI	25236	7.0	ABCD
8803	2070 *	0.8	BDEF	17266	4.8	ABCD
8802	11162	4.1	ABCD	4498	4.0	ABD
8801	28476	10.4	ABCD	6870	4.7	ABD
8800	26722	9.8	ABC	2400	3.4	BDE
8731	26284	9.6	OB	20256	5.6	BDE
8730	12950	4.7	A	22240	6.1	DEF
8729	2398	0.9	A	1518	3.2	DEFGHIJ
8728	.	.	.	28784	7.9	EFGHIJ
8727	.	.	.	27444	7.6	EFGHIJ
8726	.	.	.	25776	7.1	EFGHIJK
8725	.	.	.	32100	8.9	EFGHIJKLM
8724	.	.	.	34696	9.6	EJKLM
8723	.	.	.	18488	5.1	KL
8722	.	.	.	11764	3.2	KL
8721	.	.	.	972	0.3	L
	192786	70.6	VA 8801 - 8810	263848	72.8	VA 8724 - 8803

174   Chapter 4

Figure 4–59   Range extension occurring in the Swiss Franc, October 22-28, 1987.

	Oct 22	Oct 23	Oct 26	Oct 27	Oct 28
7046	.	.	.	.	.
7044	.	.	.	.	.
7042	.	.	.	.	J
7040	.	.	.	.	J
7038	.	.	.	.	IJ
7036	.	.	.	.	HIJ
7034	.	.	.	.	HIJ
7032	.	.	.	.	HIJ
7030	.	.	.	.	HIJ
7028	.	.	.	.	HIJ
7026	.	.	.	.	HIJK
7024	.	.	.	.	HIJ
7022	.	.	.	.	HIJ
7020	.	.	.	.	HJ
7018	.	.	.	.	H
7016	.	.	.	.	H
7014	.	.	.	.	H
7012	.	.	.	.	H
7010	.	.	.	.	H
7008	.	.	.	.	H
7006	.	.	.	.	H
7004	.	.	.	.	H
7002	.	.	.	.	GH
7000	.	.	.	.	GH
6998	.	.	.	.	GH
6996	.	.	.	.	GH
6994	.	.	.	.	G
6992	.	.	.	.	G
6990	.	.	.	.	G
6988	.	.	.	.	CG
6986	.	.	.	.	CG
6984	.	.	.	.	CDG
6982	.	.	.	.	CDG
6980	.	.	.	.	CDG
6978	.	.	.	.	CDG
6976	.	.	.	.	ZCDG
6974	.	.	.	.	YZCDG
6972	.	.	.	.	YZBCDG
6970	.	.	.	.	YZBCDG
6968	.	.	.	G	YZABCDEG
6966	.	.	.	G	YZABCDEFG
6964	.	.	.	G	YZABCDEFG
6962	.	.	.	G	YZABDEFG
6960	.	.	.	G	YZABEFG
6958	.	.	.	GH	YZABEFG
6956	.	.	.	GH	YAEF
6954	.	.	.	GH	OAE
6952	.	.	.	GH	YE
6950	.	.	.	GH	E
6948	.	.	.	GH	E
6946	.	.	.	GH	E
6944	.	.	.	GHI	.
6942	.	.	.	GHI	.
6940	.	.	.	GHI	.
6938	.	.	.	GHI	.
6936	.	.	.	FGHI	.
6934	.	.	.	FGHI	.
6932	.	.	.	FIJ	.
6930	.	.	.	FIJ	.
6928	.	.	.	FIJK	.
6926	.	.	.	EFIJ	.
6924	.	.	.	EFIJ	.
6922	.	.	.	EFIJ	.
6920	.	.	.	EFIJ	.
6918	.	.	.	EFIJ	.
6916	.	.	.	EFJ	.
6914	.	.	.	EF	.
6912	.	.	.	EF	.
6910	.	.	.	E	.
6908	.	.	.	E	.
6906	.	.	.	DE	.
6904	.	.	.	DE	.
6902	.	.	.	DE	.
6900	.	.	.	D	.
6898	.	.	.	D	.
6896	.	.	G	D	.
6894	.	.	G	D	.
6892	.	.	CG	CD	.
6890	.	.	CG	CD	.
6888	.	.	CG	C	.
6886	.	.	CG	C	.
6884	.	.	ZCDFGHI	C	.
6882	.	.	ZACDFGHI	BC	.
6880	.	.	ZACDFHI	BC	.
6878	.	.	ZACDFHI	BC	.
6876	.	.	OZACDFHIJ	YZBC	.
6874	.	.	YZACDFHIJ	YZBC	.
6872	.	.	YZABCDEFHIJ	YZB	.
6870	.	.	YZABDEFHIJK	YZAB	.
6868	.	.	YZABDEFHJ	YZAB	.
6866	.	.	YZABDEFJ	YZAB	.
6864	.	.	YZABDEF	OAB	.
6862	.	.	YZBDE	A	.
6860	.	.	YZDE	.	.
6858	.	.	YDE	.	.
6856	.	.	YD	.	.
6854	.	H	Y	.	.
6852	.	H	.	.	.

Figure 4–59
Continued

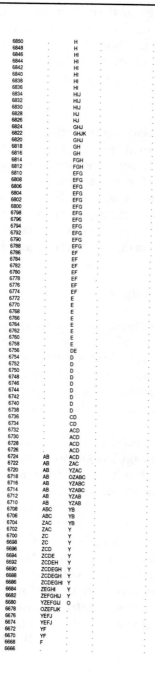

high-volume areas in anticipation of their slowing affect on price. Low volume, on the other hand, represents swift rejection. Therefore, trades should be placed or exited *in front* of that region, for the other timeframe participant that initially drove price should reject any auction attempts near the low-volume area.

High- and low-volume areas do not represent "mechanical" trades. They do, however, provide useful reference points that enable traders to visualize potential future activity. The importance of such reference points lies in the detection of market change. By monitoring activity around high- and low-volume areas, a trader can determine whether or not directional conviction has changed since the area was formed. Through the detection of fundamental change, traders can better manage their risk and identify areas offering favorable trade location.

Summary—Day Timeframe Trading

Let's pause for a moment and imagine a vast desert with nothing but sand in all directions. A man walks along, his throat dry and his lips cracked. Suddenly, he sees before him a shimmering pool of water just over the next dune. He runs towards it, relief finally in sight. He reaches the top of the sand hill and jumps—only to land in more sand. The water was a mirage created by the sun and his overwhelming desire to find water.

It is important to keep in mind at all times that the market can easily create a day timeframe "mirage" regarding longer-term market direction. When a trader is looking too hard for certain market conditions and the market exhibits some characteristics of what he seeks, the result is often a mirage that can leave a trader high and dry. For example, when a market opens substantially above the previous day's range and attempts to auction down all day, it appears as if the seller is in control. A trader with a strong bearish bias might jump into a trade, thinking his or her convictions were correct. However, if value is still established higher, then the *buyer* may actually be in control in the longer term.   In this section we discussed day timeframe control—which way the market is trying to go in the day timeframe. In the previous example, the seller was in control *in the day timeframe*. In Section II, "Long-Term Trading," we delve into an understanding of the longer term that can prevent a trader from being fooled by day timeframe mirages—an understanding that will help a trader develop the ability to take advantage of long term opportunity.

Section II: Long-Term Trading

In Section I, we compared Mike Singletary to a day timeframe futures trader. He studies charts and game films to prepare for each game, but operates solely in the *present tense* when he is on the football field. Similarly, the day timeframe trader studies recent market activity, but when the trading session begins, he or she acts purely on the day's evolving information. The academic knowledge becomes synthesized in the trader's mind to form a holistic picture, allowing for objective, intuitive decision making.

The longer-term trader, on the other hand, is more like Singletary's coach. A good coach knows that winning games, or even division titles, does not insure long-term success. A football team may go undefeated one year but could easily suffer a losing season the following year if the coach does not consider the longer-term effects of aging players, the upcoming draft, and the changing abilities of his competitors. The coach builds the strength of his team over time, bringing in new talent and constantly evaluating the long-term factors necessary to compile a winning record.

The futures market exhibits similar characteristics. The strength and duration of a trend is largely subject to the "aging" of its original participants, as well as the talent and conviction of any new business that is brought in. And, like a successful coaching career, successful long-term trading not only requires winning consistently in the day timeframe, but also a careful analysis of all the factors that affect the market's longer-term performance. The discussions in this section are designed to help traders move from focusing on each individual day timeframe situation to a more holistic, longer-term evaluation. Only through a synthesis of both can one compile a winning record.

Long-Term Directional Conviction

In Day Timeframe Trading (Section I), we studied the progression of the information generated by the market in the day timeframe. More important, we examined how a variety of structural and logical relationships produced by the day timeframe auction process help to convey the directional conviction of the other timeframe. Because each day auction is a contributing element to the longer-term auction process, these same concepts apply equally well to longer-term market analysis. Not surprisingly, our analysis of the longer term returns us to the same two all-encompassing questions: "Which way is the market trying to go," and "Is it doing a good job in its attempts to go that way?" We will first discuss a series of facts that help us gauge attempted direction. Later, we examine the methods for evaluating directional performance. Finally, we unveil an easy, simplistic Long-Term Activity Record designed to assist a trader in forming a holistic image of the Big Picture.

Attempted Direction: Which Way Is the Market Trying to Go?

When either the other timeframe buyer or seller exerts a greater influence on price, a variety of observable, longer-term directional changes are generated by the market. Each is listed below and then discussed in detail on the following pages. They are:

1. Auction Rotations
2. Range Extension
3. Long-Term Excess
4. Buying/Selling Composite Days

It is important to remember that these are merely *attempted* direction indicators. A complete understanding must incorporate longer-term directional performance, which will be covered in the latter portion of Section II.

Auction Rotations   In Day Timeframe Trading, we detailed a quick method for evaluating the cumulative directional attempts of a day's auction rotations. This method, the Rotation Factor, enables a trader to measure attempted market direction by producing a value that represents the sum of each day's half-hour auction rotations. The theory behind the Rotation Factor is simple. If a greater number of time periods auction higher than lower, then the buyer is exerting greater control over price in the day timeframe—the market is trying to move higher.

The Rotation Factor is by no means an all-conclusive indication of future market direction. It is, however, a useful tool in determining which way the market is trying to go in the day timeframe. Since a longer term auction is composed of a series of day timeframe auctions, recording and comparing the daily Rotation Factor can help traders gauge the strength and relative change in a market's longer-term directional conviction.

Range Extension   Range extension signals the entrance of the other timeframe participant beyond the initial balance set up by the locals. Persistent range extension in several time periods indicates that trade is being facilitated better in the direction of the range extension. Observing and recording continual range extension on successive days reveals a longer-term tendency in the market. In Figure 4–59 for example, five consecutive days in the Swiss franc saw strong initiative buying range extension, which alerted traders to the presence of strong other timeframe buyers fueling the bull trend.

Long-Term Excess   Earlier, we defined short-term excess as the aggressive entry of the other timeframe participant as price moves away from value, creating a tail in the day timeframe. An example of short-term excess is evident in gold on May 2, 1989 (Figure 4–60). The six tick buying tail in I period was generated by strong responsive buyers who quickly took advantage of a selling price probe (range extension) below value. Day timeframe excess not only provides continual, recordable clues regarding other timeframe directional conviction, but it also often stands as the pivot point marking a longer-term directional move. The strong buying tail in gold, for instance, supported the market during subsequent trading sessions.

Longer-term excess is caused by the same forces that create day timeframe excess. When a price level is perceived to be too low in the longer term, for instance, the other timeframe buyer will enter the market aggressively, forcing price to quickly auction higher. Prices that are deemed below longer-term value generally form one of three types of excess: an island day, a long-term tail or a gap. Refer to the daily bar chart in Figure 4–61 for the following discussion of the three types of long term excess.

Island Days   January 3, 1989 (point A) displays the first of the three types of longer term excess, the "island day." Island days are formed by aggressive initiative activity that causes price to gap above or below the previous day's range. The market spends the entire session trading at these higher or lower levels (attempting to validate price), but returns to previously established value on the following day, leaving behind an "island" of trade.

On the 3rd, the yen market opened 84 ticks above the high of December 30. After the gap higher open, the yen continued auctioning significantly higher, only to meet responsive sellers that were aggressive enough to reverse the day timeframe auction and close the yen on its lows. Because of the weak close on a day that had opened so far out of balance, the possibility was relatively high that long-term buying excess had formed. Buying excess was confirmed when the yen gapped some 50 ticks lower on the open of the following day, creating longer-term excess in the form of an island. Island days are the most extreme form of excess

Figure 4–60 Long-term excess—day timeframe tail occurring in June Gold, May 2,1989.

3813	.
3812	z
3811	z
3810	z
3809	zF
3808	yzAF
3807	yzAFJ
3806	yzADEFJK
3805	yzABDEFJK
3804	yzABDEFGJK
3803	yBCDEFGHJK
3802	BCDEFGHJK
3801	BCDGHIJK
3800	BCDHIJK
3799	BCDIJ
3798	BDIJ
3797	IJ
3796	I
3795	I
3794	I
3793	I
3792	I
3791	I
3790	.

and often provide lasting resistance against future auction attempts. Figure 4–61 displays another island day occurring in the yen on April 4 (point G).

Long-Term Tails   The second form of excess does not exhibit the violent gap activity that makes an island day so easy to identify. On a daily bar chart, this lesser form of price rejection looks more like a day timeframe tail at the end of a longer-term trend. One such long-term tail is evident in the Japanese yen on January 19 in Figure 4–61 (point B). Compare the enlarged bar chart in Figure 4–62 to the segmented Profile of the day timeframe tail we described earlier in gold (Figure 4–63). The half hour auction rotations are strikingly similar to the daily auction rotations. This is an excellent example of how the auction process applies to all timeframes. Day and longer-term excess is created by the same activity occurring over varying lengths of time.

Referring again to Figure 4–61, the yen had been in a down trend since the island day on January 3. On the 19th, the yen opened substantially below the 18th's lows. The gap lower suggested that the down trend was continuing. However, the responsive buyer perceived price to be below value and entered the market aggressively, creating an unusually strong "longer-term" buying tail. The close on the highs signified staunch rejection and that intermediate to longer term excess may have formed.

When using a standard bar chart, every new low or high, it seems, has the potential to be longer-term excess. How does one know which is excess and which is actually a developing probe to new value? Much like the formation of a potential day timeframe tail that is not confirmed until the following half-hour time period, a longer-term tail cannot be positively confirmed until the following day. However, as in the day timeframe, the market does provide reliable early clues regarding the formation of longer-term tails. For example, examine the activity of January 13 and 18 (points C and D), two days with similar ranges. Both trading sessions recorded new lows, but they also closed near their lower extremes, indicating continual seller presence. In contrast, on the 19th the yen gapped lower on the open, but closed on the *upper* extreme. The yen had overextended itself to the downside, at least temporarily. The responsive other timeframe buyer entered and quickly auctioned price higher, establishing potential intermediate to longer-term excess.

Another longer-term tail occurred three trading days later on the 24th (point E in Figure 4–61), as the seller reentered the market after a substantially higher open and closed the yen on the lows. This price reversal, occurring so soon after the relatively strong rejection on the 19th, reasserted the strength of the downward trend.

Figure 4–61   Long-term excess in the Japanese Yen. Data courtesy of Commodity Quote Graphics.

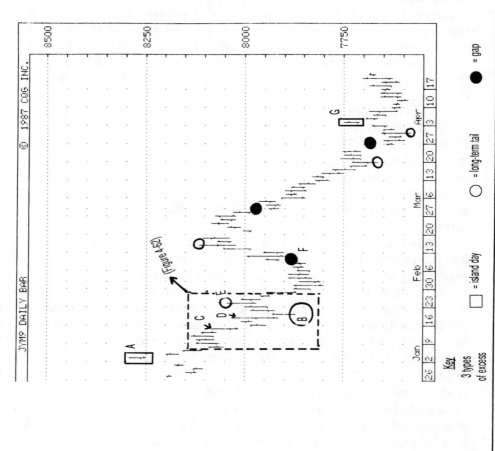

Figure 4–62 Close-up of excess in the Japanese Yen. Data courtesy of Commodity Quote Graphics.

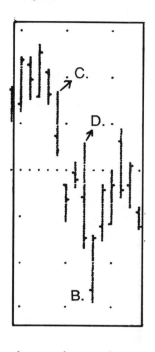

Figure 4–63 Segmented profile of excess in Gold, May 2, 1989.

Price	y	z	A	B	C	D	E	F	G	H	I	J	K
3813													
3812		z											
3811		z											
3810		z											
3809		z						F					
3808	y	z	A					F					
3807	y	z	A					F				J	
3806	y	z	A			D	E	F				J	K
3805	y	z	A	B		D	E	F				J	K
3804	y	z	A	B		D	E	F	G			J	K
3803	y			B	C	D	E	F	G	H		J	K
3802				B	C	D	E	F	G	H		J	K
3801				B	C	D			G	H	I	J	K
3800				B	C	D				H	I	J	K
3799				B	C	D					I	J	
3798				B		D					I	J	
3797											I		
3796											I		
3795											I		
3794											I		
3793											I		
3792											I		
3791											I		
3790													

Gaps   The final type of long-term excess is a gap. A gap is caused by initiative other timeframe participants who, between the market's close and the following day's open, change their perceptions of value. Price rejection, in effect, occurs overnight, as the market gaps above or below the previous day's extremes on the following day.

On February 9 (point F in Figure 4–61), for example, the yen gapped above the 8th's highs, igniting a buying auction away from the balance region that had formed from January 30 through February 8. During a gap, a market does not create the typical tail formation that so often signifies excess. Rather, the gap itself indicates swift price rejection (an "invisible tail"). In comparison to tails, gaps are actually a stronger, albeit less obvious form of excess. Note that island days are always confirmed by gaps.

Summary   Both short- and long-term excess, when properly identified, provide reliable indications of a market's directional conviction. The price levels at which the other timeframe participant enters the market and creates excess are valuable reference points for the longer-term trader. Excess is most often used as support or resistance for longer-term trade location. In addition, if the market returns and trades through the point of excess, a trader knows that the opposite activity is fueled by a high level of confidence and will most likely display continuation.

Buying/Selling Composite Days   A quick way to assess a market's attempted direction is known as composite analysis. Composite analysis simply evaluates where the majority of the day's trade took place relative to the day's open; it is performed by dividing the range into four equal parts. If the open is in the top or bottom one fourth, it is designated a "composite" day. A composite buying day occurs when the open resides in the bottom fourth of the day's range. Conversely, a composite selling day is characterized by an open within the top fourth of the range. An open in the center half indicates low directional conviction in either direction. Point B in Figure 4–61 shows a buying composite day in the yen. Figure 4–64 illustrates the composite methodology.

The logic behind this theory is relatively simple. If a market spends most of the day auctioning above the open, then the market is attempting to go higher. If the market trades below the open for most of the day, then it is trying to auction lower. Keep in mind that composite analysis does not consider the question "How good a job is it doing in its attempts to auction in that direction?" Remember the "illusion" that can arise from a market that gaps higher and auctions down all day, but develops *higher* value. Like all other directional measures, composite analysis must be evaluated in conjunction with value area relationships

Figure 4–64   Composite days.

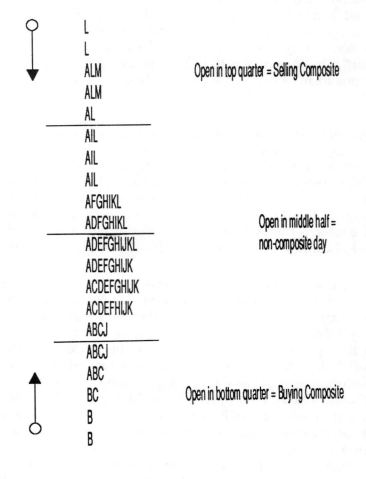

L
L
ALM   Open in top quarter = Selling Composite
ALM
AL
AIL
AIL
AIL
AFGHIKL
ADFGHIKL   Open in middle half =
ADEFGHIJKL   non-composite day
ADEFGHIJK
ACDEFGHIJK
ACDEFHIJK
ABCJ
ABCJ
ABC
BC   Open in bottom quarter = Buying Composite
B
B

and the level of trade facilitation generated by the market's attempt to auction in a given direction.

Summary   Any combination of directional measures may be present on a given day. For instance, a particular trading session might exhibit composite buying structure, a positive Rotation Factor, initiative buying tails and range extension, and higher value—unanimous indications of a market that is trying to auction higher. On some days, however, the indicators will contradict themselves. When directional measures conflict, they cancel each other out, indicating a market less confident in its directional course.

Yet, the answers to the question, "Which way is the market trying to go?" cannot stand alone. They must be considered in conjunction with the second Big Question, "Is the market doing a good job?"

Directional Performance: Is the Market Doing a Good Job in Its Attempts to Get There?

Let us return to our local grocer for a moment. Suppose that the grocer decides to expand his business by moving into a bigger building, in hopes of increasing his market share. In trading terms, his attempted direction is "up." Once the move is made, the question then becomes, "Will the expansion facilitate more trade?"

Over the ensuing weeks, the grocer finds that increased shelf space does not attract new customers. His business (and expense) has moved up, but transactional volume has not. Disappointed, the grocer realizes that the small community cannot support a larger store. Faced with rising overhead and dwindling profits, he moves back into his old building.

The futures market acts in a similar fashion. Relying solely on which way a market is trying to go can lead to financial disaster, unless you can also gauge the effectiveness of the market's attempts to go that way. Monitoring attempted direction for directional performance—determining how good of a job it is doing—is the key to a complete market understanding and longer-term trading results. Once attempted direction is known, three comparative factors are useful in evaluating a market's directional performance:

1. Volume
2. Value-Area Placement
3. Value-Area Width

Volume   As we get deeper into the longer-term forces behind directional conviction, one element stands high above the rest when it comes to evaluating directional performance—volume. Not surprisingly, volume is also the best measure of a market's ability to facilitate trade. Once attempted direction is known, volume should be used as the primary means of determining directional performance.

Put simply, the greater the volume of transactions, the better trade is being facilitated. In our grocery store example, a larger store did not generate additional volume and consequently failed. Similarly, in the futures market, a price movement that fails to generate a fair amount of volume as it auctions through time will likely not continue for very long in the same direction.

Evaluating Changes in Volume   To determine whether or not volume is increasing, it is necessary to compare each day to previous volume figures. However, there is no standard number of day timeframe transactions in any market, for volume evolves with a market's changing activity. The key to recognizing change is to think of volume more in terms of market share than in the actual number of transactions occurring (except, of course, when the number of transactions drops below that which signifies a liquid market). Therefore, a trader must keep a running record of volume to be able to detect any significant departures from the current average. This average will vary depending on your trading timeframe.

Volume as a Measure of Directional Performance   Suppose that a movie theater raises the price of admission. In the following weeks, ticket sales drop substantially. At higher ticket prices, the theater is not facilitating trade for the movie-goer. If the theater is going to stay in business, it will have to lower price. Decreased volume indicates a rejection of higher prices.

Volume plays the same role in evaluating the futures market's directional performance. For illustration, imagine that the market's attempted direction on a given day is up, based on a positive Rotation Factor and buying range extension. If the buying auctions are generating healthy or increased volume (relative to your determined norm), then the market is successfully facilitating trade with the buyer. Conversely, *lower* volume on a day attempting to move higher suggests that the market is not accepting the buying attempts.

Value-Area Placement   A structural indicator that helps us better refine the level of directional performance is value-area placement. Through an evaluation of the relationship of one day's value area to the next, we can move beyond simply determining if the market is doing a good job, to *how* good of a job it is doing. In other words, if attempted direction is up and volume is healthy, what impact does that have on value? Were buyers successful in placing value higher? How successful were they? Was value unchanged, overlapping-to-higher, or completely higher?

Let us briefly describe the different relationships that can exist between two trading session's value areas. First, value can form clearly higher or clearly lower, exhibiting obvious directional performance. Second, value can overlap to one side or the other, indicating a lesser degree of change. Third, when the value area is contained entirely within the previous day's value area, it is known as an "inside day." The market is in balance and is not facilitating trade with either participant. Finally, an "outside day" occurs when a day's value area overlaps the previous day's value area on both extremes, and represents greater trade facilitation. Much like a Neutral day, if an outside day closes in the middle of the range, the market is in balance. If it closes on an extreme, however, there is a "victor" in the day timeframe battle for control. A close on the highs, for example, would indicate directional performance favoring the buyer. Figure 4–65 illustrates these common value-area relationships.

Value-area placement often generates signals contrary to day timeframe attempted direction. Figure 4–66 demonstrates such a scenario occurring in the Treasury bond market. On September 12, bonds opened unchanged to higher and spent the entire day auctioning down. The result was a negative Rotation Factor, selling composite structure, and continued selling range extension—clearly a market trying to move lower in the day timeframe. However, higher value was still maintained. While day timeframe structure indicated seller dominance, value-area placement suggested that the buyer was still in control in the longer timeframe.

Evaluating Directional Performance through Combined Volume and Value-Area Placement   Arriving at a final evaluation of directional performance is like baking a cake—layer by layer. First, we must define attempted direction. Second, we evaluate trade facilitation according to volume. And finally, we must determine the relative success of that trade facilitation according to its impact on value-area placement.

In general, if attempted direction is up, volume is above average (or at least average) and value is higher, then the market is successfully facilitating trade at higher prices. However, if attempted direction is up and volume is *lower*, then higher prices are cutting off activity—the buying auctions are resulting in poor trade facilitation. If the buying attempts also result in lower value, then the other timeframe seller is still

Figure 4–65 Value area relationships.

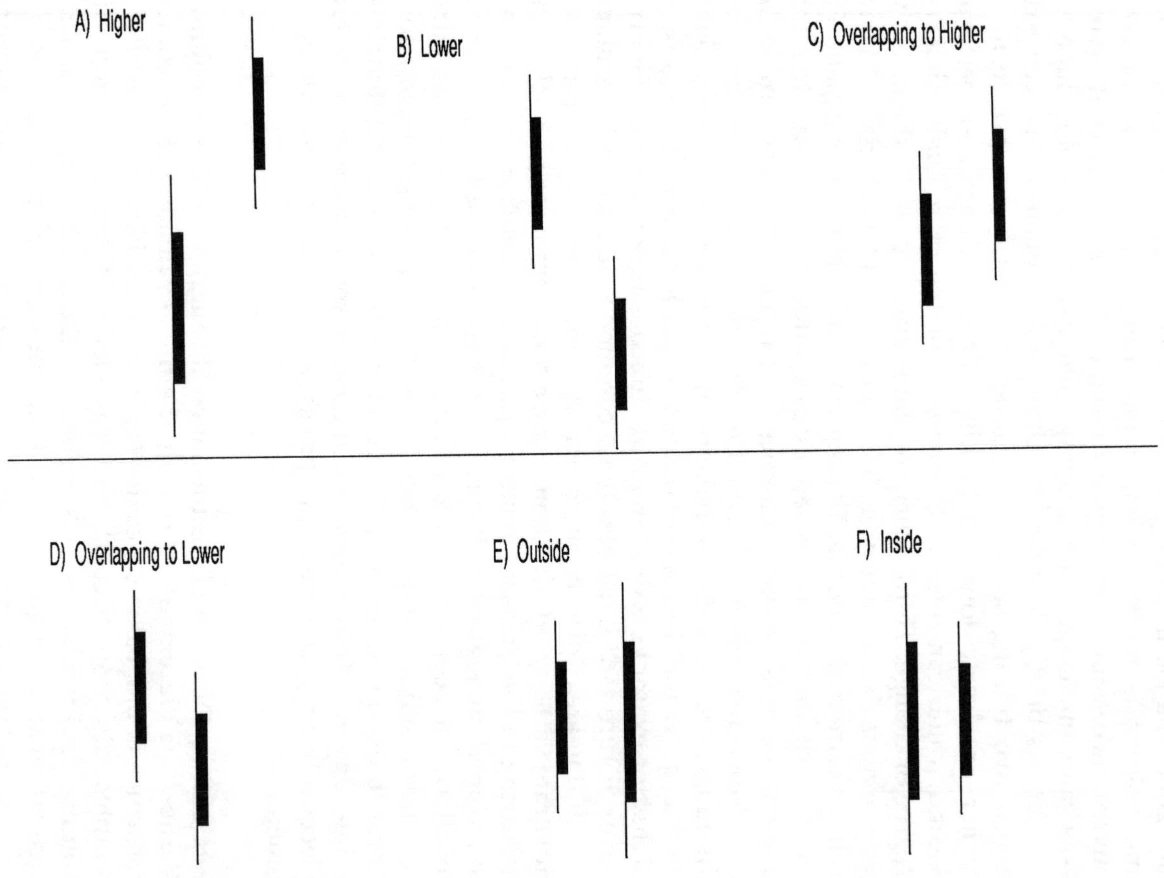

A) Higher

B) Lower

C) Overlapping to Higher

D) Overlapping to Lower

E) Outside

F) Inside

Figure 4–66 Directional performance. December Treasury Bonds, September 9 and 12, 1988.

Att Dir	Relationship	Directional Performance
Down	Lower Volume, Higher Value	Strong

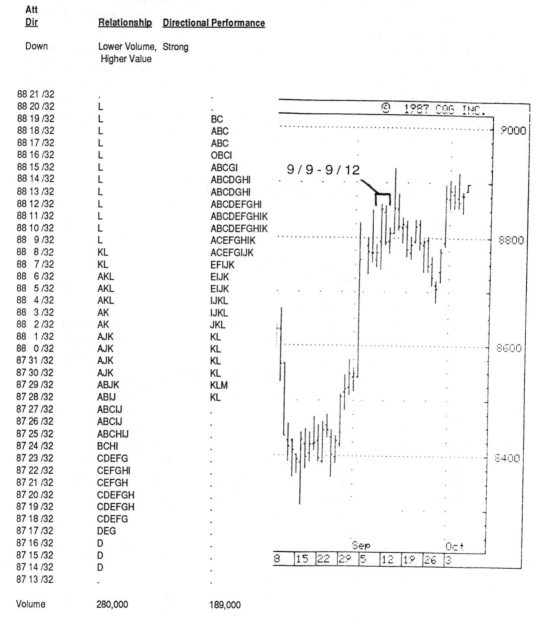

88 21 /32	.	.
88 20 /32	L	.
88 19 /32	L	BC
88 18 /32	L	ABC
88 17 /32	L	ABC
88 16 /32	L	OBCI
88 15 /32	L	ABCGI
88 14 /32	L	ABCDGHI
88 13 /32	L	ABCDGHI
88 12 /32	L	ABCDEFGHI
88 11 /32	L	ABCDEFGHIK
88 10 /32	L	ABCDEFGHIK
88 9 /32	L	ACEFGHIK
88 8 /32	KL	ACEFGIJK
88 7 /32	KL	EFIJK
88 6 /32	AKL	EIJK
88 5 /32	AKL	EIJK
88 4 /32	AKL	IJKL
88 3 /32	AK	IJKL
88 2 /32	AK	JKL
88 1 /32	AJK	KL
88 0 /32	AJK	KL
87 31 /32	AJK	KL
87 30 /32	AJK	KL
87 29 /32	ABJK	KLM
87 28 /32	ABIJ	KL
87 27 /32	ABCIJ	.
87 26 /32	ABCIJ	.
87 25 /32	ABCHIJ	.
87 24 /32	BCHI	.
87 23 /32	CDEFG	.
87 22 /32	CEFGHI	.
87 21 /32	CEFGH	.
87 20 /32	CDEFGH	.
87 19 /32	CDEFGH	.
87 18 /32	CDEFG	.
87 17 /32	DEG	.
87 16 /32	D	.
87 15 /32	D	.
87 14 /32	D	.
87 13 /32	.	.
Volume	280,000	189,000

in control of the market, despite day timeframe buyer dominance. The market must then move lower to resume balanced trade, much like the aforementioned movie theater. Figure 4–67 illustrates the combined effect of volume and value area in determining directional performance for the above two scenarios.

Listed below are 30 different relationships based on volume, value-area placement, and attempted direction. Six of them are briefly detailed in the following discussion. The accompanying figures include an inset bar chart to show the activity following the day highlighted by each example. In addition, note that the volume comparisons in these examples are relative to the previous day, not a predefined average.

Table 4–1   Directional Performance Relationships

Attempted Direction	Relationship	Directional Performance
1. Up	Higher volume, higher value (see Figure 4–68)	Very strong
2. Up	Lower volume, higher value (see Figure 4–69)	Slowing
3. Up	Unchanged volume, higher value	Strong, continuing
4. Up	Higher volume, OL*/higher value	Moderately strong
5. Up	Lower volume, OL/higher value	Slowing, balancing
6. Up	Unchanged volume, OL/higher value	Mod. strong, balancing
7. Up	Higher volume, unchanged value	Balancing
8. Up	Lower volume, unchanged value	Balancing, weakening
9. Up	Unchanged volume, unchanged value	Balancing
10. Up	Higher volume, lower value	Unclear
11. Up	Lower volume, lower value	Weak
12. Up	Unchanged volume, lower value	Weak, balancing
13. Up	Higher volume, OL/lower value	Weakening
14. Up	Lower volume, OL/lower value (see Figure 4–70)	Moderately weak
15. Up	Unchanged volume, OL/lower value	Weakening, balancing
16. Down	Higher volume, lower value	Very weak
17. Down	Lower volume, lower value	Slowing
18. Down	Unchanged volume, lower value	Weak, continuing
19. Down	Higher volume, OL*/lower value	Moderately weak
20. Down	Lower volume, OL/lower value	Slowing, balancing

Table 4–1 continues

Table 4–1   Directional Performance Relationships
Continued

Attempted Direction	Relationship	Directional Performance
21. Down	Unchanged volume, OL/lower value (see Figure 4–72)	Mod. weak, balancing
22. Down	Higher volume, unchanged value	Balancing
23. Down	Lower volume, unchanged value	Balancing, strengthening
24. Down	Unchanged volume, unchanged value	Balancing
25. Down	Higher volume, higher value	Unclear
26. Down	Lower volume, higher value (see Figure 4–66)	Strong
27. Down	Unchanged volume, higher value	Strong, balancing
28. Down	Higher volume, OL/higher value	Strengthening
29. Down	Lower volume, OL/higher value	Moderately strong
30. Down	Unchanged volume, OL/higher value	Strengthening, balancing

* OL = overlapping

Figure 4–68, Treasury Bonds on September 1 and 2, 1988   Treasury bonds gapped open above the previous day's range and drove sharply higher. Attempted direction was clearly up, as witnessed by an initiative buying tail, initiative buying range extension, a positive Rotation Factor and buying composite structure. Substantially higher volume and the resulting higher value confirmed that the directional performance of the buyer was strong.

Figure 4–69, Gold on July 28 and 29, 1988   The gold market on the 29th was clearly attempting to auction higher. And, although the buying auctions managed to build higher value, volume declined, indicating poor directional performance. Underlying market conditions were weakening. The inset bar chart shows the subsequent return to seller control.

Figure 4–70, Treasury Bonds on April 14 and 15, 1988   After a lower opening on April 15, bonds spent most of the day attempting to auction higher. Longer-term traders relying solely on attempted direction might have bought, perceiving day timeframe buyer control and an opportunity to acquire relatively good intermediate-term trade location. However, the upward auction attempts actually discouraged trade and were unable to

Figure 4–67   Volume/value area relationships.

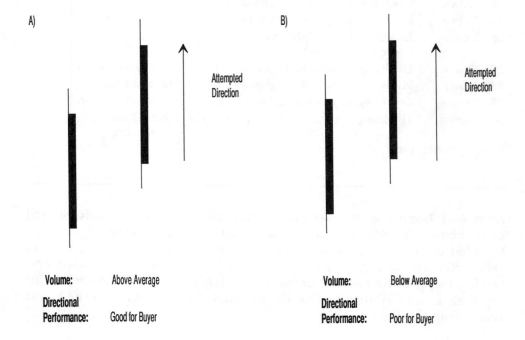

Figure 4–68   Directional performance. December Treasury Bonds, September 1 and 2, 1988. Data courtesy of Commodity Quote Graphics.

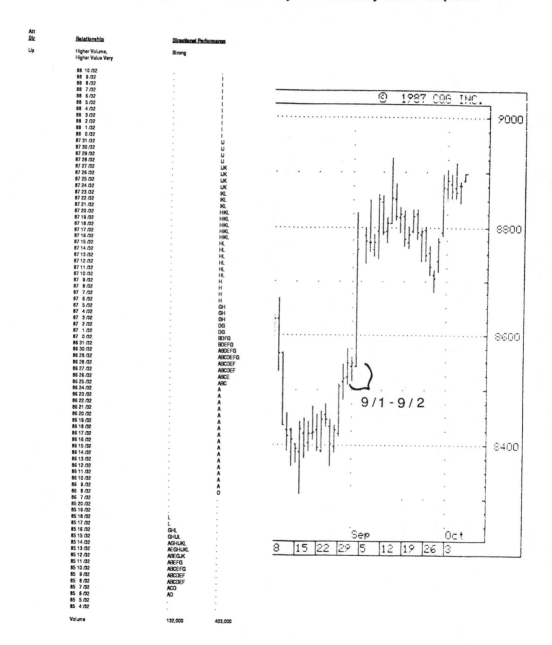

Figure 4–69 Directional performance. August Gold, July 28 and 29, 1988. Data courtesy of Commodity Quote Graphics.

Att Dir	Relationship	Directional Performance
Up	Lower Volume, Higher Value	Strong

4378	.	.
4376	.	C
4374	.	AC
4372	.	ABC
4370	.	ABC
4368	.	ABC
4366	.	ABC
4364	.	ABCDK
4362	.	ABCDFK
4360	.	ABDFJKL
4358	.	ADFJK
4356	.	ADFJK
4354	.	ADEFGJK
4352	.	ADEFGIJ
4350	.	AEFGHIJ
4348	.	AEFGHI
4346	.	AEFGHI
4344	.	AFGH
4342	A	ZAFG
4340	A	ZAFG
4338	A	Z
4336	AFI	Z
4334	YABEFIJ	YZ
4332	YZABEFIJ	YZ
4330	YZABEFGIJK	O
4328	YZABDEFGHIJK	.
4326	YZABCDEFGHIJK	.
4324	YZABCDEGHIJKL	.
4322	YZACDEGHJK	.
4320	YZCDEHJK .	.
4318	YCDHJ	.
4316	YC	.
4314	Y	.
4312	Y	.
4310	O	.
4308	Y	.
4306	Y	.
4304	Y	.
4302	Y	.
4300	Y	.
4298	Y	.
4296	.	.
Volume	56,000	37,000

Figure 4–70 Directional performance. June Treasury Bonds, April 14 and 15, 1988.

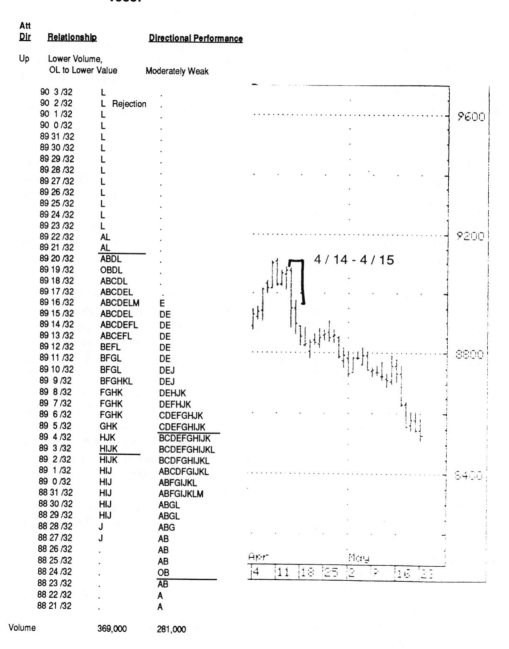

Att Dir	Relationship	Directional Performance
Up	Lower Volume, OL to Lower Value	Moderately Weak

90 3 /32	L	.
90 2 /32	L Rejection	.
90 1 /32	L	.
90 0 /32	L	.
89 31 /32	L	.
89 30 /32	L	.
89 29 /32	L	.
89 28 /32	L	.
89 27 /32	L	.
89 26 /32	L	.
89 25 /32	L	.
89 24 /32	L	.
89 23 /32	L	.
89 22 /32	AL	.
89 21 /32	AL	.
89 20 /32	ABDL	.
89 19 /32	OBDL	.
89 18 /32	ABCDL	.
89 17 /32	ABCDEL	.
89 16 /32	ABCDELM	E
89 15 /32	ABCDEL	DE
89 14 /32	ABCDEFL	DE
89 13 /32	ABCEFL	DE
89 12 /32	BEFL	DE
89 11 /32	BFGL	DE
89 10 /32	BFGL	DEJ
89 9 /32	BFGHKL	DEJ
89 8 /32	FGHK	DEHJK
89 7 /32	FGHK	DEFHJK
89 6 /32	FGHK	CDEFGHJK
89 5 /32	GHK	CDEFGHIJK
89 4 /32	HJK	BCDEFGHIJK
89 3 /32	HIJK	BCDEFGHIJKL
89 2 /32	HIJK	BCDFGHIJKL
89 1 /32	HIJ	ABCDFGIJKL
89 0 /32	HIJ	ABFGIJKL
88 31 /32	HIJ	ABFGIJKLM
88 30 /32	HIJ	ABGL
88 29 /32	HIJ	ABGL
88 28 /32	J	ABG
88 27 /32	J	AB
88 26 /32	.	AB
88 25 /32	.	AB
88 24 /32	.	OB
88 23 /32	.	AB
88 22 /32	.	A
88 21 /32	.	A
Volume	369,000	281,000

return value to the levels of the previous day. The buyer's directional performance on this day was very poor and indicated longer term control was in the hands of the other timeframe seller.

Figure 4–71, Gold on September 19 and 20, 1988   On the 20th, gold opened and tested above the previous day's highs. When no continuation developed, other timeframe sellers entered the market and auctioned price lower all day. Attempted direction was down, accompanied by lower value and higher volume. Directional performance on this day clearly favored the seller.

Figure 4–72, S&P 500 on August 3 and 4, 1988   Attempted direction was obviously down on this Open-Drive selling day. However, the day's selling attempts only managed overlapping to lower value and basically unchanged volume. This scenario generally indicates a market that is continuing but slowing and coming into balance or a market that is in the midst of gradual transition. Subsequent trading sessions should be monitored carefully for signs of directional conviction.

Value-Area Width   One drawback to day trading is that exact volume figures are usually not available until after the trading session is over. However, one practical way to gauge the level of volume as the day develops is through the value-area width. On days where volume is relatively low, the value area and the length of the range tend to be narrow. For example, in Treasury bonds on April 17, 1989 (Figure 4–73), the value area was only two ticks wide. Volume was at a scarce 120 thousand contracts. In this particular case, the lack of facilitation was due to the fact that traders had balanced their positions in anticipation of the Producer Price Index figure to be released on the following day. Conversely, value areas tend to widen on days exhibiting higher volume (Figure 4–74). On April 27, the value area was a healthy 16 ticks wide. Volume on this day was just short of 600,000 contracts.

The logic behind this theory is that the wider the value area, the greater the range of prices at which trade is being conducted. This results in increased participation, for as price auctions higher and lower, different timeframes are "brought in" to the market as they perceive price to be away from value. The farther price travels, the better the possibility that new activity will enter the market, thus creating greater trade facilitation (and higher volume).

We conducted a limited study comparing total volume with average value area width for Treasury Bonds from December 14, 1988, through June 22, 1989 (Figure 4–75). The data clearly showed a marked increase in volume on days with larger value areas. For example, the average

Figure 4–71 Directional performance. December Gold, September 19 and 20, 1988.

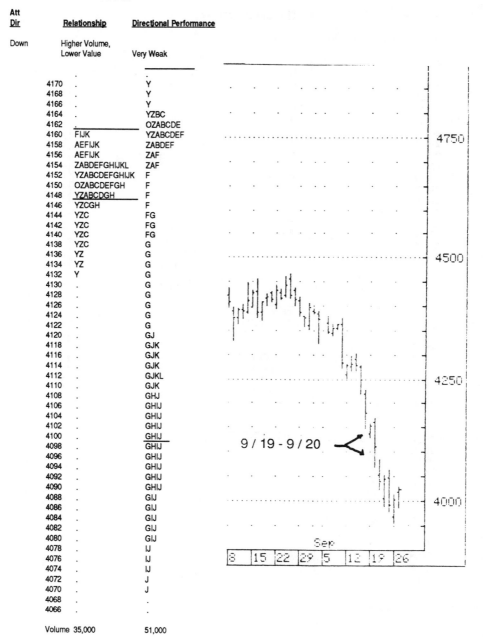

Att Dir	Relationship	Directional Performance
Down	Higher Volume, Lower Value	Very Weak

4170	.	Y
4168	.	Y
4166	.	Y
4164	.	YZBC
4162	.	OZABCDE
4160	FIJK	YZABCDEF
4158	AEFIJK	ZABDEF
4156	AEFIJK	ZAF
4154	ZABDEFGHIJKL	ZAF
4152	YZABCDEFGHIJK	F
4150	OZABCDEFGH	F
4148	YZABCDGH	F
4146	YZCGH	F
4144	YZC	FG
4142	YZC	FG
4140	YZC	FG
4138	YZC	G
4136	YZ	G
4134	YZ	G
4132	Y	G
4130	.	G
4128	.	G
4126	.	G
4124	.	G
4122	.	G
4120	.	GJ
4118	.	GJK
4116	.	GJK
4114	.	GJK
4112	.	GJKL
4110	.	GJK
4108	.	GHJ
4106	.	GHIJ
4104	.	GHIJ
4102	.	GHIJ
4100	.	GHIJ
4098	.	GHIJ
4096	.	GHIJ
4094	.	GHIJ
4092	.	GHIJ
4090	.	GHIJ
4088	.	GIJ
4086	.	GIJ
4084	.	GIJ
4082	.	GIJ
4080	.	GIJ
4078	.	IJ
4076	.	IJ
4074	.	IJ
4072	.	J
4070	.	J
4068	.	.
4066	.	.

| Volume 35,000 | | 51,000 |

9 / 19 - 9 / 20

Figure 4–72 Directional performance. September S&P 500, August 3 and 4, 1988. Data courtesy of Commodity Quote Graphics.

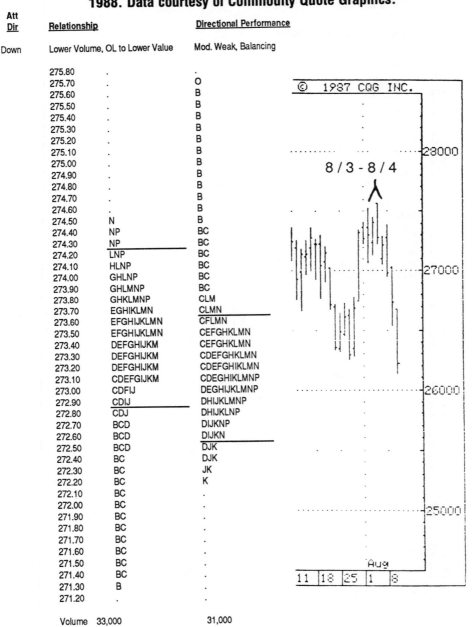

Att Dir	Relationship	Directional Performance
Down	Lower Volume, OL to Lower Value	Mod. Weak, Balancing

275.80	.	.
275.70	.	O
275.60	.	B
275.50	.	B
275.40	.	B
275.30	.	B
275.20	.	B
275.10	.	B
275.00	.	B
274.90	.	B
274.80	.	B
274.70	.	B
274.60	.	B
274.50	N	B
274.40	NP	BC
274.30	NP	BC
274.20	LNP	BC
274.10	HLNP	BC
274.00	GHLNP	BC
273.90	GHLMNP	BC
273.80	GHKLMNP	CLM
273.70	EGHIKLMN	CLMN
273.60	EFGHIJKLMN	CFLMN
273.50	EFGHIJKLMN	CEFGHKLMN
273.40	DEFGHIJKM	CEFGHKLMN
273.30	DEFGHIJKM	CDEFGHKLMN
273.20	DEFGHIJKM	CDEFGHIKLMN
273.10	CDEFGIJKM	CDEGHIKLMNP
273.00	CDFIJ	DEGHIJKLMNP
272.90	CDIJ	DHIJKLMNP
272.80	CDJ	DHIJKLNP
272.70	BCD	DIJKNP
272.60	BCD	DIJKN
272.50	BCD	DJK
272.40	BC	DJK
272.30	BC	JK
272.20	BC	K
272.10	BC	.
272.00	BC	.
271.90	BC	.
271.80	BC	.
271.70	BC	.
271.60	BC	.
271.50	BC	.
271.40	BC	.
271.30	B	.
271.20	.	.
Volume 33,000		31,000

Figure 4–73 Narrow value area. Treasury Bonds, April 17, 1989.

VOLUME/FUTURES SUMMARY REPORT FOR 04 17 89

COMMODITY -- T-BOND (CBOT) DAY   JUN 89

Volume Summary

Price	Volume	%Vol	%Cti1	%Cti2	%Cti3	%Cti4	Brackets
8828	774	0.7	31.0	27.5	25.3	16.1	CD
8827	12866	10.9	52.9	23.2	7.2	16.6	Z$ABCDK
8826	46552	39.6	55.9	16.0	5.2	22.9	Z$ABCDEFIJKL
8825	42452	36.1	55.1	15.0	6.2	23.8	Z$ABCDEFGHIJKLM
8824	15050	12.8	48.7	18.4	3.1	29.7	Z$BCFGHJLM

70%	8826	89004	75.6	55.5	15.5	5.7 23.3	ABCDEFGHIJKLMZ$
V-A	8825						

Volume for T-BOND (CBOT) DAY   JUN 89   117694
Volume for all T-BOND (CBOT) DAY   120250 <-- LOW VOLUME

Figure 4–74 Wide value area. Treasury Bonds, April 27, 1989.

VOLUME/FUTURES SUMMARY REPORT FOR 04 27 89

COMMODITY -- T-BOND (CBOT) DAY   JUN 89

Volume Summary

	Price	Volume	%Vol	%Cti1	%Cti2	%Cti3	%Cti4	Brackets
	9011	1660	0.3	51.3	0.3	0.0	48.4	H
	9010	6538	1.1	56.3	16.2	3.3	24.1	FH
	9009	21786	3.8	49.2	13.4	4.4	33.0	FH
	9008	21462	3.7	58.9	16.1	4.4	20.6	FGH
	9007	19646	3.4	56.6	17.6	4.6	21.1	EFGH
	9006	38296	6.6	58.8	20.0	5.2	16.1	EFGHIJKL
	9005	49836	8.6	56.2	17.5	8.0	18.3	EFGHIJKL
	9004	53246	9.2	56.0	15.7	6.3	22.1	EFGHIJKL
	9003	64348	11.1	56.9	16.5	8.3	18.3	DEFGIJKL
	9002	36050	6.2	56.1	12.3	7.6	24.0	DEFIJKL
	9001	14354	2.5	55.1	15.0	4.9	25.0	DEFJL
	9000	9616	1.7	56.2	13.3	6.3	24.2	DLM
	8931	12282	2.1	57.3	12.1	2.6	27.9	DLM
	8930	21772	3.8	54.9	17.8	3.0	24.3	DL
	8929	18898	3.3	58.3	11.6	3.0	27.1	DL
	8928	3542	0.6	55.3	10.2	4.6	29.9	D
	8927	3576	0.6	53.1	22.0	4.7	20.2	D
	8926	12284	2.1	57.6	17.2	5.0	20.2	$CD
	8925	25928	4.5	59.3	19.6	3.0	18.1	$CD
	8924	21430	3.7	60.9	15.4	3.9	19.8	Z$CD
	8923	21782	3.8	62.4	12.2	5.4	20.1	Z$C
	8922	26662	4.6	53.0	19.2	7.3	20.4	Z$ABC
	8921	27352	4.7	59.8	18.7	3.9	17.5	Z$ABC
	8920	38648	6.7	58.0	14.9	7.9	19.1	ZABC
	8919	4298	0.7	57.8	14.4	5.4	22.5	ZABC
	8918	1472	0.3	37.0	11.6	3.4	48.0	AC
	8917	560	0.1	52.0	1.4	12.9	33.8	C
70%	9011	409192	70.9	56.3	15.9	5.9	21.9	CDEFGHIJKLM$
V-A	8926							

				%CTI1	%CTI2	%CTI3	%CTI4
Volume for T-BOND (CBOT) DAY JUN 89			577324	56.9	16.1	5.8	21.2
Volume for all T-BOND (CBOT) DAY			598492	56.5	16.1	6.1	21.2

Figure 4–75   Value area width relative to volume. Treasury Bonds, December 14, 1988-June 22,1989. Data courtesy of CISCO and Commodity Quote Graphics.

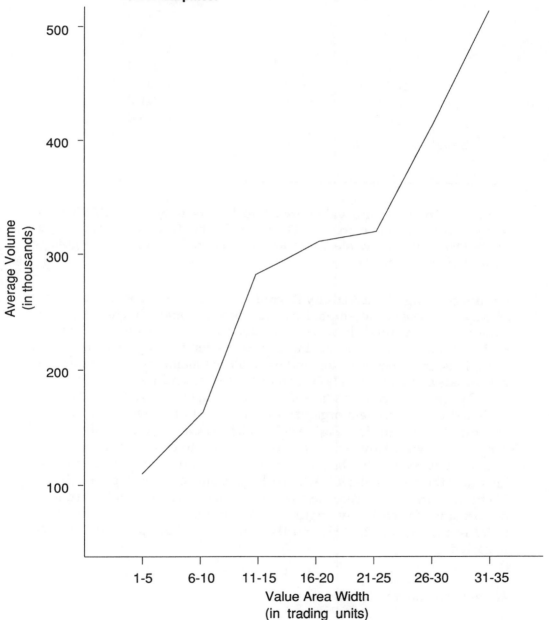

Table 4–2   Results for Six-Month Period in Treasury Bonds

Value-Area Width	Average Volume
1–5	127,000
6–10	188,000
11–15	284,000
16–20	310,000
21–25	313,000
26–30	417,000*
31–35	417,000*

* Small sample size

volume on days with a value area 1 to 5 ticks wide was 127,000 contracts. Days with value areas of 11 to 15 ticks, however, averaged roughly 284,000 contracts, while value areas of 21 to 25 ticks were regularly around 313,00 contracts.

Summary: Long-Term Activity Record   We have now covered a variety of ways to measure attempted market direction and directional performance. Keep in mind, however, that focusing on just one method can lead to tunnel vision and an incomplete understanding of true market conditions. It is necessary to synthesize all the elements of direction and performance to arrive at a holistic market understanding.

Figure 4–76 contains a simplified "Long-Term Activity Record" designed to help traders organize the answers to the two Big Questions addressed in this section. Figure 4–76 is left blank for you to pull out and copy if you wish. However, we encourage you to create your own long-term activity record that better fits your needs and trading timeframe. To illustrate the use of the LTAR, we have isolated a brief period in the Soybean market, and recorded the attempted direction and directional performance for each day. Figures 4–77 through 4–85 show Soybean activity from May 16-22, 1989, and the completed LTAR's that correspond to each day.

Long-Term Auction Rotations

The auction process is akin to a vertical tug-of-war, with price moving higher when buyers are in control and lower when sellers are in control.

Figure 4–76   Long-term activity record.

---

*Market:*_____   *Date:*_____

Attempted Direction: *Buyer*   *Seller*

1. Rotation Factor (   )
2. Range Extension
3. Tails
4. Buying/Selling Composite

Overall Attempted Direction: *Higher*   *Lower*   *Neutral*

Comments:

Directional Performance:

1. Volume:
Daily: (   )   Higher   Lower   Unchanged
Auction Average: (   )   Higher   Lower   Unchanged

2. Value-Area Placement:
                            Higher OL/High Lower OL/Low Unchgd.

3. Value-Area Width: Wider   Average   Narrower

Comments:

Expected Results:

Figure 4–77   July Soybeans, May 16, 1989.

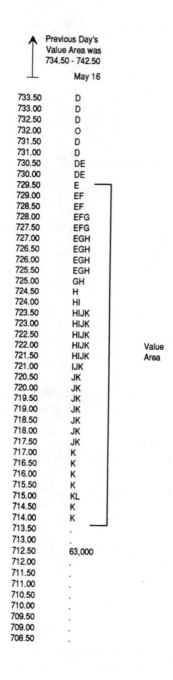

Previous Day's
Value Area was
734.50 - 742.50

May 16

733.50	D
733.00	D
732.50	D
732.00	O
731.50	D
731.00	D
730.50	DE
730.00	DE
729.50	E
729.00	EF
728.50	EF
728.00	EFG
727.50	EFG
727.00	EGH
726.50	EGH
726.00	EGH
725.50	EGH
725.00	GH
724.50	H
724.00	HI
723.50	HIJK
723.00	HIJK
722.50	HIJK
722.00	HIJK
721.50	HIJK
721.00	IJK
720.50	JK
720.00	JK
719.50	JK
719.00	JK
718.50	JK
718.00	JK
717.50	JK
717.00	K
716.50	K
716.00	K
715.50	K
715.00	KL
714.50	K
714.00	K
713.50	.
713.00	.
712.50	63,000
712.00	.
711.50	.
711.00	.
710.50	.
710.00	.
709.50	.
709.00	.
708.50	.

Value
Area

Figure 4–78   Long-term activity record for July Soybeans, May 16, 1989.

Market: _Soybeans_   Date: _5-16-89_

Attempted Direction: *Buyer*   *Seller*

1. Rotation Factor   (-11)   ✗
2. Range Extension (Selling Trend day)   ✗
3. Tails   ✗
4. Buying/Selling Composite   ✗

Overall Attempted Direction: *Higher*   (*Lower*)   *Neutral*

Comments: **Strong Selling Trend day structure.**

Directional Performance:

1. Volume:
   Daily: (63,000)   (Higher) Lower   Unchanged
   Auction Average: (40,000)   (Higher) Lower   Unchanged

2. Value-Area Placement:
   Higher   OL/High (Lower) OL/Low   Unchgd.

3. Value-Area Width: (Wider)   Average   Narrower

Comments:
   Extremely high volume - trade facilitated with
        seller all day.

Expected Results:
   - Weak markets may balance after such an extreme selling
      day — should develop lower value Tomorrow.
   - Longer term sellers should hold short.

Figure 4–79 July Soybeans, May 16-17, 1989.

	May 16	May 17
	.	.
733.50	D	.
733.00	D	.
732.50	D	.
732.00	D	.
731.50	D	.
731.00	D	.
730.50	DE	.
730.00	DE	.
729.50	E	.
729.00	EF	.
728.50	EF	.
728.00	EFG	.
727.50	EFG	.
727.00	EGH	.
726.50	EGH	.
726.00	EGH	.
725.50	EGH	.
725.00	GH	.
724.50	H	.
724.00	HI	.
723.50	HIJK	.
723.00	HIJK	.
722.50	HIJK	.
722.00	HIJK	.
721.50	HIJK	.
721.00	IJK	.
720.50	JK	.
720.00	JK	.
719.50	JK	.
719.00	JK	J
718.50	JK	J
718.00	JK	J
717.50	JK	JK
717.00	K	JK
716.50	K	JK
716.00	K	OJK
715.50	K	DJK
715.00	K	DJK
714.50	K	DJK
714.00	K	DIJK
713.50	.	DIK
713.00	.	DHIK
712.50	.	DHIKL
712.00	.	DHIK
711.50	.	DFHIK
711.00	.	DEFHK
710.50	.	DEFGH
710.00	.	DEFGH
709.50	.	DEFG
709.00	.	EG
708.50	.	EG
708.00	.	E
707.50	.	E
707.00	.	E
706.50	.	.
	63,000	53,000

Figure 4–80   Long-term activity record for July Soybeans, May 17, 1989.

Market: **Soybeans**   Date: **5-17-89**

Attempted Direction: *Buyer*   *Seller*

1. Rotation Factor **(+2)**   ✗
2. Range Extension   ✗
3. Tails   ✗   ✗
4. Buying/Selling Composite   ✗

Overall Attempted Direction: *Higher*   *Lower*   (Neutral)

Comments:

Balancing day — expected.

Directional Performance:

1. Volume:
Daily: **(53,000)**   Higher (Lower) Unchanged
Auction Average: **(42,600)**   (Higher) Lower Unchanged

2. Value-Area Placement:
            Higher OL/High Lower (OL/Low) Unchgd.

3. Value-Area Width: Wider (Average) Narrower

Comments:
**Volume is still healthy, though no clear directional
conviction. Weak close.**

Expected Results:
**– Monitor for developing conviction Tomorrow.
– Longer term sellers should hold short.
– Shorter term sellers should be flat.**

Figure 4–81   July Soybeans, May 16-18, 1989.

	May 16	May 17	May 18
733.50	D	.	.
733.00	D	.	.
732.50	D	.	.
732.00	D	.	.
731.50	D	.	.
731.00	D	.	.
730.50	DE	.	.
730.00	DE	.	.
729.50	E	.	.
729.00	EF	.	.
728.50	EF	.	.
728.00	EFG	.	.
727.50	EFG	.	.
727.00	EGH	.	.
726.50	EGH	.	.
726.00	EGH	.	.
725.50	EGH	.	.
725.00	GH	.	.
724.50	H	.	.
724.00	HI	.	.
723.50	HIJK	.	.
723.00	HIJK	.	.
722.50	HIJK	.	.
722.00	HIJK	.	K
721.50	HIJK	.	K
721.00	IJK	.	KL
720.50	JK	.	K
720.00	JK	.	K
719.50	JK	.	K
719.00	JK	J	K
718.50	JK	J	EFGJK
718.00	JK	J	DEFGJK
717.50	JK	JK	DEFGHJK
717.00	K	JK	DEFGHIJK
716.50	K	JK	DEGHIJK
716.00	K	DJK	DEHIJK
715.50	K	DJK	DHJK
715.00	K	DJK	D
714.50	K	DJK	D
714.00	K	DIJK	D
713.50	.	DIK	D
713.00	.	DHIK	D
712.50	.	DHIK	O
712.00	.	DHIK	D
711.50	.	DFHIK	D
711.00	.	DEFHK	.
710.50	.	DEFGH	.
710.00	.	DEFGH	.
709.50	.	DEFG	.
709.00	.	EG	.
708.50	.	EG	.
708.00	.	E	.
707.50	.	E	.
707.00	.	E	.
706.50	.	.	.
		53,000	24,000

Figure 4–82   Long-term activity record for July Soybeans, May 18, 1989.

Market: _Soybeans_   Date: _5-18-89_

Attempted Direction: _Buyer_   _Seller_

1. Rotation Factor   (**+1**)   ✗
2. Range Extension   ✗
3. Tails   ✗   (K period is final period —
4. Buying/Selling Composite   ✗   does not count)

Overall Attempted Direction: (Higher)   _Lower_   _Neutral_

Comments:
Clearly attempting to auction higher. Early development of "P" formation looks like short covering (up to K period) — poor buyer facilitation.

Directional Performance:

1. Volume:
Daily: (**24,000**)   Higher   (Lower)   Unchanged
Auction Average: (**43,100**)   Higher   Lower   Unchanged

2. Value-Area Placement:
                 Higher (OL/High) Lower   OL/Low   Unchgd.

3. Value-Area Width: Wider   Average   (Narrower)

Comments:
Drastically lower volume accompanying the attempted higher auction indicates underlying weakness.

Expected Results:
Higher prices will probably continue to cut off activity, seller should soon resume control. "K" period buying price probe is suspect. Watch for buyer continuation.

Figure 4–83 July Soybeans, May 16-19, 1989.

	May 16	May 17	May 18	May 19
	.	.	.	.
733.50	D	.	.	.
733.00	D	.	.	.
732.50	D	.	.	.
732.00	D	.	.	.
731.50	D	.	.	.
731.00	D	.	.	.
730.50	DE	.	.	.
730.00	DE	.	.	.
729.50	E	.	.	.
729.00	EF	.	.	.
728.50	EF	.	.	.
728.00	EFG	.	.	.
727.50	EFG	.	.	.
727.00	EGH	.	.	.
726.50	EGH	.	.	.
726.00	EGH	.	.	.
725.50	EGH	.	.	.
725.00	GH	.	.	.
724.50	H	.	.	.
724.00	HI	.	.	GI
723.50	HIJK	.	.	FGI
723.00	HIJK	.	.	EFGHIJ
722.50	HIJK	.	K	EFGHIJK
722.00	HIJK	.	K	DEFGHIJK
721.50	HIJK	.	K	DEFHIJK
721.00	IJK	.	K	DEJKL
720.50	JK	.	K	DEJK
720.00	JK	.	K	OJK
719.50	JK	.	K	DJK
719.00	JK	J	K	DJ
718.50	JK	J	EFGJK	D
718.00	JK	J	DEFGJK	D
717.50	JK	JK	DEFGHJK	D
717.00	K	JK	DEFGHIJK	D
716.50	K	JK	DEGHIJK	.
716.00	K	DJK	DEHIJK	.
715.50	K	DJK	DHJK	.
715.00	K	DJK	D	.
714.50	K	DJK	D	.
714.00	K	DIJK	D	.
713.50	.	DIK	D	.
713.00	.	DHIK	D	.
712.50	.	DHIK	D	.
712.00	.	DHIK	D	.
711.50	.	DFHIK	D	.
711.00	.	DEFHK	.	.
710.50	.	DEFGH	.	.
710.00	.	DEFGH	.	.
709.50	.	DEFG	.	.
709.00	.	EG	.	.
708.50	.	EG	.	.
708.00	.	E	.	.
707.50	.	E	.	.
707.00	.	E	.	.
706.50	.	.	.	.
			24,000	27,000

Figure 4–84   Long-term activity record for July Soybeans, May 19, 1989.

Market: **Soybeans**   Date: **5-19-89**

Attempted Direction: Buyer   Seller

1. Rotation Factor (**+3**)   **X**

2. Range Extension   **X**

3. Tails   **X**

4. Buying/Selling Composite   **N/A**

Overall Attempted Direction: (Higher)   Lower   Neutral

Comments:

The market is still trying to auction higher, but the buyer looks weak – no continuation.

Directional Performance:

1. Volume:
Daily: (**27,000**)   Higher   Lower   (Unchanged)
Auction Average: (**41,400**)   Higher   Lower   Unchanged

2. Value-Area Placement:
     (Higher) OL/High Lower OL/Low Unchgd.

3. Value-Area Width: Wider   Average   (Narrower)

Comments:

Higher prices continue to cut off activity – low volume indicates the market is not facilitating trade at higher prices.

Expected Results:

The market needs to go lower to facilitate trade – the buyer has failed to take control of activity – look for an opportunity to short while monitoring seller entry

Figure 4–85 July Soybeans, May 16-20, 1989.

	May 16	May 17	May 18	May 19	May 20
	.	.	.	.	.
733.50	D	.	.	.	.
733.00	D	.	.	.	.
732.50	D	.	.	.	.
732.00	D	.	.	.	.
731.50	D	.	.	.	.
731.00	D	.	.	.	.
730.50	DE	.	.	.	.
730.00	DE	.	.	.	.
729.50	E	.	.	.	.
729.00	EF	.	.	.	.
728.50	EF	.	.	.	.
728.00	EFG	.	.	.	.
727.50	EFG	.	.	.	.
727.00	EGH	.	.	.	.
726.50	EGH	.	.	.	.
726.00	EGH	.	.	.	.
725.50	EGH	.	.	.	.
725.00	GH	.	.	.	.
724.50	H	.	.	.	.
724.00	HI	.	.	GI	.
723.50	HIJK	.	.	FGI	.
723.00	HIJK	.	.	EFGHIJ	.
722.50	HIJK	.	.	EFGHIJ	.
722.00	HIJK	.	K	DEFGHIJK	.
721.50	HIJK	.	K	DEFHIJK	.
721.00	IJK	.	K	DEJK	.
720.50	JK	.	K	DEJK	.
720.00	JK	.	K	DJK	.
719.50	JK	.	K	DJK	.
719.00	JK	J	K	DJ	.
718.50	JK	J	EFGJK	D	.
718.00	JK	J	DEFGJK	D	.
717.50	JK	JK	DEFGHJK	D	.
717.00	K	JK	DEFGHIJK	D	.
716.50	K	JK	DEGHIJK	.	.
716.00	K	DJK	DEHIJK	.	.
715.50	K	DJK	DHJK	.	.
715.00	K	DJK	D	.	D
714.50	K	DJK	D	.	D
714.00	K	DIJK	D	.	D
713.50	.	DIK	D	.	D
713.00	.	DHIK	D	.	D
712.50	.	DHIK	D	.	D
712.00	.	DHIK	D	.	D
711.50	.	DFHIK	D	.	D
711.00	.	DEFHK	.	.	O
710.50	.	DEFGH	.	.	D
710.00	.	DEFGH	.	.	D
709.50	.	DEFG	.	.	D
709.00	.	EG	.	.	D
708.50	.	EG	.	.	D
708.00	.	E	.	.	D
707.50	.	E	.	.	D
707.00	.	E	.	.	D
706.50	.	.	.	.	D
706.00	.	.	.	.	D
705.50	.	.	.	.	D
705.00	.	.	.	.	D
704.50	.	.	.	.	D
704.00	.	.	.	.	D
703.50	.	.	.	.	D
703.00	.	.	.	.	D
702.50	.	.	.	.	D
702.00	.	.	.	.	D
701.50	.	.	.	.	D
701.00	.	.	.	.	D
700.50	.	.	.	.	D
700.00	.	.	.	.	D
699.50	.	.	.	.	DE
699.00	.	.	.	.	DE
698.50	.	.	.	.	DE
698.00	.	.	.	.	DE
697.50	.	.	.	.	DE
697.00	.	.	.	.	DEH
696.50	.	.	.	.	DEGH
696.00	.	.	.	.	EGH
695.50	.	.	.	.	EFGHI
695.00	.	.	.	.	EFGHI
694.50	.	.	.	.	EFGHIJK
694.00	.	.	.	.	EFGIJK
693.50	.	.	.	.	EFGIJKL
693.00	.	.	.	.	EFGIJK
692.50	.	.	.	.	EFGIJK
692.00	.	.	.	.	FGJ
691.50	.	.	.	.	GJ
691.00	.	.	.	.	.
				27,000	44,000

Figure 4–86   Volatility.

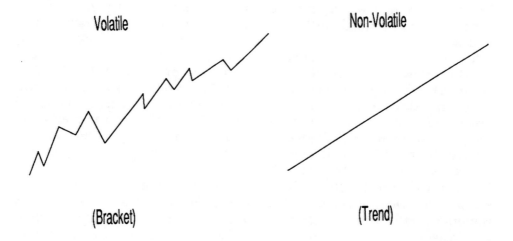

The auction rotations are, in a sense, the structural footprints of the rotational struggle between the other timeframe participants. In the day timeframe, the auctions take the form of either one-timeframe or two-timeframe market conditions. Long-term auction rotations are composed of the same form of activity. However, the "footprints" are recorded over a longer period of time. A bracket, for example, is a long-term two-timeframe market, while a trend is a long-term one-timeframe market.

Just as a day trader must be aware of timeframe control, it is crucial for a longer-term trader to know whether the market is trending or in a bracket. The following discussion details the longer-term trade applications of bracketed and trending markets. Our goal is to arrive at methods to objectively assess long term market movement.

Brackets   In review, markets spend approximately 70 percent of the time in a trading range, or bracket, in which the other timeframe buyer and seller become *responsive parties*. When a market is bracketing, the other timeframe participants have similar views of value, and the prices at which they are willing to do business grow much closer together. As price nears the top of the perceived bracket, the seller responds and auctions price downward. In turn, the responsive buyer enters at the lower bracket extreme and rotates price back to the upside. As the market attempts to facilitate trade between the buyer and seller, price movements tend to be volatile, auctioning back and forth with no real longer-term directional conviction (Figure 4–86).

It is difficult to define a bracket in absolute terms. As with a trend, seldom do two traders have the same definition of a bracket, for all traders operate with a different timeframe in mind. The daily bar chart for Treasury bonds in Figure 4–87 can be broken down into a myriad of individual brackets. For example, the entire bar chart could be considered a bracket by a longer-term trader, spanning some six months (point 1 in Figure 4–87). The longer-term participant might seek to buy below 87:00 and sell above 91:00.

A shorter-term swing trader, on the other hand, might break the bond market down into a smaller bracket, as shown by point 2 in Figure 4–88. This balanced region encompasses roughly a month. The swing trader would attempt to place longs around 88–00, then exit and go short above 89–16.

Figure 4–89 illustrates some of the many possible brackets contained within the bond market over this particular six-month period. There are brackets within brackets . . . within brackets, depending on your trading timeframe. At point 5 in Figure 4–89, a shorter-term trader might consider six days of overlapping value to be a bracket. A longer-term trader,

Figure 4–87 A six-month bracket in Treasury Bonds. Data courtesy of Commodity Quote Graphics.

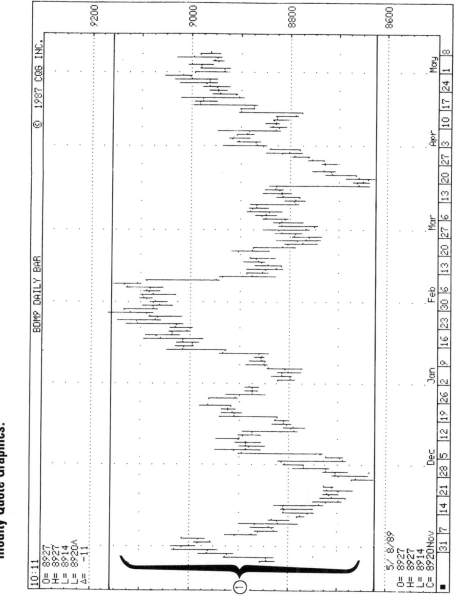

Figure 4–88   A one-month bracket in Treasury Bonds. Data courtesy of Commodity Quote Graphics.

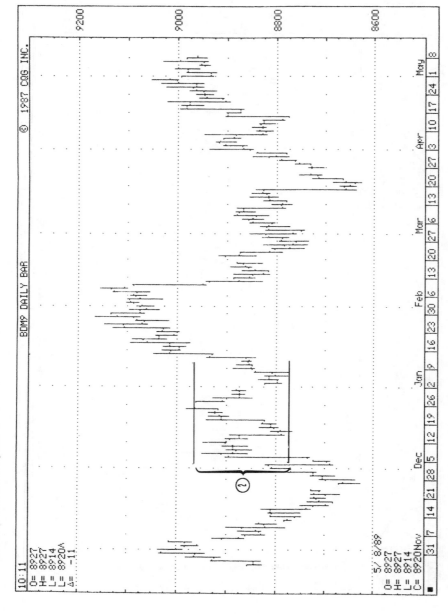

Figure 4–89   Multiple brackets in Treasury Bonds. Data courtesy of Commodity Quote Graphics.

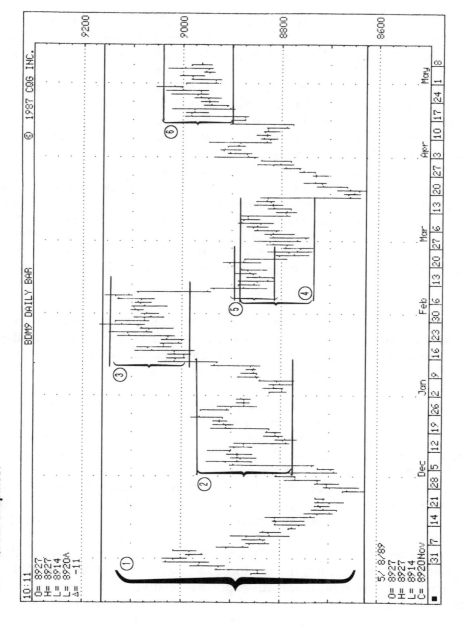

however, would consider that region to be a part of the longer-term bracket at point 4.

Even if two traders agree on a balance area, they still may differ on the actual extremes of the bracket. In Figure 4–90, one swing trader might consider the bracket extremes to be created by recurring value-area tops and bottoms. Another swing trader might use price extremes (excess) to define the bracket, as in Figure 4–91. The point is, bracket definition is largely a product of time. There is no perfect bracket, just as there is no perfect trend. *The important concept to remember is that to successfully trade in a bracketed market, it is necessary to clearly define the bracket in which you are trading according to your timeframe.*

It is helpful to literally "draw in" the bracket extremes as you perceive them. This allows you to visualize future auction rotations and ideal trade location. When you clearly define a bracket, you are, in effect, testing your market understanding. Brackets do evolve, however, and it is important to constantly monitor for fundamental changes. By observing and continually reevaluating your view of the bigger picture, you will gain experience and further the learning process that is necessary to becoming an expert trader.

Trade Location in a Bracketed Market Once you realize that you are in a bracketed market and have defined the bracket extremes, several guidelines can help you secure proper trade location, improve your trading performance and manage your trade risk.

Rule 1: Monitor market direction and location within the current bracket All trades in a bracketed market should be placed *responsively*. We use the term "responsive" here in a more generic sense than has been previously discussed. Consider it this way: the distance from the top of the bracket to the bottom, regardless of the bracket's size, is similar to a day's range. Therefore, the "value area" is contained within the middle of the bracket. Longs placed below the bracket value area are considered responsive, as are shorts placed above. Any trade positioned in the middle of the balance area is initiative and offers poor bracket trade location.

At point 1 in Figure 4–92, for example, the responsive seller responds to price approaching the top of a bracket. Shorts entered at this point result in minimum upside exposure relative to downside profit potential. If the market continues up, movement to the upside should be slowed by resistance at the top of the bracket. This would allow a trader time to evaluate the trade and, if necessary, exit the short at minimal loss.

Figure 4–90   Bracket extremes in Treasury Bonds. Data courtesy of Commodity
Quote Graphics.

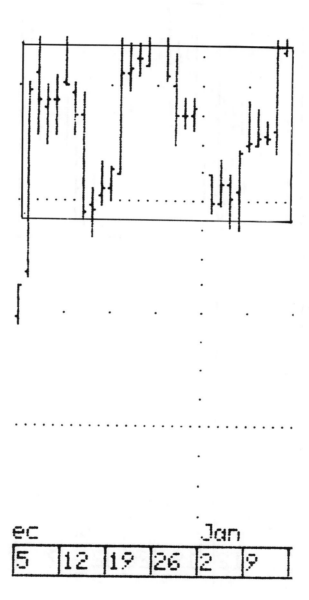

Figure 4–91   Bracket extremes in Treasury Bonds. Data courtesy of Commodity Quote Graphics.

Figure 4–92 Simulated movement within a bracket.

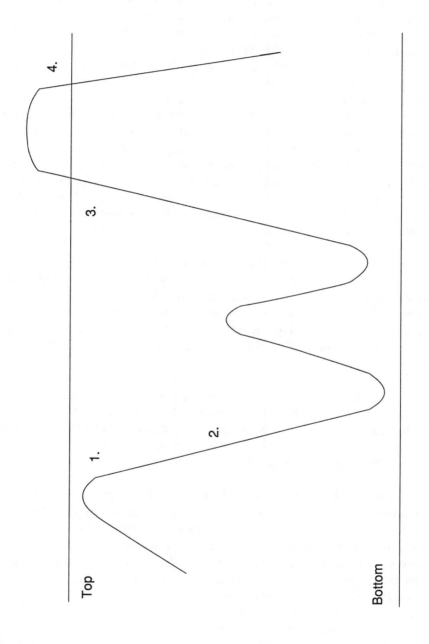

At point 2, however, activity is initiative and trade location is poor for short positions. Immediate upside exposure is equal to downside profit potential. A long placed here embodies even greater risk, for the current medium term auction is down.

The market eventually auctions back to the top of the bracket at point 3. Longs placed here with the initiative buyer offer little upside potential with the risk of price returning to bracket lows. Shorts should be entered at the upper extreme with the expectation that longer-term sellers will respond to price above value. If price auctions above the bracket top, however (point 4), the market may be poised to break-out of the balanced area. If price is accepted above the bracket, shorts should be exited and longs placed with the break-out activity. Conversely, if the upper extreme offers resistance and price is returned within the bracket, shorts offer excellent trade location. In both cases, trades should be monitored carefully, for movement is often swift coming off a bracket.

Rule 2: Markets generally test the bracket extreme more than once   If you miss an opportunity to sell a bracket top (or buy a bracket bottom), do not scramble to enter a trade for fear that you will not get another chance. Chasing a bracketed market only results in poor trade location. Over a large sample size, the market will return to test the bracket extreme on the average of three to five times before moving to new levels with confidence.

Rule 3: Markets fluctuate within bracketed regions   A market generally will not auction from one extreme of a bracket to the other in a "beeline." Rather, price fluctuates within the balanced area: from top to middle, middle to top, middle to bottom, etc. Due to the price fluctuations, swing trades placed in the middle of a bracket offer poor trade location.

Rule 4: Monitor activity near the bracket extremes for acceptance/rejection   When price auctions near a bracket low, it is easy to let objectivity slip and begin to anticipate that the market will travel through the bracket. After all, recent activity has been to the downside—why should it stop now? However, it is extremely dangerous to place a short at the bracket low before the market has exhibited acceptance and follow-through below the bracket. If you are wrong, you have positioned yourself with the worst possible trade location, in a market that will most likely auction back to the bracket's upper extreme.

Remember, in a bracketed market, both the other timeframe buyer and seller are *responsive participants*. Responsive activity is generally much slower and more gradual to develop. A trader usually has time to monitor the bracket extremes for rejection or follow-through.

Transition: Bracket to Trend   All brackets eventually evolve into some form of a trend, just as all trends end in a balancing area, or bracket. It is an ongoing cycle. Because of the vast difference in trading techniques during a trend and a bracket, it is necessary to be able to identify when such a transition is occurring. Again, because every trader operates within a different timeframe, it is impossible to positively define a perfect "transition rule." Traders with exceptionally long timeframes might consider a year-long trend to be part of a larger bracket. Conversely, a swing trader might consider a week of consecutively higher value areas to be a trend. Identifying the transition from a bracket to a trend is a product of your personal timeframe.

In Day Timeframe Trading, we discussed transition in terms of one-timeframe and two-timeframe conditions. The same concept can be applied to the longer-term auctions. When a market is in a bracket, both the other timeframe buyer and seller are present and active (over a longer period of time). There is no clear longer-term directional conviction. A transition occurs when the initiative participants exert more control over price than the responsive participants.

In the longer-term, transition is marked by the formation of excess confirmed by sustained follow-through in the opposite direction. The beginning of an up trend, for example, is usually marked by the aggressive entry the other timeframe buyer, creating excess in the form of a longer-term buying tail or a buying gap. The responsive buyer overwhelms the seller, and the market begins to trend upward, turning initiative as it passes through previously established value. In Figure 4–93, the buyer entered responsively at point 1 within a balanced area. The subsequent initiative buying gaps at points 2, 3, and 4 established strong long-term excess and confirmed the conviction of the initiative other timeframe buyer. This gapping activity began an upward trend that spanned some four months.

In the intermediate term, a transition might take the form of a balance-area break-out. In Figure 4–94, for instance, the S&P had developed three days of overlapping value (February 1–3). On February 7, the S&P "broke-out" of the balance area, indicating a transition to a trending scenario. The result was a Double Distribution Buying Trend day. Similarly, Treasury bonds exhibited an intermediate-term transition from bracket to trend on April 9 (Figure 4–95). After eight days of overlapping value, a multiple-distribution Trend day signaled the reentry of an initiative other timeframe seller with strong directional conviction.

Trends   A trend is the result of clear control and directional conviction by either the other timeframe buyer or seller. The stronger the conviction underpinning the trend, the greater the excess that usually sparks the

Figure 4-93   Transition from bracket to trend in Crude Oil. Data courtesy of Commodity Quote Graphics.

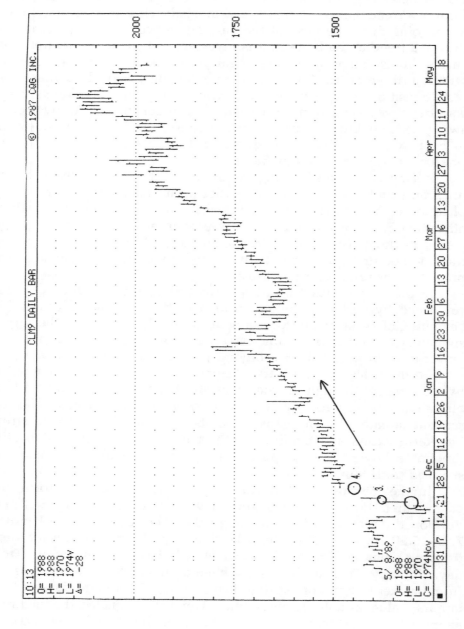

trend's beginning. In other words, a trend of great magnitude will typically have an elongated longer-term tail and/or a large gap (invisible tail) that creates a firm base from which the trend begins (Figure 4–96). It follows that early trend activity will tend to be more dramatic and pronounced, witnessed by more range extensions, elongated Profiles and substantial tails.

Trade Location in a Trending Market   There is no such thing as good trade location during the early stages of a trend. If the market is truly trending, price will continually lead value. The key to trade location is simply to "get on board early" and then monitor the market for continuation. If a trend is strong, your position should soon be rewarded with follow-through and your trade location should improve. If not, then the trend is suspect and trades should be exited.

Early entry in a trending market is more difficult than it sounds, for it means that a trader must buy considerably *above* recent perceptions of value. Picking up the phone and saying "buy it" when price is quickly auctioning above the last several days' value areas can be a nerve-wracking experience, even for the trader who is usually calm and objective. When a trend emerges after a prolonged balance area, a trader must quickly reverse his or her trading perspective. It is very difficult to change from a responsive mode to the go-with, trail-blazing mentality of the initiative trader.

Later in the life of a trend, however, trades should be placed responsively, or when the market temporarily breaks during an up trend (or rallies in a down trend). Regardless of "where you are" within a longer-term trend, *it is safest to trade with the trend*. You will save the cost of this book ten times over if you simply do not trade against a trend.

Monitoring Trends for Continuation   One useful way to monitor a trend for signs of continuation and/or slowing by comparing activity on up days against activity occurring on down days. While in an up trend, for example, determine which way each individual trading session is attempting to go. Then, compare the volume generated on down days versus the up days. If a trend is strong, up days should exhibit greater trade facilitation by generating higher volume than down days. When volume begins to increase on days *against* the trend, then the trend is aging and may soon begin to balance, or enter a bracket.

Transition: Trend to Bracket   A trend is officially over when the responsive participant is able to exert as much influence on price as the initiator. An up trend has ended, for instance, when the responsive other

Figure 4-94 Balance area break-out occurring in the June S&P 500, January 31-February 7, 1989.

Price	January 31	February 1	February 2	February 3	February 6	February 7
302.70						M
302.60						LM
302.50						LM
302.40						LM
302.30						LM
302.20						LM
302.10						LM
302.00						KLM
301.90						KLMN
301.80						KLMN
301.70						JKLMN
301.60						JKLMN
301.50						JKLNP
301.40						JKLNP
301.30						JKNP
301.20						HJKP
301.10						HJK
301.00						HJK
300.90						HJK
300.80						HJK
300.70						HJ
300.60						HI
300.50						H
300.40						H
300.30		C				FH
300.20		CD				FGH
300.10		CD				FGH
300.00		CD				FGH
299.90		CD	K			FGH
299.80		CD	K			FG
299.70	N	CD	K			CFG
299.60	N	CDM	JK			CDFG
299.50	N	CDM	JK	C		CDFG
299.40	N	CDEM	BJK	C		CDF
299.30	NP	CELMN	BJK	BC		CDEF
299.20	NP	CELMNP	BJKL	BC	B	CDEF
299.10	NP	CELMNP	BJKL	BCDN	BC	CDEF
299.00	NP	CELMNP	BJKL	BCDMN	BC	CDE

Price					
298.90	NP	CEFIJLMNP	BCDMN	BC	CDE
298.80	MNP	CEFIJLMNP	BCDEMNP	BC	CDE
298.70	MNP	BCEFHIJLMNP	BDEHLMNP	BC	BCD
298.60	MNP	BCEFHIJLMNP	BDEGHLMNP	BC	BC
298.50	M	BCEFHIJLMN	BDEFGHIJLMNP	BC	BC
298.40	LM	BCEFGHIJKLM	BEFGHIJLN	BCI	BC
298.30	LM	BEFGHIJKLM	BEFGHIJKL	BCHI	BC
298.20	LM	BEFGHIJKLM	BEFGHIJKL	BCHI	B
298.10	LM	BEGHIJKL	BFGHIJK	BCHIM	B
298.00	LM	BEGIJK	CFGHIMN	BCDHIM	B
297.90	KL	BEGK	CEFGHMN	BDHIJLMP	B
297.80	KL	BGK	CDEFGM	BDHJLMNP	B
297.70	KL	BGK	CDEFM	BDGHJLMNP	B
297.60	HKL	GK	DEFM	BDGHJLMNP	B
297.50	HKJL	GK	DEM	DGHJKLMNP	B
297.40	BHJK	G	DE	DFGJKLMNP	B
297.30	BHJK	.	D	DEFGJKLMN	B
297.20	BCHJK	.	D	DEFGJKLMN	.
297.10	BCHJK	.	.	DEFGKLMN	.
297.00	BCHJK	.	.	DEFGKMN	.
296.90	BCGHIJ	.	.	DEFGMN	.
296.80	BCGHIJ	.	.	DEGM	.
296.70	BCGHIJ	.	.	DEM	.
296.60	CGHI	.	.	EM	.
296.50	CGI	.	.	E	.
296.40	CFGI	.	.	E	.
296.30	CFGI	.	.	.	.
296.20	CFGI	.	.	.	.
296.10	CEFG	.	.	.	.
296.00	CEFG	.	.	.	.
295.90	CEFG	.	.	.	.
295.80	CEG	.	.	.	.
295.70	CDE	.	.	.	.
295.60	CDE	.	.	.	.
295.50	CDE	.	.	.	.
295.40	DE	.	.	.	.
295.30	D	.	.	.	.
295.20	D	.	.	.	.
295.10	.	.	.	.	.
295.00	.	.	.	.	.

Figure 4–95 Balance area break-out occurring in June Treasury Bonds, March 30–April 9, 1987.

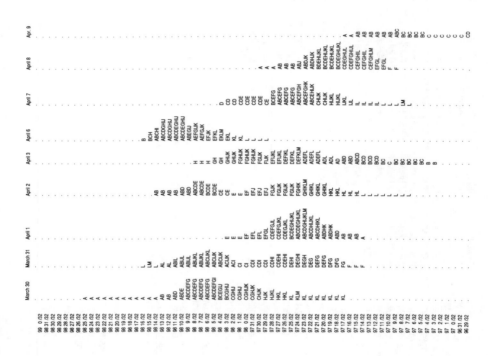

Price	TPO
96 28 /32	CO
96 27 /32	CO
96 26 /32	CO
96 25 /32	CO
96 24 /32	D
96 23 /32	DE
96 22 /32	DE
96 21 /32	DEF
96 20 /32	DEF
96 19 /32	DEFH
96 18 /32	EFGH
96 17 /32	EFGH
96 16 /32	FGH
96 15 /32	FGH
96 14 /32	FGHIJ
96 13 /32	FGHIJ
96 12 /32	GHIJ
96 11 /32	GHIJ
96 10 /32	HIJ
96 9 /32	HIJ
96 8 /32	IJ
96 7 /32	IJ
96 6 /32	J
96 5 /32	J
96 4 /32	J
96 3 /32	J
96 2 /32	J
96 1 /32	J
96 0 /32	J
95 31 /32	J
95 30 /32	J
95 29 /32	J
95 28 /32	JL
95 27 /32	JKL
95 26 /32	JKL
95 25 /32	JKLM
95 24 /32	JKL
95 23 /32	JKL
95 22 /32	JKL
95 21 /32	JKL
95 20 /32	JKL
95 19 /32	JKL
95 18 /32	JKL
95 17 /32	KL
95 16 /32	KL
95 15 /32	KL
95 14 /32	KL
95 13 /32	KL
95 12 /32	KL
95 11 /32	KL
95 10 /32	KL
95 9 /32	KL
95 8 /32	KL
95 7 /32	KL
95 6 /32	KL
95 5 /32	KL
95 4 /32	KL
95 3 /32	KL
95 2 /32	KL
95 1 /32	KL
95 0 /32	K
94 31 /32	K
94 30 /32	K
94 29 /32	K
94 28 /32	K
94 27 /32	K
94 26 /32	K
94 25 /32	K
94 24 /32	K
94 23 /32	K
94 22 /32	K
94 21 /32	K

Figure 4–96   The beginning of a trend occurring in Crude Oil. Data Courtesy of Commodity Quote Graphics.

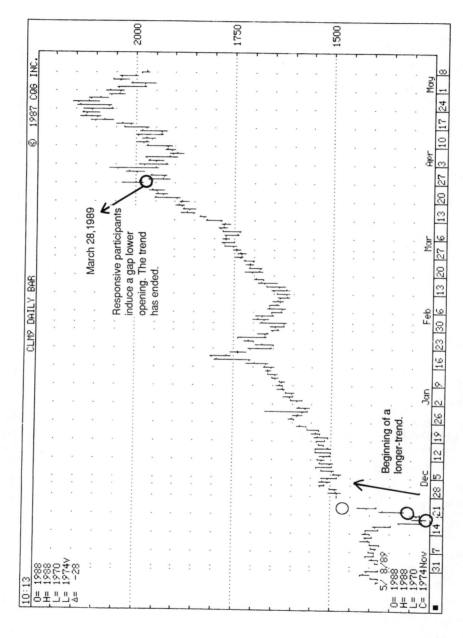

timeframe seller is able to create significant excess at the top of the trend. Once the trend is over, the market will begin to balance. As a market begins the bracketing process, traders should revert to a responsive mode, seeking to sell the top of the bracket and buy the bottom.

Examine Figure 4–96 containing the daily bar chart for crude oil. The longer term trend that began in late November 1988 began to balance when the responsive seller was strong enough to induce a gap lower opening on March 28, 1989. Although the resulting excess did not last for long, it indicated that the initiative buyer was weakening and a trading range was developing.

Figure 4–97 provides a second example of a transition from trend to bracket, although over a much shorter period of time. After two strong buying days on January 19 and 20, the Japanese yen began to balance. The inability of the buyer to establish continually higher value indicated the presence of the responsive seller. The yen had entered a short-term bracketing period as evidenced by responsive activity on both extremes of the bracket (see circled areas).

Detailed Analysis of a Developing Market   To bring the concepts of a bracketed market to life, we will now take a detailed look at the developing Treasury bond market from late October 1988 to early May 1989. We have specifically chosen this time period for its volatility. A volatile, bracketing market is a complex and emotionally difficult market to trade. In a trend, trade location is simply a matter of "Am I too late?" and "Can I buy above or sell below value?" Trading in a bracketed market, however, is much more challenging. To be successful, traders must mentally change gears quickly—literally trade from several different states of mind. Since markets generally spend between 70 and 80 percent of the time bracketing, such a challenge is the norm—not the exception—in futures trading.

In a bracketed market, the other timeframe buyer and seller are much closer together in their perception of value (see Bracketed Markets in Chapter 3). Both are actively probing to determine the condition of the marketplace. As an illustration, consider the development of the computer chip industry. Early on, when microchips were suddenly in great demand but only produced by a few suppliers, prices trended steadily higher. However, as new producers entered the marketplace and existing suppliers increased their output, the computer chip market entered a bracketing phase. Price began to auction back and forth between the long-term participants as their perceptions of value started to narrow. Buyers and sellers, in effect, were testing each other to determine the condition of the market. Attempts by producers to raise price were sometimes rejected as buyers found alternative, less expensive sources. Con-

Figure 4–97   Coming into balance. March Japanese Yen, January 19-29, 1988.

	January 19	January 20	January 21	January 22	January 25	January 26	January 27	January 28	January 29
7920	.	.	.	.	.	.	.	.	.
7918	.	.	.	.	.	.	.	.	.
7916	.	.	.	.	.	.	.	.	.
7914	.	.	.	.	.	.	.	.	.
7912	.	.	.	.	.	.	.	J	.
7910	.	.	.	.	.	.	.	J	.
7908	.	.	Z	.	.	.	.	J	.
7906	.	.	YZ	.	.	.	.	YJ	.
7904	.	.	YZJ	.	.	.	H	YZJK	.
7902	.	.	YZFJK	I	.	.	H	YZJ	.
7900	.	.	YZFJ	IJ	.	.	H	YZJ	.
7898	.	.	YZFIJ	IJ	.	.	GH	YZIJ	.
7896	.	.	YZFGIJ	IJ	.	.	GHI	YZHIJ	.
7894	.	J	YZFGHIJ	IJ	.	.	GHIJ	OZFGHIJ	.
7892	.	JK	YZFGHIJ	GIJ	.	.	GHIJK	YZAFGHI	.
7890	.	J	YZFGHI	GHIJ	.	.	GHIJ	ZACEFGH	.
7888	.	J	OZFGHI	GHIJ	.	.	GHIJ	ZABCDEF	.
7886	.	J	YZDEFGHI	GHIJ	.	.	GHIJ	ZABCDEF	.
7884	.	J	YZDEFGHI	GHIJK	.	.	GIJ	ZABCD	.
7882	.	OEJ	YZCDEFGHI	GHIJ	.	.	GIJ	AB	.
7880	.	YEJ	ZCDEFGH	GHJ	.	.	GI	AB	.
7878	.	YEIJ	ZACDEGH	GH	.	.	DG	B	.
7876	.	YAEFIJ	ZACDEH	G	.	Y	ABDG	.	.
7874	.	YAEFIJ	ZACD	G	.	Y	ABDEFG	.	.
7872	.	YADEFIJ	ZABCD	G	Y	O	YABDEF	.	.
7870	.	YADEFIJ	ZABCD	BG	O	Y	YABDEF	.	.
7868	.	YABDEFIJ	ZABCD	YBCG	Y	Y	YZABDEF	.	.
7866	.	YZABDEFHI	ZABC	YBCFG	YZ	YBC	YZABCD	.	.
7864	.	YZABDEFHI	ZAB	OBCDFG	YZA	YABCDG	YZABCD	.	.
7862	.	YZABDEFHI	AB	YZBCDFG	YZAF	YABCDFGJ	YZABCD	.	.
7860	.	YZABCDEFHI	AB	YZABDEFG	YZABFH	YABCDFGHIJ	YZAC	.	.
7858	.	ZABCDEFGHI	AB	YZABDEF	YZABCFGHJ	YZABCDEFGHIJK	YZA	.	.
7856	.	ZABCDEFGH	A	YZADEF	YZBCEFGHIJK	YZACDEFGHIJ	YA	.	C
7854	.	ZABCDFGH	A	ZADEF	BCEFGHIJ	YZEFGHIJ	Y	.	BCEJ
7852	.	ZBCDGH	A	ZADEF	BCDEGHIJ	YZEFH	Y	.	BCEFJ
7850	.	BCGH	A	ZDE	BCDEGHIJ	YZEF	Y	.	ABCEFGJ
7848	.	CGH	A	ZDE	CDEHIJ	YZEF	Y	.	ZABCDEFGJ
7846	.	CGH	.	DE	DE	EF	Y	.	ZABCDEGJ
7844	.	CGH	.	D	DE	EF	Y	.	ZABDEGHIJ
7842	.	C	.	D	DE	.	Y	.	YZAGHIJ
7840	.	C	.	.	D	.	Y	.	OZAHIJ
7838	.	C	.	.	.	.	Y	.	YZHIJK
7836	I	C	.	.	.	.	Y	.	YJ
7834	IJ	C	.	.	.	.	Y	.	Y
7832	IJ	C	.	.	.	.	Y	.	Y
7830	HIJ	.	.	.	.	.	Y	.	.
7828	HIJ	.	.	.	.	.	Y	.	.
7826	HIJ	.	.	.	.	.	Y	.	.
7824	HIJ	.	.	.	.	.	Y	.	.
7822	FHIJ	.	.	.	.	.	Y	.	.
7820	FHIJ	.	.	.	.	.	Y	.	.
7818	FHIJ	.	.	.	.	.	Y	.	.
7816	EFHIJ	.	.	.	.	.	Y	.	.
7814	EFGHIJK	.	.	.	.	.	Y	.	.
7812	EFGHIJ	.	.	.	.	.	Y	.	.
7810	EGHIJ	.	.	.	.	.	Y	.	.
7808	EG	.	.	.	.	.	.	.	.
7806	EG	.	.	.	.	.	.	.	.
7804	E	.	.	.	.	.	.	.	.
7802	E	.	.	.	.	.	.	.	.
7800	E	.	.	.	.	.	.	.	.
7798	E	.	.	.	.	.	.	.	.
7796	E	.	.	.	.	.	.	.	.
7794	DE	.	.	.	.	.	.	.	.
7792	DE	.	.	.	.	.	.	.	.
7790	DE	.	.	.	.	.	.	.	.
7788	DE	.	.	.	.	.	.	.	.
7786	DE	.	.	.	.	.	.	.	.
7784	BD	.	.	.	.	.	.	.	.
7782	BCD	.	.	.	.	.	.	.	.
7780	BCD	.	.	.	.	.	.	.	.
7778	BCD	.	.	.	.	.	.	.	.
7776	BCD	.	.	.	.	.	.	.	.
7774	BCD	.	.	.	.	.	.	.	.
7772	BCD	.	.	.	.	.	.	.	.
7770	ABCD	.	.	.	.	.	.	.	.
7768	ZABCD	.	.	.	.	.	.	.	.
7766	ZACD	.	.	.	.	.	.	.	.
7764	ZA	.	.	.	.	.	.	.	.
7762	ZA	.	.	.	.	.	.	.	.
7760	ZA	.	.	.	.	.	.	.	.
7758	ZA	.	.	.	.	.	.	.	.
7756	ZA	.	.	.	.	.	.	.	.
7754	ZA	.	.	.	.	.	.	.	.
7752	YA	.	.	.	.	.	.	.	.
7750	O	.	.	.	.	.	.	.	.
7748	Y	.	.	.	.	.	.	.	.
7746	Y	.	.	.	.	.	.	.	.
7744	Y	.	.	.	.	.	.	.	.
7742	Y	.	.	.	.	.	.	.	.
7740	Y	.	.	.	.	.	.	.	.
7738	Y	.	.	.	.	.	.	.	.
7736	Y	.	.	.	.	.	.	.	.
7734	.	.	.	.	.	.	.	.	.
7732	.	.	.	.	.	.	.	.	.
7730	.	.	.	.	.	.	.	.	.

versely, sometimes higher prices were accepted due to a temporary flux of buyers.

Bracket Reference Points   To successfully trade a bracketed market, you must first recognize that the market lacks long-term directional conviction and, consequently, become more *selective* in your trading. In other words, it is essential that you develop both a "hands-on" strategy and a "minds-on" approach to evaluating the market's auctions. Because of the closeness of timeframes, the market's probes for acceptance of value appear to be extremely disorganized, often to the point of random rotation. We will show that in some cases this is actually true. However, there are many other times when the "footprints" of the market's auctions provide valuable information regarding short-term conviction, enabling alert traders to identify change in its early stages.

The key to selective trading lies in the understanding, recognizing, and recording of a few very basic reference points. Not surprisingly, these reference points are generated by many of the market forces we have already discussed—forces such as market balance, Nontrend days, balance break-outs and auction failures. Before we delve into our detailed Treasury bond example, let us first recap a few of the forces that shape a bracketed market.

A market that lacks directional conviction spends the majority of its time in very short-term balance areas. Intermittently, the market will break-out of the balance region and make a swift directional move to a new price level, whereupon it again returns to balance. This chain of events happens again and again, until conditions change significantly and sustained other timeframe conviction surfaces. Until then, it is wise to maintain a relatively short trading timeframe. Generally, a trade should be held overnight only if there is substantial structural evidence in its favor.

There is little opportunity in the short-term balance regions, for they usually lack any semblance of directional conviction. The sharp price spurts between balance areas, on the other hand, last for a short period of time but offer a high degree of opportunity for the trader who is alert and prepared to take advantage of them. Because of the swift nature of a break-out, traders must not only be able to recognize the auction behavior that leads to a probe away from balance, but also have the foresight to enter orders ahead of time to take advantage of the potential break-out.

The key to early identification of a break-out lies in the concept of market balance. In a bracket, the market develops a series of short term balance areas (brackets within brackets), or consecutive days of overlapping value. In most cases, the direction that the market "breaks-out" of these short term balance areas proves to be the beginning of at least a short-term auction. The salient concept is follow-through. Monitoring a break-out for continuation is the key to identifying other timeframe control.

In the large majority of cases, a break-out will begin with either a gap or an auction failure. After several days of overlapping value, a gap opening indicates that the market is out of balance and could be breaking out in the direction of the gap. A more subtle form of break-out occurs when the market tests one extreme, fails to follow through, and breaks-out in the opposite direction, forming an "outside" day—a day that extends beyond both of the previous session's extremes. For example, consider a market that develops overlapping value on six consecutive days. On the seventh day, the market tests below the balance area lows, fails to follow-through and then auctions quickly to the upside, forming an outside day. The initial auction failure is the first indication that the market has the potential to break out of balance, for it forms excess and establishes a known reference point. The frequency of this behavior is witnessed by the great number of substantial day timeframe price movements that are also outside days.

We emphasize, however, that observing market behavior and actually placing the trade are two entirely different actions. After several days of overlapping value, for example, it is easy to grow accustomed to the seemingly random, back-and-forth balancing. When the market finally tests below the short-term bracket low and fails to follow through, it is relatively easy to recognize the potential for an outside day. However, the ensuing auction back through the balance area appears to be the same activity that has lulled the trader to sleep during previous days. As one trader put it, "I can identify the auction failure and I know that there is a good possibility that the market will move substantially higher, but . . . I just can't pull the trigger. The phone gets extremely heavy."

Trading a bracketed market is by no means easy, even with clearly defined reference points. As we stated earlier, you must "do the trade" in order to build the experience and confidence necessary to take advantage of a sound market understanding.

As you proceed through our dissection of the Treasury bond market, one fact should ring loud and clear. Overlapping value regions, auction failures, break-outs, and the resulting outside days happen over and over again. They literally form the backbone of a bracketed market. As you become more familiar with their formations and consistent behavior, what once seemed to be virtually random, unorganized behavior will begin to take on a new meaning, to make sense. You will realize that through these apparently random auctions, the market is actually organizing itself, fulfilling its purpose—facilitating trade. For the trader, these behaviors and resulting structural features draw the road map that is so critical to selectively taking advantage of the dynamic short-term price movements that characterize a bracketed market. The points discussed below are highlighted in Figures 4–98 through 4–101.

Region A (Figure 4–98)   After a strong buying auction, the Treasury bond market recorded potential buying excess at 90–12 on November 1. The selling gap denoted by point 1 confirmed the excess and set into motion a sustained move to the downside. Excess, in this case a long-term selling tail and a selling gap, should act as resistance to future long-term buying auctions. If price trades back through these areas of rejection, the condition of the market will have changed (the other timeframe sellers that initially drove price are no longer present).

At point 2, the Bond market came into short-term balance, as is evidenced by two days of overlapping value. On the third day, a probe above the balance failed to attract buying and was swiftly rejected. Armed with the knowledge that there was no interest in buying, the bond market then broke below the balance area to start a new selling auction. The result was a dynamic outside day. When it comes to being selective in your trades, these are the conditions that you should be looking for. Identify overlapping value/balance regions. Then, monitor the probes beyond these regions for acceptance or rejection. If they are accepted, the market will probably continue to auction in that direction, at least for a few days. If they are rejected, however, stay alert and get ready to reverse your trading state of mind.

Note that the failed auction created short-term excess on the day's high—remember, markets need to auction too high to know that they have gone high enough. Point 3 shows the same behavior occurring all over again. After three days of overlapping value, an auction above the previous two days' highs failed, resulting in yet another outside selling day. Following the break-out at point 3, bonds once again settled into balance, recording five days of narrowing, overlapping value (point 4). The bond market gapped sharply below the balance area on the following day, but failed to continue. Point 5 shows aggressive responsive buyers closed the market very near its high on this day, signaling the potential formation of selling excess. To confirm the excess at 89–06, buyers should show continuation out of this region.

Region B (Figure 4–99)   The day following the selling gap at point 5 opened higher, then auctioned down to test the at 89–06 low. Aggressive other timeframe buyers were still present and they again closed the day on its highs, confirming the selling excess at 89–06. This new buying was fueled by strong directional conviction, as was evidenced by the fact that

Figure 4–98   Detailed analysis of a developing market, June Treasury Bonds. Region A. Data Courtesy of Commodity Quote Graphics.

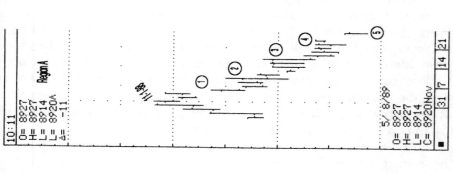

Figure 4–99 Detailed analysis of a developing market, June Treasury Bonds. Region B. Data Courtesy of Commodity Quote Graphics.

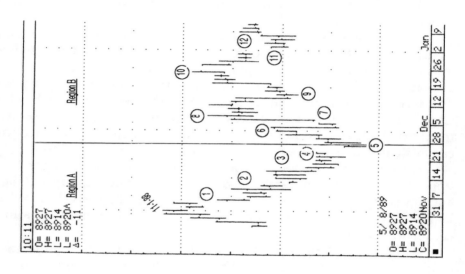

buyers were able to auction price completely through the previous day's selling gap.

After a quick upward swing auction, point 6 shows that bonds opened and attempted to auction higher, but failed to "take out" the short-term excess that had previously been formed at point 3. On this day, bonds had opened above the previous day's range—*out of balance.* When the buying auction failed and bonds returned down into the previous day's range, traders were alerted that the market possessed unlimited downside potential. Anyone still long at this point should have exited. Versatile traders might even have entered short positions, monitoring carefully for seller continuation. The result was a dynamic, outside selling day.

Point 7 demonstrates how important it is to be able to mentally switch gears. After the swift outside selling day, sellers were unable to muster continuation. Bonds gapped higher, erased the short-term excess at points 3 and 6, and stopped directly at the excess created at point 2. The fact that the bond market stopped at this level is no coincidence. Gaps and other forms of excess are important reference points. By monitoring activity around them for follow-through or rejection, a trader can evaluate the market's directional attempts.

On the next day (point 8), bonds opened higher and began to auction into the selling gap established at point 1. However, buyers failed to auction completely through the selling gap and the market closed near its lows. The resistance provided by the gap created more than a month earlier was still intact.

After establishing potential buying excess at point 8, the market quickly came into balance, as is shown by the development of overlapping value on the following two days. On the third day, a test of the excess at point 8 failed (bonds closed on the low), which fueled an intermediate bracketing period bounded by excess at points 9 and 10. Note that in the bracketing process the selling gap at point 1 was erased. The only remaining long-term reference point to the upside was the 90–12 long-term high established on November 1.

Points 11 and 12 show the familiar overlapping value/balance formation, followed by a failed auction in one direction and the resulting dramatic price move in the other. Known reference points come into play again at Point 11. In this case, the outside day was a result of the seller's failure to attract new selling business below the previous day's low, and also the short term selling excess generated back at point 9.

Region C (Figure 4–100)   The buying auction at point 13 erased the 90–12 long-term high, negating any probability of a long term top to the bond market. Treasury bonds then entered a period of extreme volatility. Although price was migrating higher, there was a total lack of directional conviction. Traders should have day timeframe traded only until clear signs of conviction appeared. Bonds finally gapped sharply lower at point 14—the first indication of directional conviction in nearly a month. Point 15 shows a similar nonconviction period occurring in February and March.

The areas marked by points 15 and 16 exhibit a clear lack of excess supporting their lower reaches—another characteristic of a nonconviction market. Even though the market began a gradual buying auction at point 15, it was unlikely that buyers would move price substantially until high-conviction selling excess was recorded.

Think back to the last time you got into a heated argument with a good friend. Remember how the issues became emotional rather than rational? Market behavior during times of nonconviction is much the same. It is not clear which way the market's "argument" is heading, nor when the directional issue will be solved. A lot of unintentional hurt can be dealt when an argument reaches the emotional level. Similarly, an irrational, nonconviction market can inflict severe financial pain on those who are too stubborn to stand aside and wait for clear signs of conviction.

Point 16 highlights a balance period which was again "tipped over" by a failed auction. After six days of overlapping value, bonds opened higher (out of balance) but failed to follow through. Price returned to value and the market broke to the downside on the next day.

Point 17 is yet another outstanding example of the importance of known reference points. After breaking below the non-conviction region designated by Point 16, the market came into balance just above the long term lows created at Point 5. Sellers were unable to generate continuation below the 89-06 low, which attracted the responsive buyer. Bonds closed in the upper half of the range on this day, signalling the potential formation of longer term selling excess. Note, once again, that the dynamic outside day was sparked by a failed auction.

Region D (Figure 4–101)   Region D provides several additional examples of why it is so important to be selective in your trading during bracketed conditions. Points 18, 19, 20, and 21 show dynamic outside days—two buying and two selling—occurring within a 10-day period. If positioned the wrong way, each could have dealt a serious financial blow. However, note that all four were preceded by the characteristic clues that often signal their formation: (1) overlapping value/balance, and (2) an auction failure.

Figure 4–100 Detailed analysis of a developing market, June Treasury Bonds. Region C. Data Courtesy of Commodity Quote Graphics.

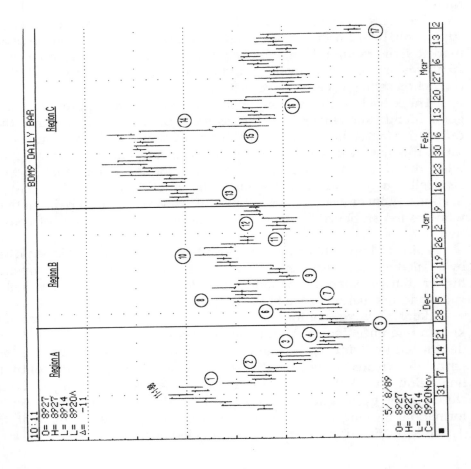

Figure 4-101 Detailed analysis of a developing market, June Treasury Bonds. Region D. Data Courtesy of Commodity Quote Graphics.

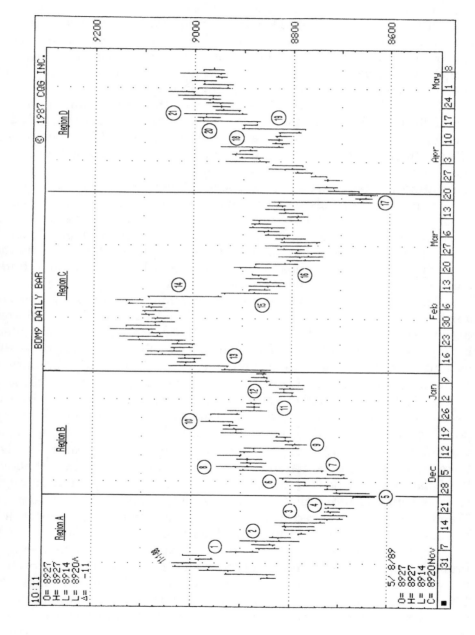

Long-Term Auction Failures An auction failure, for any timeframe, occurs when a market auctions above or below a known reference point
and fails to follow through. Day Timeframe Trading detailed the forces
that contribute to an auction failure and the characteristics of the rejection that often follows. The principal difference between a day and
longer-term auction failure lies in the magnitude of the tested reference
point and, therefore, the magnitude of the subsequent rejection.

In Day Timeframe Trading, we described the implications of an auction failure—swift rejection and the opportunity to secure good day
timeframe trade location during a day with the potential to generate significant price movement. We also mentioned that longer timeframe auction failures are usually followed by ensuing activity of greater
magnitude. Suppose that a market auctions below a low that has held for
several months but fails to attract new business. The ensuing reaction
caused by the auction failure will often involve all timeframes and continue in the opposite direction for days, weeks, or even longer. Traders
who are aware of the longer-term reference points that exist in the
marketplace are better prepared to secure good longer timeframe trade
location in the event that a failure should occur.

The daily bar chart in Figure 4–102 illustrates two good examples of
auction failures occurring in the Treasury bond market. The boxed area
designated by point 1 highlights the activity leading up to an intermediate-term auction failure that occurred on February 21. Figure 4–103
expands the boxed area to include the daily Profiles for February 9
through 22. After aggressive other timeframe selling activity on February
9 and 10, the bond market came into balance, as is evidenced by the
development of six days of overlapping value. On the 21st, Treasury
bonds opened above the intermediate term bracket and attempted to
auction higher but failed to generate continuation to the upside. Traders
were alerted to the potential for an auction failure, because the test above
the balance area failed to attract new, initiative buying. In addition, a
narrow initial balance indicated the possibility for a Double-Distribution
Trend day. Shorts entered during the B period selling-range extension
offered good day, swing, and intermediate-term trade location.

Point 2 in Figure 4–102 identifies an auction failure following a
probe below a longer-term reference point. And, as would be expected,
the subsequent activity is of much greater magnitude. On November 25,
1988, Treasury bonds recorded a long-term low at 86–09, forming long-
term excess. After rallying to as high as 91–21 in late January, bonds
eventually traded back down and approached the 86–09 excess on March
21, 1989—some four months later. On the 21st, price auctioned down and
stopped *precisely at* 86–09. The selling probe failed to stimulate new activity, and the same responsive buyers were there quickly to buy below

Figure 4–102 Auction failure occurring in Treasury Bonds. Data courtesy of Commodity Quote Graphics.

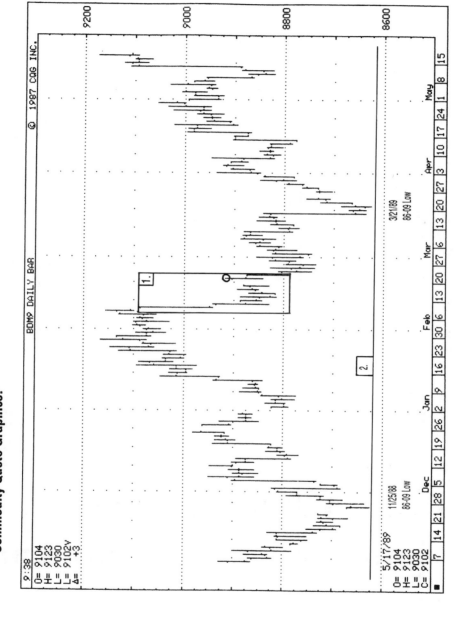

Figure 4–103 Auction failure in March Treasury Bonds, February 9-22, 1989.

	Feb. 9	Feb. 10	Feb. 13	Feb. 14	Feb. 15	Feb. 16	Feb. 17	Feb. 21	Feb. 22
9024	.	.	.	.	.	.	.	.	.
9023	Y								
9022	Y								
9021	YZ								
9020	YZ								
9019	YZ								
9018	YZAB								
9017	YZABC								
9016	YZABCE								
9015	YABCDEF								
9014	ABCDEF								
9013	ABCDEF								
9012	ADEFG								
9011	ADEFG								
9010	ADGH								
9009	ADGH								
9008	GH								
9007	GH								
9006	GH								
9005	H								
9004	H								
9003	H								
9002	H								
9001	H								
9000	H								
8931	H								
8930	H								
8929	H								
8928	HI								
8927	HIJK								
8926	HIJK								
8925	HIJK								
8924	HIJKL								
8923	IJKL								
8922	IJKL								
8921	IJL								
8920	IJL								
8919	J								
8918	.	.	.	.	.	.	.	.	.
8917									
8916									
8915									

Market Profile — Chicago Board of Trade

Price						
8914						
8913						
8912						
8911	Y					
8910	Y					
8909	Y					
8908	Y					
8907	Y					
8906	Y					
8905	Y					
8904	Y					
8903	Y					
8902	YHJ			Y	Y	
8901	YHJ			YZ	YZ	Y
8900	YCHJ			YZ	Y	Z
8831	YCFHJ		A	YZAC	Y	BJ
8830	YCDFGHIJK		A	YZABCFG	YHIL	BJ
8829	YCDEFGHIJKL	A	ABC	YZABCDEFGH	YFHIKL	BCDJK
8828	YCDEFGHIJKL	AF	ZABC	F · YZABCDEFGH	YFGHIJKL	BCDJK
8827	YCDEFGHIJK	ABEFGH	ZABC	FG · YZABCDEFGH	YEFGHIJK	BCDJKL
8826	YCEFGHIJK	ZABEFGHIJ	ZABC	EFG · YZBDEFHI	YEFGIJK	CDJKL
8825	YCEFK	YZABCDEFGHIJK	YZACDE	DEFG · YBHIKL	YAEFG	DJKL
8824	YZACEFK	YZBCDFGHIJK	YZCDEFH	ZDEFGH · YHIJKL	YABCDE	DJK
8823	YZABCE	YZBCDFIJKL	YZDEFGHI	ZDEFGH · YIJKL	YABCDE	DIJ
8822	YZABE	YZCDJKL	YDEFGHI	ZBDEFGHJ · YIJK	YZABCD	DGHIJ
8821	YZAB	YL	YDEFGHI	ZBDEHIJ · YJ	YZABCD	DGHIJ
8820	YZAB	Y	YEFGHI	ZBCDEHIJKL · YJ	YZAB	DEFGHI
8819	YZA	Y	YFGI	ZBCDHIJKL	YZA	DEFGH
8818	YZA		YFIJ	YZABCIKL	YZ	DEF
8817	ZA		YIJ	YZABCKL	YZ	DEF
8816	ZA		YIJK	YZABKL	YZ	DE
8815	ZA		YIJKL	YAB	YZ	D
8814	Z		YIJKL	YAB	Z	
8813	Z		YIJKL	YAB	Z	
8812			YJKL	YAB		
8811			YKL	AB		
8810			YK	A		YZA
8809			Y	A		YZAB
8808						YZABC
8807						YZABC
8806						YZABC
8805						YZABCD
8804						YZBCDE
8803						YBCDE
8802						YCDEKL
8801						YCDEFKL
8800						EFGKL

EFGJK
EFGHJK
EFGHJK
GHJK
HIJ
HIJ
HIJ
HI

longer-term value. In this particular case, the long term auction failure sparked the beginning of a major longer-term buying trend.

To experienced traders, known reference points serve as checkpoints on the "market map." By observing market behavior at key locations, it is possible to determine the market's directional conviction before opportunity has slipped away.

Long-Term Short Covering and Long Liquidation

We discussed day timeframe short covering and long liquidation in Section I. The same forces that cause short covering and its obverse, long liquidation, are also present in the longer timeframe. After a sustained down trend, for example, the "anxiety" level of participants who have been short for an extended period of time often begins to increase as their profits grow. Should something trigger covering, the ensuing rally could last for several days as traders scramble to buy back their short positions. Such swift buying can easily be interpreted to mark the end of the trend or even the beginning of a new trend in the opposite direction. However, if the buying is not accompanied by continuation and elongated Profile structure, the cause is probably short covering. Short covering is a result of old business covering positions placed with the original trend, not by new initiative buyers. The resulting Profiles tend to be short and narrow, often developing into the familiar "P" formation, indicating a lack of facilitation with the other timeframe buyer.

Figure 4–104 illustrates the beginning of long term short covering in soybeans that was sparked by a selling auction failure on January 26, 1989. Following a 70 cent ($3,500 per contract) down trend, sellers auctioned price near the longer-term 740 lows (Figure 4–105) and were confronted by the responsive buying that commonly occurs at longer-term reference points. This "knee-jerk" type of buying, combined with the seller's inability to extend price below 740, triggered a wave of aggressive buying that eventually developed into a Double-Distribution Buying Trend day.

The rally on January 26 put sellers of all timeframes in a tenuous position. Imagine having the longer-term foresight and discipline to build up a 60 or 70 cent gain in a trade, only to watch the market reclaim 20 cents in just a few hours. Or even worse, suppose that you sold into the trend late and had gains of only a nickel, and then suddenly found yourself 15 cents "underwater." In the face of a move as dynamic as that which occurred in soybeans on the 26th, it is likely that many traders exited in order to conserve gains or to limit loss.

Figure 4–104 Long-term short covering in Soybeans, January 25-February 7,

	Jan. 25	Jan. 26	Jan. 28	Jan. 31	Feb. 1	Feb. 2	Feb.3	Feb. 6	Feb. 7
777.50	.	.	.	.	.	FG	.	.	.
777.00	.	.	.	.	.	FG	.	.	.
776.50	.	.	.	.	.	EFG	.	.	.
776.00	.	.	.	.	.	EFG	.	.	.
775.50	.	.	.	.	.	EFG	.	.	.
775.00	.	.	.	.	.	EFG	.	.	.
774.50	.	.	.	.	.	EFGH	.	.	.
774.00	.	.	.	.	K	DEFGH	.	.	.
773.50	.	.	.	.	K	DEGHJ	.	.	.
773.00	.	.	.	.	JK	DEHIJ	.	.	.
772.50	.	.	.	.	JK	DEHIJ	.	.	.
772.00	.	.	.	.	JK	DEHIJ	.	.	.
771.50	.	.	.	.	EIJK	DHIJ	.	.	.
771.00	.	.	.	.	EFIJ	DHIJK	.	HIK	.
770.50	.	.	.	.	EFIJ	DHIJK	.	HIK	.
770.00	.	.	.	.	EFIJ	DHIJK	.	HIK	.
769.50	.	.	.	.	DEFGHIJ	DIJK	.	HIJK	.
769.00	.	.	.	.	DEFGHIJ	DJK	.	HIJK	D
768.50	.	.	.	.	DEFGHI	K	.	HIJK	D
768.00	.	J	.	.	DEFGHI	K	.	HIJK	D
767.50	.	J	.	.	DEGH	K	K	DHIJK	D
767.00	.	J	.	.	DEGH	K	K	DHIJK	D
766.50	.	J	.	.	DEG	K	DK	DHI	D
766.00	.	JK	.	.	DE	K	DEGHK	DH	D
765.50	.	JK	.	.	DE	K	DEGHIJK	DEH	D
765.00	D	JK	.	.	D	K	DEFGHIJK	DEGH	D
764.50	D	JK	.	.	.	.	DEFGHIJK	DEFGH	D
764.00	D	JK	.	K	.	.	DEFGHIJK	DEFGH	D
763.50	D	JK	D	K	.	.	DEFGHIJK	DEFGH	D
763.00	D	JK	D	GK	.	.	EFHIJK	DEFH	D
762.50	D	JK	D	FGK	.	.	EFIJ	DEF	D
762.00	D	JK	D	FGK	.	.	F	E	D
761.50	DH	JK	DE	FGIK	.	.	F	E	D
761.00	DHI	JK	DEFK	FGIK	.	.	.	.	DE
760.50	DEHI	JK	DEFK	EFHIJK	.	.	.	.	DEF
760.00	DEFGHI	JK	DEFK	EFHIJK	.	.	.	.	DEFG
759.50	DEFGHI	IJ	DEFK	EFHIJK	.	.	.	.	DEFGHI
759.00	DEFGHIJ	IJ	DEFGHJK	EFHIJK	.	.	.	.	DEFGHI
758.50	DEFGHIJ	IJ	DEFGHJK	EFHIJK	.	.	.	.	EFGHI
758.00	DEGHIJ	I	DEFGHJK	EFHIJK	.	.	.	.	EFGHIJ
757.50	DHIJ	I	DEFGHIJK	EFIJ	.	.	.	.	EFGHIJ
757.00	J	I	DEFGHIJK	EFIJ	.	.	.	.	EHIJ
756.50	J	I	EGHIJK	DEFJ	.	.	.	.	IJK
756.00	J	HI	EGHIJK	DF	.	.	.	.	IJK
755.50	J	HI	HIJK	D	.	.	.	.	JK
755.00	J	DHI	HIJK	D	.	.	.	.	JK
754.50	J	DHI	HIJK	D	.	.	.	.	JK
754.00	J	DHI	HJK	D	.	.	.	.	JK
753.50	J	DHI	HJK	D	.	.	.	.	JK
753.00	J	DHI	HJK	D	.	.	.	.	.
752.50	JK	DHI	K	D	.	.	.	.	.
752.00	JK	DHI	K	D	.	.	.	.	.
751.50	JK	DH	K	D	.	.	.	.	.
751.00	JK	DH	K	D	.	.	.	.	.
750.50	JK	DH	.	D	.	.	.	.	.
750.00	JK	DEH	.	.	.	.	.	.	.
749.50	JK	DEH	.	.	.	.	.	.	.
749.00	JK	DEH	.	.	.	.	.	.	.
748.50	K	DEFH	.	.	.	.	.	.	.
748.00	K	EFH	.	.	.	.	.	.	.
747.50	.	EFH	.	.	.	.	.	.	.
747.00	.	EFGH	.	.	.	.	.	.	.
746.50	.	EFGH	.	.	.	.	.	.	.
746.00	.	EFGH	.	.	.	.	.	.	.
745.50	.	EFGH	.	.	.	.	.	.	.
745.00	.	EGH	.	.	.	.	.	.	.
744.50	.	EGH	.	.	.	.	.	.	.
744.00	.	EGH	.	.	.	.	.	.	.
743.50	.	GH	.	.	.	.	.	.	.
743.00	.	GH	.	.	.	.	.	.	.
742.50	.	GH	.	.	.	.	.	.	.
742.00	.	H	.	.	.	.	.	.	.
741.50	.	H	.	.	.	.	.	.	.
741.00	.	H	.	.	.	.	.	.	.
740.50	.	H	.	.	.	.	.	.	.

Once you have been forced out of a market by such a violent move, it is difficult to muster the confidence to place a new trade. However, it is during times like these, when market confidence is lowest, that some of the greatest opportunities are created.

When a market begins to move counter to the major auction, what is most important is not a lone day's structure; rather, how successful the market is at moving counter to the trend. The initial day of counteractivity may show directional conviction, but are subsequent days facilitating trade and exhibiting follow-through? In other words, "Is the market doing a good job in its attempts to go that way?" If not, the activity may be due to long-term short covering (or long liquidation).

Figure 4–104 shows the soybean rally on January 26, as well as the Profiles for the next seven trading days. After the strong rally, January 27 and 30 developed overlapping value areas just below the upper distribution of the 26th. If the soybean market was truly as strong as it had appeared to be on the 26th, these balancing days would have developed closer to, or even above, the January 26th 768 highs. February 1 and February 2 did manage to auction higher and establish value above 768. However, after soybean buyers had gained 30 cents in just one day, four more days of work netted only 9½ cents more. In addition, the fourth day (February 2) closed on its lows *below the January 26 highs*. Figure 4–104 illustrates the selling that continued through February 6. By the 9th, soybeans were again trading near the 740 lows.

If you look at January 26 through February 2 in isolation and without the benefit of hindsight, the short-term trend does appear to be up and higher value is developing. However, by "overlaying" the activity of each day onto the previous day (beginning with the start of the rally), a different picture begins to form. In Figure 4–106, we have combined the individual day timeframe Profiles into a *Long-Term Profile*.

Figure 4–106 shows the gradual development of longer-term value in the soybean market, beginning on January 26 and running through February 9. These particular Long-Term Profiles were formed using the price/volume data from the Liquidity Data Bank, although they may just as easily be formed using TPOs. The number of Xs at a given price represents the volume that occurred at that price, relative to the volumes occurring at all other prices traded during the period selected. Thus, the Long-Term Profile for the January 26–31 period (four market days) shows the greatest value (volume) building around 760. In addition, we have drawn a line separating trade above and below 768, the January 26 high. Remember, the salient feature to observe in order to identify short covering in any timeframe is continuation. Any activity above the high for the 26th is indicative of buyer continuation.

Figure 4–105 Long-term short covering in Soybeans. Data courtesy of Commodity Quote Graphics.

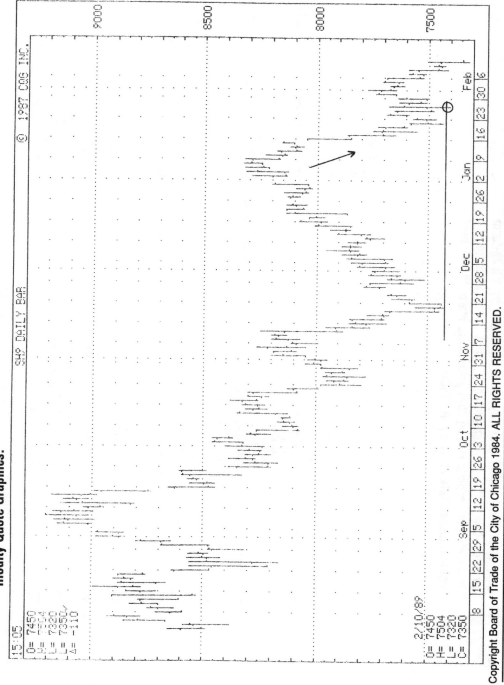

Figure 4–106 Long-term short covering in Soybeans illustrated by a long-term profile. The "X"'s corresponding to each price indicate the level of volume occurring at that price, relative to the highest volume price. Data courtesy of CISCO.

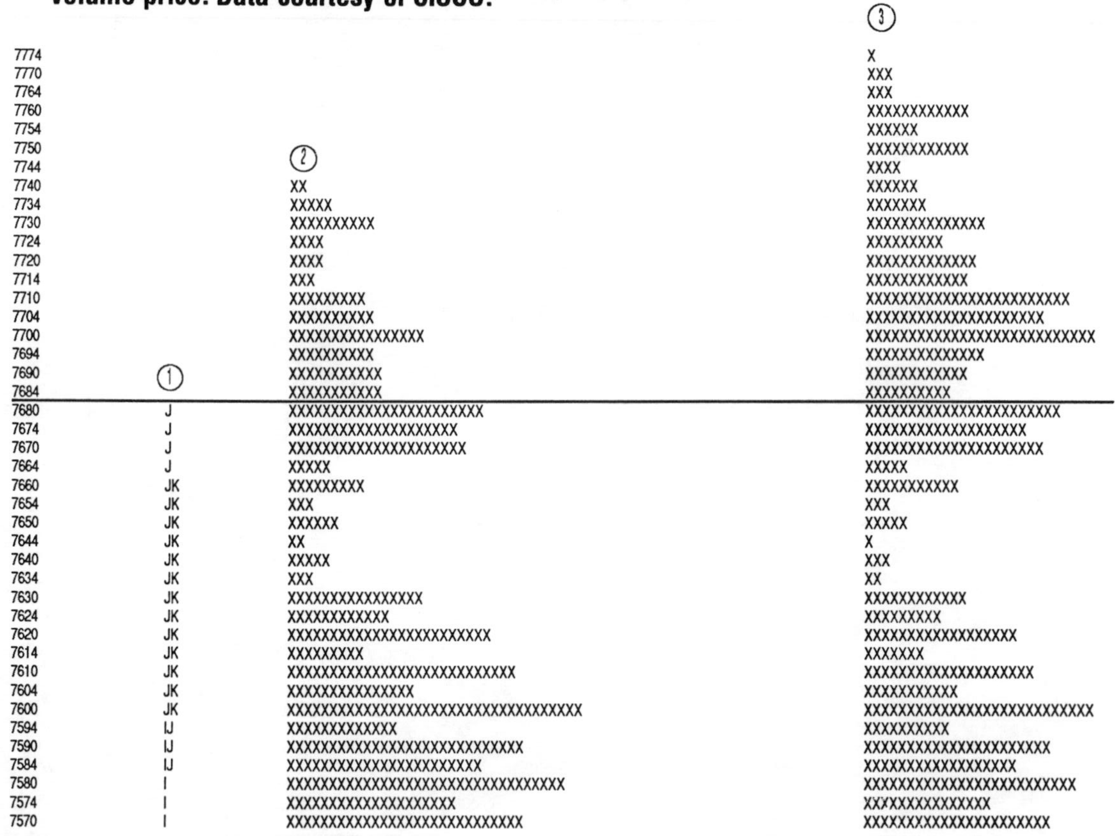

	①	②	③
7564	I	XXXXXXXXXX	XXXXXXXXX
7560	HI	XXXXXXXXXXXXXXXXXX	XXXXXXXXXXXX
7554	HI	XXXXXXXXXX	XXXXXXXX
7550	DHI	XXXXXXXXXXXX	XXXXXXXX
7544	DHI	XXXXXXX	XXXXX
7540	DHI	XXXXXXXXXXXXXXXX	XXXXXXXXXXXX
7534	DHI	XXXXXXXXXXXXXX	XXXXXXXXXXXXX
7530	DHI	XXXXXXXXXXXXXXXXXX	XXXXXXXXXXXXXX
7524	DHI	XXXXXXXXXXXX	XXXXXXXX
7520	DH	XXXXXXXXXXXXXXXXXXXXXX	XXXXXXXXXXXXXXXXXXXX
7514	DH	XXXXXXX	XXXXXX
7510	DH	XXXXXXXXXXX	X
7504	DEH	XX	XXXXXX
7500	DEH	XXXXXXXX	XXXXXXXX
7494	DEH	XXX	XXX
7490	DEFH	XXXX	XXXXX
7484	EFH	XXX	XXX
7480	EFH	XXXXX	XXX
7474	EFGH	XXXXXXX	XXXXXX
7470	EFGH	XXXXXXX	XXXXX
7464	EFGH	XXXXX	XXXXX
7460	EFGH	XXXXXXXXXXX	XXXXXXXXX
7454	EGH	XXXXXXX	XXXXX
7450	EGH	XXXXXXXXXXXXXX	XXXXXXXXXXX
7444	EGH	XXXX	XXX
7440	GH	XX	X
7434	GH	X	X
7430	GH	XXX	XX
7424	GH	XXX	XXX
7420	H	XXXXX	XXXX
7414	H	XXX	XX
7410	H	XX	XX
7404	H	X	X
	1/ 26	1/26-1/31	1/26-2/1

Figure 4-106
Continued

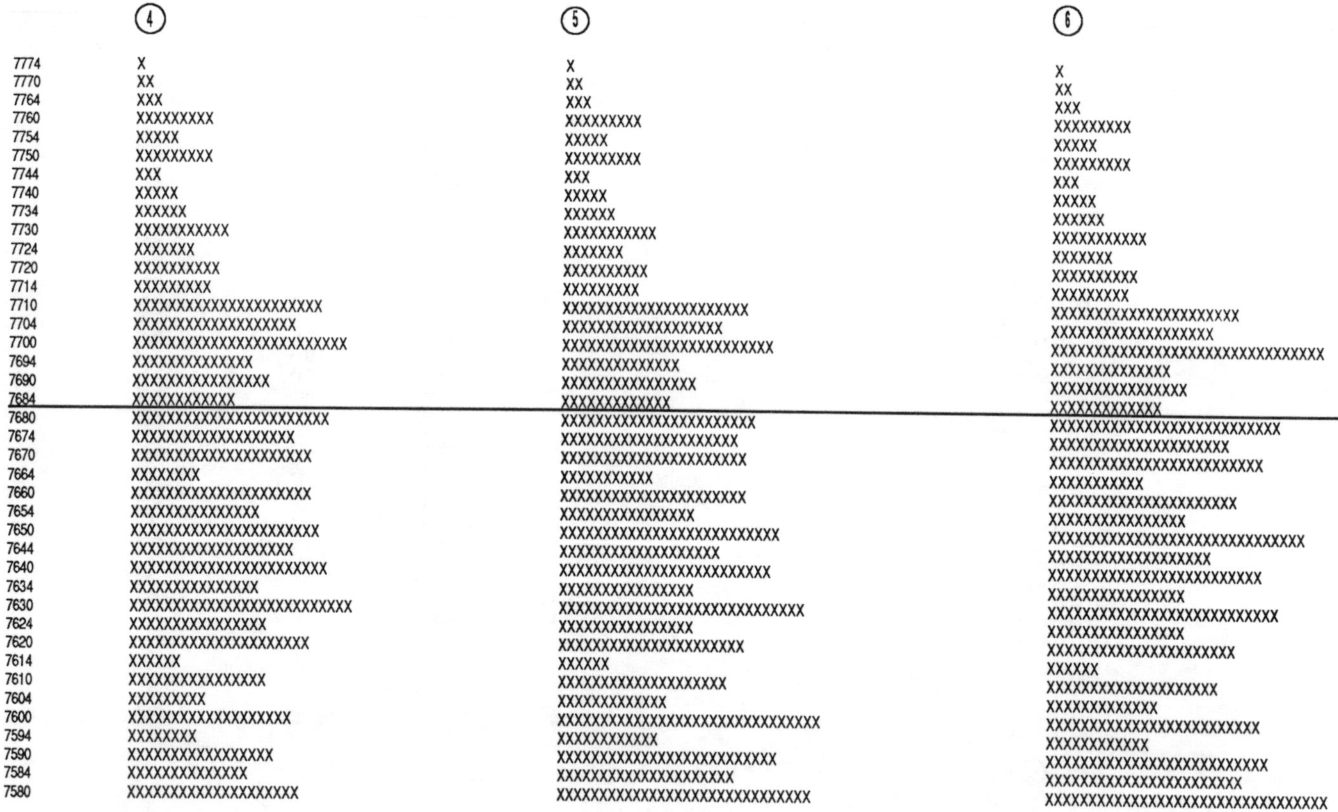

④

```
7574   XXXXXXXXXX
7570   XXXXXXXXXXXXXXXX
7564   XXXXXXXXXX
7560   XXXXXXXXX
7554   XXXXX
7550   XXXXXXXX
7544   XXXXXXXX
7540   XXXXXXXXXXXXX
7534   XXXXXXXXXX
7530   XXXXXXXXXXXXXX
7524   XXXXXX
7520   XXXXXXXXXXXXXX
7514   XXXXX
7510   XXXXX
7504   X
7500   XXXXX
7494   XX
7490   XXXX
7484   XXX
7480   XXX
7474   XXXX
7470   XXXXX
7464   XXXX
7460   XXXXXXX
7454   XXXX
7450   XXXXXXXXX
7444   XX
7440   X
7434   X
7430   X
7424   XX
7420   X
7414   X
7410   X
7404   X

1/26 - 2/6
```

⑤

```
XXXXXXXXXXXX
XXXXXXXXXXXXXXXXX
XXXXXXXX
XXXXXXX
XXXXXXXX
XXXXXXXXXXXXXXXX
XXXXXXXXXXXXXXXXXXX
XXXXXXXXXXXX
XXXXXXXXXXX
XXXXXXX
XXXXXXXXXXXX
XXXXX
XX
XXXXX
XX
XXXX
XXX
XXX
XXXX
XXXXX
XXXX
XXXXXXX
XXXX
XXXXXXXXX
XX
X
X
XX
XXX
X
X

1/26 - 2/7
```

⑥

```
XXXXXXXXXXXXXXXXXXXXXXXXXX
XXXXXXXXXXXXX
XXXXXXXXXX
XXXXXXXXXXXXX
XXXXXXXXXXXXXXXXXXXXXXXX
XXXXXXXXXXXXXXXXXXXXX
XXXXXXXXXXXX
XXXXXXXXXXX
XXXXXXX
XXXXXXXXXXXXXX
XXXXXX
XXXXXX
X
XXXXX
XX
XXX
XXX
XXXX
XXXX
XXXXXXX
XXXX
XXXXXXXXX
XX
X
X
XX
XXX
X
X

1/26 - 2/8
```

Figure 4–106
Continued

①

7574	XXXXXXXXXXXXXXXXXXXX
7570	XXXXXXXXXXXXXXXXXXXXXXXXXXXX
7564	XXXXXXXXXXXXXX
7560	XXXXXXXXXXXXXXXXXXX
7554	XXXXXXXXXXXXXXXXX
7550	XXXXXXXXXXXXXXXXXXXXXXXXXXX
7544	XXXXXXXXXXXXXXXXXXXXXXXXXX
7540	XXXXXXXXXXXXXXXXXXXXXXXXXXXX
7534	XXXXXXXXXXXXXX
7530	XXXXXXXXXXXXXXXX
7524	XXXXXXXX
7520	XXXXXXXXXXXXXXXXX
7514	XXXXXX
7510	XXXXXXXX
7504	XX
7500	XXXXXXXXXXXXXXXXXX
7494	XX
7490	XXXXX
7484	XXX
7480	XXXXX
7474	XXXXX
7470	XXXXXXXXX
7464	XXXXXXXXX
7460	XXXXXXXXXXXXXXX
7454	XXXXXXXXX
7450	XXXXXXXXXXXXXXXX
7444	XXXXXX
7440	XXXXXX
7434	XXXX
7430	XXXXXXXXX
7424	XXXXXX
7420	XXXXXXXXXXXXXX
7414	XXX
7410	X
7404	X

1/26 - 2/9

Figure 4–107   Corrective action in September Treasury Bonds, August 25-31, 1988.

	AUG. 25	AUG.26	AUG. 29	AUG. 30	AUG.31
86 10/32	.	.	.	.	A
86 9/32	.	.	.	.	O
86 8/32	.	.	.	.	A
86 7/32	.	.	.	.	A
86 6/32	.	.	.	.	A
86 5/32	.	.	.	.	ABC
86 4/32	.	.	.	.	ABC
86 3/32	.	.	.	.	ABCLM
86 2/32	.	.	.	.	BCLM
86 1/32	.	.	.	A	CDL
86 0/32	.	.	.	A	CDEFIL
85 31/32	.	.	.	A	CDEFHIL
85 30/32	.	.	.	A	CDEFHIJKL
85 29/32	.	.	.	OC	DEFGHIJKL
85 28/32	.	.	.	ABC	EFGHIJKL
85 27/32	.	.	.	ABCKL	EFGJKL
85 27/32	.	.	.	ABCKL	FGJK
85 25/32	.	.	.	BCKLM	FJK
85 24/32	.	.	.	CKL	J
85 23/32	.	.	L	CDK	J
85 22/32	.	.	L	CDJK	.
85 21/32	.	.	KLM	CDEJK	.
85 20/32	.	.	KL	CDEJ	.
85 19/32	.	.	KL	DEFHIJ	.
85 18/32	.	.	JK	DEFHIJ	.
85 17/32	.	.	JK	FGHIJ	.
85 16/32	.	.	IJK	FGHIJ	.
85 15/32	.	.	IJ	FGHIJ	.
85 14/32	.	.	IJ	FGIJ	.
85 13/32	.	.	IJ	G	.
85 12/32	.	.	I	.	.
85 11/32	.	.	HI	.	.
85 10/32	.	.	CHI	.	.
85 9/32	.	.	CGHI	.	.
85 8/32	.	.	ABCDEFGH	.	.
85 7/32	.	.	ABCDEFG	.	.
85 6/32	.	.	ABCDEFG	.	.
85 5/32	.	.	AB	.	.
85 4/32	.	.	A	.	.
85 3/32	.	.	A	.	.
85 2/32	.	.	A	.	.
85 1/32	.	.	A	.	.
85 0/32	.	.	A	.	.
84 31/32	.	.	A	.	.
84 30/32	.	DJ	A	.	.
84 29/32	.	DJK	O	.	.
84 28/32	.	DFIJKLM	A	.	.
84 27/32	.	CDEFGIJKL	.	.	.
84 26/32	.	CDEFGHIKL	.	.	.
84 25/32	.	CGHIKL	.	.	.
84 24/32	.	CGHL	.	.	.
84 23/32	.	CG	.	.	.
84 22/32	.	C	.	.	.
84 21/32	K	C	.	.	.
84 20/32	KL	C	.	.	.
84 19/32	JKL	C	.	.	.
84 18/32	JKL	OBC	.	.	.
84 17/32	BJKL	ABC	.	.	.
84 16/32	BCIJK	ABC	.	.	.
84 15/32	ABCDEIJ	A	.	.	.
84 14/32	ABCDEIJ	.	.	.	.
84 13/32	ABCDEFGHI	.	.	.	.
84 12/32	ABEFGH	.	.	.	.
84 11/32	AEFGH	.	.	.	.
84 10/32	AFG	.	.	.	.
84 9/32	AFG	.	.	.	.
84 8/32	AF	.	.	.	.
84 7/32	.	.	.	.	.

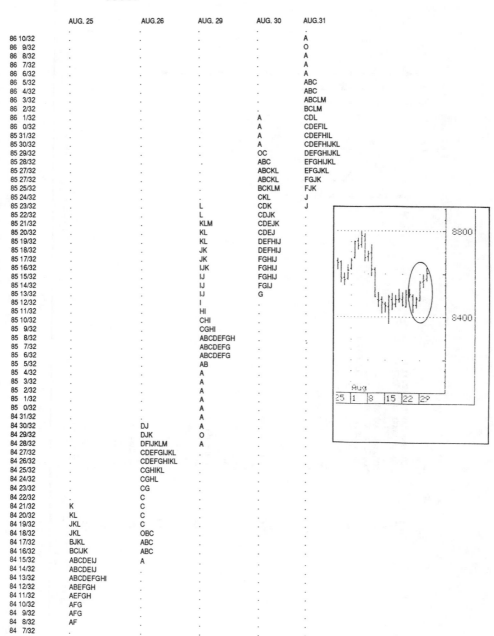

Through February 1, soybeans auction higher and begin to build value above 768. However, continuation remains low relative to the magnitude of the initial rally. By February 2, there has been no further buyer follow-through, relative volume is beginning to decline above 768, and most notable, a "P" formation is beginning to form. In effect, longer term buying auctions are stalling, thus creating the noncontinuation structure found in day timeframe short covering. Higher prices are cutting off activity as old business has covered their shorts and new buyers have not entered the market. This is the first long-term structural indication of poor buyer continuation. The buying in the soybean market, in this case, was likely longer term short covering, not healthy new initiative buying.

Applications   Suppose that you are one of the traders forced out of the market by the covering. It has only been a few days, and the memory of the swift rally is no doubt still fresh in your mind. If your intent is to reestablish your short position, by February 3 the Long-Term Profile provides some of the longer term information you need in order to enter the market:

1. Risk is identified. If the soybean market returns up to trade above 777½ (7774), it is most likely caused by the actions of new, initiative other timeframe buyers. Thus, shorts should be exited if price returns above 777½.

2. By February 2 and 3, buying auctions are subsiding as the short covering diminishes and control reverts back to the other timeframe seller. This transition phase is evidenced by the return of value below 768.

3. If the short covering is genuine, then soybeans should auction down to "take another look" at the 740 lows.

At the right side of Figure 4–106, we have created a sequential Profile in which each time period represents a day (instead of half-hour auctions). This longer-term Profile clearly exhibits the similarities between day and longer-term short covering. The quick initial rally in "1" period is followed by weak buying-range extension attempts. Short covering activity wanes and the seller resumes control in "8" period, eventually filling in the lower half of the Profile.

Corrective Action

Most great scientific discoveries are brought forth by a creative individual who looks at something old in a new and innovative way. Often using the same information that others have studied and researched for years, the inventor simply sees the data in a different light. It is easy to become entrenched in a mode of thinking or behavior. By locking our minds into a single mindset, however, we often fail to question what we think are the obvious answers.

Before we enter our discussion, take a minute to write down your first reaction to the following questions:

1. What do we mean when we say that a market needs to correct itself (assuming that the current auction is up)?

2. What forms can this corrective action take?

A common dictionary definition of the term "correction" is *counteraction*. For something to be corrected, an opposite action must take place. If your thinking is locked into the generally accepted definition, you might conceptualize a correction to be a situation where the market auctions lower after a sustained rally, resulting in lower prices. Or, in a larger timeframe sense, you may see a correction as a gradual sell-off resulting in several days of lower prices. The point is, a typical "stimulus" response to the question "what is correction after an up auction" is often simply that price needs to move lower. We, however, define correction as "counteraction." When viewed as counteraction, you will begin to see that corrective action can take a more subtle, and perhaps more powerful, form.

Traditionally, a correction after an up auction is assumed to be selling, or profit taking, that results in lower prices. This is not always true. Even though there are sellers in the market covering longs after an up auction, *price does not necessarily have to fall*. For example, a market may open higher and sell off all day, resulting in higher prices, higher value and a higher close. On such a day, correction can still be taking place even though lower prices are not evident.

This sort of correction occurs when old buyers sell, taking their profits at the same time new buyers are just deciding to enter the market. Thus, responsive selling (profit taking) is met by initiative buyers entering new positions. If the initiative buying is strong enough, price may remain higher despite old business liquidating their original positions. Remember, however, that when the responsive seller is able to exert more influence on price than the initiative buyer, the up auction may be over (refer to Bracketed Markets in Chapter 3).

The Function of Corrective Action   Corrective action serves several purposes. First, it allows for profit-taking—a vital ingredient in maintaining a healthy market. Profit-taking eases the anxiety level of the market. Naturally, traders with well-placed trades often build up high levels of anxiety about being able to keep their profits. The way to reduce this worry and nervousness is to lock in your profit—to sell if price has been going up or to buy if price has been going down.

More important, counteraction also serves as a test of the strength of the buyer (or seller). If a correction is occurring in an up auction and the market still manages to establish higher value, then the underlying market conditions are very strong. A textbook example of such corrective action is provided by Treasury bonds in Figure 4–107.

Following a higher opening, traders holding longs were given ample time to sell all they wanted. The resulting selling-range extension and Normal Variation selling structure suggests that this is exactly what happened. Although lower prices were not the result, this selling is nonetheless a "counteraction" to the buying that had been occurring over the previous three days. Reviewing the Treasury bond activity prior to August 30, excess was created on August 25, which ultimately marked the beginning of an up auction. As the bar chart windowed inside Figure 4–107 shows, the buying auction continued with a break-out above a previous short-term high at 85–11. On August 30, the market opened above value and attempted to trade lower most of the session (until J period). However, the resulting value area and close were actually higher than the previous day. As the activity of subsequent days proved, within the sell-off of August 30 was the well-disguised correction for which alert buyers had been waiting.

Corrective action is important to the health of a trend. The fact that corrective selling attempts occurred at the same time value was being established higher indicated that the bond market was exceptionally strong. Old buyers had ample time to liquidate their positions at a favorable price, and new buyers had plenty of opportunity to place longs with good day timeframe trade location. Conventional traders relying mainly on price might not have recognized the correction, and instead reacted to the sell-off after the open by entering short positions. As Figure 4–107 shows, any short positions on this day soon became losing trades.

Whether talking about corrective action or any other natural market function, it is important to keep in mind that the most obvious behavioral clues, such as lower prices, are not always available. On August 30, creative, open-minded traders probably recognized that price did not have to go lower for a correction to take place.

Summary   Being able to identify corrective action without the benefit of an obvious price break or rally requires a level of creativity that can only come from the trader who is willing and able to look at the same information from more than one angle. Objectivity stretches far beyond this one isolated instance, however. Futures trading presents us with a formidable variety of such situations every day. As we gain more experience and draw closer to the levels of Proficient and Expert, our goal is to begin to consistently see the unusual—to develop the open-mindedness that allows us to identify and take advantage of the unique trading opportunities that arise when the market deviates from the norm.

Long-Term Profiles

> *The truth knocks on the door and you say, "Go away, I'm looking for the truth," and so it goes away.*

From *Zen and the Art of Motorcycle Maintenance*, by Robert Pirsig

In today's complex world, we are continually confronted by the ever-changing demands and influences of society. It is difficult to remain cooly objective in the face of the shifting images produced by public opinion, the media, and noted financial experts. Occasionally, everyone gets caught up and loses sight of the "big picture"—whether it be in one's profession, family life, or trading. In such cases, it is easy to miss the proverbial forest for the trees, to tell truth to go away when it should be as obvious as a knock on the door.

How many times have you gotten so involved with the individual, day-to day auctions that you lost sight of the real market? When you focus on the individual "trees," you lose the longer-term big picture. What is needed is a consistent method of recording the longer-term auctions so that they can be observed objectively. A Long-Term Profile simply plots greater units of time in relation to price in order to form a long-term version of the day timeframe Market Profile.

The salient concept behind the Long-Term Profile is the fact that the principles of the market's auction process apply to all timeframes, from the shortest time period to the longer-term auctions. Just as each day's Profile is composed of a series of half-hour auctions, a week-long Profile would be composed of five-day timeframe Profiles. It follows then, that a Long-Term Profile develops the same structural manifestations of market activity, such as gaps, brackets, trends, high and low volume areas, excess, and tails.

Shown in Figure 4–108 are a typical day timeframe Profile, a 10-day "Swing Profile," and a one month Long-Term Profile. Notice the striking-

Figure 4–108   Profiles across timeframes.

```
.                 .                 .
.                 .                 .
.                 .                 .
.                 .                 .
.                 XX                .
.                 XX                X
.                 XXX               XX
.                 XXXX              XXXXXXXX
.                 XXXX              XXXXXXXXX
.                 XXXXX             XXXXX
X                 XXXXXXX           XXXXXXXXXXX
X                 XXXXXXXX          XXXXXXXXXX
X                 XXXXXXX           XXXXXXXXXXXXXXXXXXXXX
X                 XXXXXXX           XXXXXXXXXXXXXXXXXXXXXXXXXXXX
X                 XXXXXXX           XXXXXXXXXXXXXXXX
X                 XXXXXX            XXXXXXXXXXXXXXXXXXXXXXXXXXX
X                 XXXXXXXXX         XXXXXXXXXXXXXXXXXXXXXXXXXXXXXXX
XX                XXXXXXXXXXXX      XXXXXXXXXXXXXXXXXXXXXX
XX                XXXXXXXXXX        XXXXXXXXXXXXXXXXXXXXXXXXXXXXXXXX
XX                XXXXXXXXXXX       XXXXXXXXXXXXXXXXXXXXXXXXXXXX
XXXX              XXXXXXXXXXX       XXXXXXXXXXXXXXXXXXXXXXXXXXXXXXXXX
XXXXX             XXXXXXXXXXX       XXXXXXXXXXXXXXXXXXXXXXXXXX
XXXXX             XXXXXXXXXXXX      XXXXXXXXXXXXXXXXXXXXXX
XXXXXXX           XXXXXXXXXXXXX     XXXXXXXXXXXXXXXXXXXXXXXXXXXXXXXXX
XXXXXXX           XXXXXXXXXXX       XXXXXXXXXXXXXXXXXXXXXXXXXXXXX
XXXXX             XXXXXXXX          XXXXXXXXXXXXXXXXXXXXXXXXXXXXXXXXXXXXXX
XXXX              XXXXXXXXX         XXXXXXXXXXXXXXXXXXXXXXXXXXXXXXXX
XXXXXX            XXXXXXX           XXXXXXXXXXXXXXXXXXXXXXXXXX
XXXXX             XXXXXXX           XXXXXXXXXXXXXXXXXXXXXXXXXXXXXXXXXXXX
XXXXX             XXXXXXX           XXXXXXXXXXXXXXXXXXXXXXXXXXXXXXXXXXX
XXXXX             XXXXXXX           XXXXXXXXXXXXXXXXXXXXX
XXXXX             XXXXX             XXXXXXXXXXXXXXXXXXXXXX
XXXX              XXXXXX            XXXXXXXX
XXXX              XXXXX             XXXXXXXXXXXXXXXXXXXX
XXX               XXXX              XXXXX
XX                XXXX              XXXXX
XX                X X               XXXXXXXXXX
X                 XX                XXXXXXXXXXXXXXXXXXXX
X                 XXXX              XXXXXXXXXXXXXXXXXXX
X                 XXXXX             XXXXXXXX
X                 XXXXXX            XXXXXXXXXXXX
X                 XXXXXX            XXXXXXXXXXX
X                 XXXXXXX           X
X                 XXXXXXX           .
X                 XXXXXXXX          .
X                 XXXXXXXX          .
X                 XXXXXXXX          .
X                 XXXXXXXXX         .
.                 XXXXXXXX          .
.                 XXXXXXXXX         .
.                 XXXXX             .
.                 XXXXX             .
.                 XXXXX             .
.                 XXX               .
.                 XXX               .
.                 XXX               .
.                 XXX               .
.                 X                 .
.                 .                 .
One  Day          Ten Days          One Month
```

ly similar characteristics. To make the distributions appear more generic, the individually lettered TPOs have been replaced with common "Xs."

Using Long-Term Profiles The main strength of the Long-Term Profile lies in the clear definition of brackets and the migration of value. It not only provides a visual picture of the longer-term structures of the market but also enables you to easily monitor elements that signify change. By identifying changing conditions through the Long-Term Profile, longer-term traders are prepared to act in the early stages of opportunity.

Theoretically, if a Long-Term Profile was "accumulated" indefinitely, the ultimate result would be a giant, normal distribution curve that is of little value to anyone. Thus, to use the Long-Term Profile effectively, you need to begin building the Profile when a significant long-term change has occurred, such as a long-term high or low. As you witness significant market changes that influence your particular timeframe, you might consider a "running Long-Term Profile" starting at the point of change in order to better evaluate continuation. When the market enters a new period marked by confirmed long term change, you should begin a new Long-Term Profile. It is wise to keep your past Profiles as well in order to keep track of long-term reference points that might have an affect on future auctions.

The Long-Term Profile in Action We have illustrated the similarities between the day, swing, and longer timeframes throughout the book. In this section, we present an ongoing analysis of a Long-Term Profile for the Japanese yen during the first few months of 1989. The aim is to demonstrate how the Long-Term Profile accurately pinpoints the key longer-term reference points that traders commonly attempt to glean from a daily bar chart. In addition, we show that through the added dimension of time (TPOs), the *success* of the longer-term auction is easily discernable through a Long Term Profile.

This period in the yen is particularly useful, because it also illustrates how markets evolve from trend, to bracket, then back to trend again (see Trending versus Bracketed Markets in Chapter 3). The example displays the usefulness of the Long-Term Profile during both types of market conditions.

The analysis is segmented into two regions. Each region is accompanied by a Long-Term Profile and the daily bar chart for the corresponding period of time.

Region A (Figures 4–109 & 4–110) Region A displays a longer-term selling trend that began with a break-out of a short-term bracket and then slowed when the market eventually came into balance near the .7600 level. Point 1 in the bar chart shows several volatile but basically over-lapping days occurring in the .8000–.8100 region. Point 1 on the Long-Term Profile vividly depicts the bracket resulting from this balancing process. Notice how the Long-Term Profile displays the bracket in a well-defined high volume area bound by longer-term tails (points 1a and 1b). Just like a day timeframe Profile, high volume represents acceptance and serves to attract price. The low-volume extremes indicate strong responsive other timeframe presence at the bracket top and bottom.

The yen broke below the bracket with the sharp selling gap denoted by point 2. The gap is represented on the Long-Term Profile by the single prints directly below the bracketed region at point 1. (This particular Long-Term Profile assumes that some degree of trade took place and therefore records "single prints" in the area of the gap.) The excess created by the gap gave other timeframe sellers the confidence they needed to initiate the selling trend denoted by point 3. During a trend, the Long-Term Profile exhibits relatively low volume and elongated structure. In the bar chart, the trend is witnessed by the steady progression of lower prices.

After another selling gap at point 4 (the gap is less evident through the Long Term Profile, because the yen had actually traded in the region of the gap four days earlier), the yen entered the second balanced area (point 5) evidenced by a high-volume region in the Long-Term Profile. This particular bracketing phase was caused by central bank intervention to slow the U.S. dollar's rise (which had a supportive affect on the yen). Note, however, that the long-term point of control continued to fall (points 5a, b and c in the Long-Term Profile), indicating the long-term seller remained in control and was gradually establishing lower value. While strong excess above the bracket is shown by the Long-Term Profile through the gap and accompanying low volume at point 4, the lower extreme of the bracket does not display the aggressive rejection indicative of a high-confidence low.

Region B (Figures 4–111 & 4–112)   The Long-Term Profile in Figure 4–112 displays the entire down auction for February 15 through May 24. Readers should note that the price intervals used are now tens instead of fours so that the selling auction can be represented in its entirety on one page. At point 6 in region B, the yen gapped below the bracket established at point 5, reigniting the strong selling auction and confirming the control of the other timeframe seller. After a short term balancing period at point 7, the long-term selling trend resumed as other timeframe sellers auctioned price substantially lower. Much like a Trend day, when the long-term trend denoted by point 8 was underway, the Long-Term

Figure 4-109   Region A, Japanese Yen. Data courtesy of Commodity Quote Graphics.

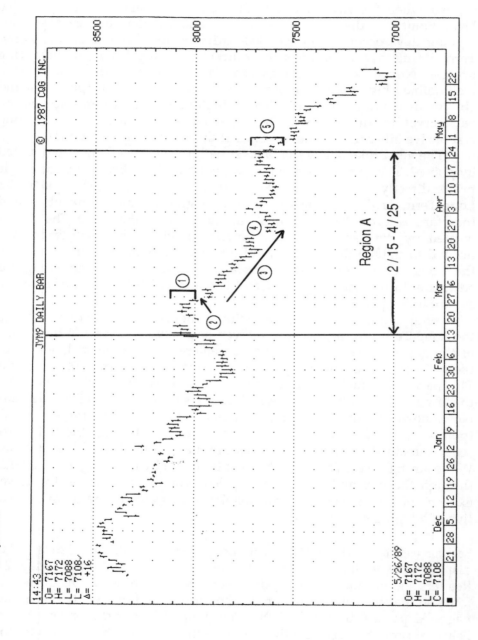

Figure 4–110   Region A, long-term profile for Japanese Yen. The "X"'s corresponding to each price indicate the relative number of TPO's occurring at that price, relative to the highest TPO price. Data courtesy of CISCO.

COMBINED TPO PLOT. IF ACTUAL TPO COUNT EXCEEDS 50 THE PLOT IS NORMALIZED TO 50

PRICE	DYS	TPO (TPO DENSITY)
8116	1	1 X
8112	1	2 XX <-- ①A
8108	2	3 XXX
8104	2	4 XXX
8100	2	4 XXX
8092	2	3 XXX
8088	2	5 XXXX
8084	3	8 XXXXXX
8080	3	12 XXXXXXXXXX
8076	3	11 XXXXXXXXXX
8072	4	12 XXXXXXXXXX
8068	5	18 XXXXXXXXXXXXXX
8064	5	19 XXXXXXXXXXXXXXX
8060	6	18 XXXXXXXXXXXXXX
8056	6	25 XXXXXXXXXXXXXXXXXXXX
8052	6	24 XXXXXXXXXXXXXXXXXXX
8048	6	16 XXXXXXXXXXXX
8044	7	18 XXXXXXXXXXXXXX
8040	6	17 XXXXXXXXXXXXX
8036	6	15 XXXXXXXXXXXX
8032	5	15 XXXXXXXXXXXX
8028	6	19 XXXXXXXXXXXXXXX
8024	4	15 XXXXXXXXXXXX
8020	2	10 XXXXXXXX
8016	2	12 XXXXXXXXXX
8012	2	9 XXXXXXX
8008	2	7 XXXXX
8004	2	5 XXXX
8000	2	4 XXX
7996	2	3 XXX
7992	2	4 XXX <-- ①B
7988	2	4 XXX
7984	1	1 X
7980	1	1 X
7976	1	1 X <-- ② SELLING GAP; LOW VOLUME
7964	1	1 X
7960	1	2 XX

① BRACKET; HIGH VOLUME

**Figure 4–110
Continued**

```
7956 │ 1     2 XX
7952 │ 1     3 XXX
7948 │ 2     7 XXXXX
7944 │ 2    14 XXXXXXXXXXXX
7940 │ 3    22 XXXXXXXXXXXXXXXXXXXX
7928 │ 3    22 XXXXXXXXXXXXXXXXXXXX
7924 │ 2    11 XXXXXXXXX
7920 │ 2     2 XX
7916 │ 1     1 X
7908 │ 1     1 X
7904 │ 1     3 XXX
7900 │ 1     2 XX
7896 │ 3    12 XXXXXXXXXX
7892 │ 3    17 XXXXXXXXXXXXXXX
7888 │ 3    14 XXXXXXXXXXXX
7884 │ 3    13 XXXXXXXXXXX
7880 │ 4    18 XXXXXXXXXXXXXXXX
7876 │ 4    16 XXXXXXXXXXXXXX
7872 │ 4    11 XXXXXXXXX
7868 │ 3     8 XXXXXXX
7864 │ 4    10 XXXXXXXXX
7860 │ 4    12 XXXXXXXXXX
7856 │ 4    13 XXXXXXXXXXX
7852 │ 4     9 XXXXXXXX
7848 │ 2     5 XXXX
7844 │ 1     9 XXXXXXXX
7840 │ 1     7 XXXXXX
7836 │ 2    13 XXXXXXXXXXX
7832 │ 2    11 XXXXXXXXX
7828 │ 3    10 XXXXXXXXX
7824 │ 3    17 XXXXXXXXXXXXXX
7820 │ 3    12 XXXXXXXXXX
7816 │ 2    15 XXXXXXXXXXXX
7812 │ 2    15 XXXXXXXXXXXX
7808 │ 2     5 XXXX
7804 │ 3     4 XXX
7800 (3) 2     3 XXX
7796 │ 2     4 XXX
7792 │ 2     5 XXXX
7788 │ 1     5 XXXX
7784 │ 1     4 XXX  <-- ( 4 ) SELLING GAP; LOW VOLUME
7780 │ 2     5 XXXX
7776 │ 2     2 XX
7772 │ 2     6 XXXXX
7768 │ 2     5 XXXX
7764 │ 2     9 XXXXXXXX
```

**Figure 4–110
Continued**

```
7760      2     4 XXX
7756      3     5 XXXX
7752      3     7 XXXXXX
7748      5    17 XXXXXXXXXXXXXXX
7744      5    20 XXXXXXXXXXXXXXXXXX
7740      5    19 XXXXXXXXXXXXXXXX
7736      5    24 XXXXXXXXXXXXXXXXXXXXX
7732      6    30 XXXXXXXXXXXXXXXXXXXXXXXXXX   (5A)
7728      7    28 XXXXXXXXXXXXXXXXXXXXXXXX
7724      7    29 XXXXXXXXXXXXXXXXXXXXXXXXX
7720      6    23 XXXXXXXXXXXXXXXXXXXX
7716      6    21 XXXXXXXXXXXXXXXXXX
7712      5    14 XXXXXXXXXXX
7708      4    11 XXXXXXXXX
7704      2    13 XXXXXXXXXXX
7700      3    11 XXXXXXXXXX
7696      5    14 XXXXXXXXXXX
7692      5    24 XXXXXXXXXXXXXXXXXXXXX
7688      6    25 XXXXXXXXXXXXXXXXXXXXXX
7684      8    34 XXXXXXXXXXXXXXXXXXXXXXXXXXXXXX
7680      9    39 XXXXXXXXXXXXXXXXXXXXXXXXXXXXXXXXX
7676     10    40 XXXXXXXXXXXXXXXXXXXXXXXXXXXXXXXXXX
7672     10    44 XXXXXXXXXXXXXXXXXXXXXXXXXXXXXXXXXXXXXX   (5B)
7668      9    33 XXXXXXXXXXXXXXXXXXXXXXXXXXX
7664      6    24 XXXXXXXXXXXXXXXXXXXXX
7660      7    20 XXXXXXXXXXXXXXXXX
7656      9    20 XXXXXXXXXXXXXXXXX
7652     11    29 XXXXXXXXXXXXXXXXXXXXXXXXX
7648     12    36 XXXXXXXXXXXXXXXXXXXXXXXXXXXXXX
7644     12    42 XXXXXXXXXXXXXXXXXXXXXXXXXXXXXXXXXXXX
7640     11    46 XXXXXXXXXXXXXXXXXXXXXXXXXXXXXXXXXXXXXXXX
7636     12    57 XXXXXXXXXXXXXXXXXXXXXXXXXXXXXXXXXXXXXXXXXXXXXXXXXXX   (5C)
7632     11    47 XXXXXXXXXXXXXXXXXXXXXXXXXXXXXXXXXXXXXXXX
7628     10    40 XXXXXXXXXXXXXXXXXXXXXXXXXXXXXXXXXX
7624     11    45 XXXXXXXXXXXXXXXXXXXXXXXXXXXXXXXXXXXXXXX
7620      9    48 XXXXXXXXXXXXXXXXXXXXXXXXXXXXXXXXXXXXXXXXXX
7616      9    34 XXXXXXXXXXXXXXXXXXXXXXXXXXXX
7612      9    26 XXXXXXXXXXXXXXXXXXXXX
7608      5    15 XXXXXXXXXXXXX
7604      3     7 XXXXXX
7600      3     9 XXXXXXXX
7596      2    10 XXXXXXXXX
7592      2     8 XXXXXX
7588      1     3 XXX
7584      1     1 X    <-- (5D)
```

(5) Bracket High Volume

Figure 4-111   Region B, Japanese Yen. Data courtesy of Commodity Quote Graphics.

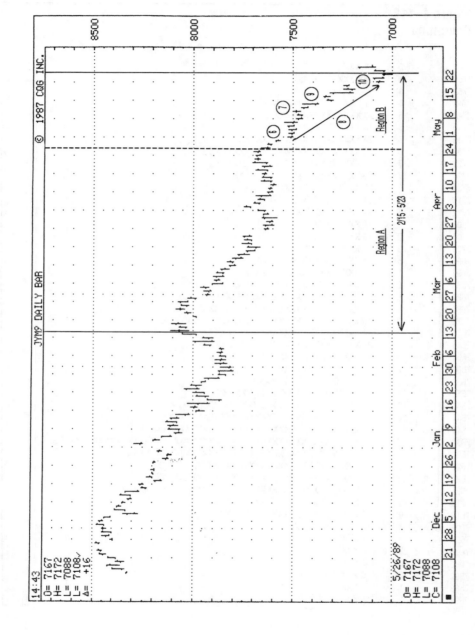

Figure 4–112 Region B, long-term profile for Japanese Yen. The "X"'s corresponding to each price indicate the relative number of TPO's occurring at that price, relative to the highest TPO price.

```
JUN 89 JAP YEN (CME-IMM)
15 02 89 TO 23 05 89

COMBINED TPO PLOT. IF ACTUAL TPO COUNT EXCEEDS 50 THE PLOT IS NORMALIZED TO 50

PRICE      DYS TPO (TPO DENSITY)

8110        1   2 XX
8100        2   4 XXXX
8090        2   4 XXXX
8080        3  12 XXXXXXXXXXX
8070        5  17 XXXXXXXXXXXXXXX
8060        6  18 XXXXXXXXXXXXXXXXX
8050        6  21 XXXXXXXXXXXXXXXXXXXXX
8040        6  17 XXXXXXXXXXXXXXXX
8030        5  20 XXXXXXXXXXXXXXXXXXXX
8020        2  10 XXXXXXXXX
8010        2   7 XXXXXX
8000        2   4 XXXX
7990        2   4 XXXX
7980        1   1 X
7960        1   2 XX
7950        1   6 XXXXX
7940        2  13 XXXXXXXXXXXX
7930        3  25 XXXXXXXXXXXXXXXXXXXXXXXX
7920        2   2 XX
7900        1   2 XX
7890        3  18 XXXXXXXXXXXXXXXXX
7880        4  18 XXXXXXXXXXXXXXXXX
7870        3  11 XXXXXXXXXX
7860        4  12 XXXXXXXXXXXX REGION  A
7850        3   8 XXXXXXXX
7840        1   7 XXXXXX
7830        3   7 XXXXXX
7820        3  12 XXXXXXXXXXX
7810        2  10 XXXXXXXXX
7800        2   3 XXX
7790        2   4 XXXX
7780        2   5 XXXXX
7770        2   4 XXXX
7760        2   4 XXXX
7750        3  12 XXXXXXXXXXX
7740        5  19 XXXXXXXXXXXXXXXXXX
7730        7  29 XXXXXXXXXXXXXXXXXXXXXXXXXXXX
7720        6  23 XXXXXXXXXXXXXXXXXXXXXX
7710        5  12 XXXXXXXXXXX
7700        3  11 XXXXXXXXXX
7690        5  24 XXXXXXXXXXXXXXXXXXXXXXX
7680        9  39 XXXXXXXXXXXXXXXXXXXXXXXXXXXXXXXXXXXXXX
7670       10  43 XXXXXXXXXXXXXXXXXXXXXXXXXXXXXXXXXXXXXXXXXXX
7660        8  21 XXXXXXXXXXXXXXXXXXXX
7650       13  36 XXXXXXXXXXXXXXXXXXXXXXXXXXXXXXXXXXX
7640       12  48 XXXXXXXXXXXXXXXXXXXXXXXXXXXXXXXXXXXXXXXXXXXXXXXXX
7630       12  49 XXXXXXXXXXXXXXXXXXXXXXXXXXXXXXXXXXXXXXXXXXXXXXXXXX
7620       11  55 XXXXXXXXXXXXXXXXXXXXXXXXXXXXXXXXXXXXXXXXXXXXXXXXXXXXXXX
7610        9  22 XXXXXXXXXXXXXXXXXXXXX
7600        3   9 XXXXXXXX
7590        2   5 XXXXX
7580        1  11 XXXXXXXXXX                    REGIONS
7570        1   2 XX
7560        1   1 X   <-- (6) SELLING GAP          A & B
7530        2   3 XXX
7520        4  18 XXXXXXXXXXXXXXXX
7510        5  16 XXXXXXXXXXXXXXX
7500        5   6 XXXXX          (7)
7490        3  18 XXXXXXXXXXXXXXXXX
7480        3   6 XXXXX
7470        3  14 XXXXXXXXXXXXX
7460        3   8 XXXXXXX
7450        2   2 XX
7440        2   8 XXXXXXX
7430        2   9 XXXXXXXX
7420        1   2 XX
7410        1   4 XXXX
7400        1   4 XXXX
7390        1   3 XXX
7380        1   2 XX
7350        1   1 X   <-- (9)          REGION B
7340        1   5 XXXXX
7330  (8)   2   7 XXXXXX
7320        2  11 XXXXXXXXXX
7310        2   2 XX
7300        1   1 X
7290        1   1 X
7280        1   1 X
7270        1   1 X
7260        1   2 XX
7250        1   2 XX
7240        3  11 XXXXXXXXXX
7230        3  20 XXXXXXXXXXXXXXXXXXX
7220        3  22 XXXXXXXXXXXXXXXXXXXXX
7210        2   5 XXXXX
7200        1   1 X
7100        1   1 X   <-- (10)
7090        1   6 XXXXX
7080        2   7 XXXXXX
7070        2  14 XXXXXXXXXXXXX
7060        2   9 XXXXXXXX
7050        2   5 XXXXX
```

Profile never showed a significant accumulation of volume at any lone price. The trend is obvious in the bar chart. Two "acceleration" selling gaps at points 9 and 10, present in both the bar chart and via the low volume areas in the Long-Term Profile, illustrate just how quickly this market is auctioning through time.

Summary   The Long-Term Profile vividly illustrates how the auction process is the same in all timeframes. Just as changes in other timeframe control are evident in day timeframe auctions and structural development, the Long-Term Profile reveals other timeframe activity in a big-picture sense through the evaluation of high- and low-volume areas.

Special Situations

A high school teacher tells the story of a frustrating day in his career. He was lecturing on the bravery of the American soldiers during the fight for independence. On this particular day, he became quite dramatic and descriptive, vividly portraying the battle fields and the courage of our forefathers. He described the freezing cold winter, the meager rations, and the eloquent words of Washington that kept the men's spirits high. The teacher was trying to give his students a feeling for what it was like to fight for one's country, the self-sacrifice that led to our freedom from England so many years ago.

The class was nearing its end when a student raised his hand. "Yes," the teacher said.

"Will this be on the test?" he asked.

The teacher was trying to give his students an understanding of the cost of freedom, but the boy who raised his hand was so worried about what he had to know for the test that he missed the point entirely. The student wanted to be given the answers. He did not want to have to actively think for himself. By focusing on what he thought he had to know, he did not hear what the instructor was really teaching.

It would be nice to know the answers, to rely on a little certainty. We would all be rich and successful if someone would come up with an answer that would tell us when to buy and when to sell. But if we are dogmatically given the answers, we will never truly *understand* their roots. In the words of Heraclitus, "Much learning does not teach understanding." Many traders do not want to actively think and make their own decisions. They want steadfast rules to guide their trading.

However, market-generated information, when observed and interpreted through the Market Profile, will at times reveal unique situations that offer a high degree of certainty. We call these high-probability occurrences "Special Situations." We will introduce six of these market-created opportunities. They are:

1. 3–I Days
2. Neutral-Extreme Days
3. The Value-Area Rule
4. Spikes
5. Balance-Area Break-outs
6. Gaps

There are no guarantees, but one of the comforts of a Special Situation is the identification of a *mechanical trade*—a trade which almost has to be done (under the right market conditions). And, while the limited studies that we have performed reveal encouraging results, it is important to note that the success of a Special Situation trade lies in the trader's *understanding* of the market conditions influencing that trade.

3–I Days

Probably the best known Special Situation is the 3–I day. A 3–I day is characterized by an initiative tail, TPO count, and range extension. Thus, a 3–I buying day would show an initiative buying tail, initiative buying TPOs and initiative buying range extension. Figure 4–113 displays a 3–I Buying Trend day in Soybeans (TPOs always favor the trend).

Over a large sample size, the trading session following a 3–I buying day should open within value or higher. Thus, traders holding longs placed within the previous day's value area should have an opportunity to exit within the same region (the opposite applies to a 3–I selling day). In sum, 3–I days often provide an opportunity to hold a highly leveraged position while incurring minimal risk.

We conducted a limited study evaluating the opportunity embodied in 3–I days by observing their continuation into the first 90 minutes of the following trading session as well as through to the day's close. Specifically, we recorded whether the subsequent day's trading took place at prices better than, within, or worse than the previous day's value area. For example, if the day following a 3–I Buying day opened higher, then activity was given a "better" reading for the initial 90 minutes of trade. Conversely, if the session following a 3–I Buying day closed below the previous day's value area, then it was given a "worse"

Figure 4–113   3-I day occurring in Soybeans, May 4-8, 1989.

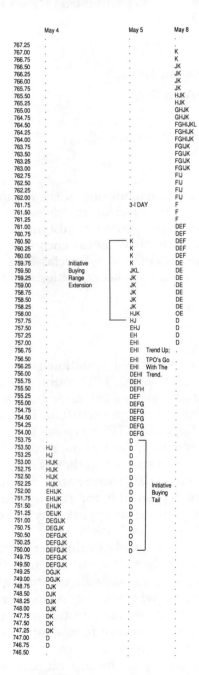

Next Day Initial 90 Minute

Day Type	Price Movement Better Than Prev. VA	Within Prev. VA	+ Worse Than Prev. VA
3–I	94%	6%	0%
2I–1R	71%	29%	0%

Day Type	Next Day Close Better Than Prev. VA	Within Prev. VA	Worse Than Prev. VA
3–I	59%	38%	3%
2I–1R	46%	36%	18%

reading in the "Next Day's Close" category. For purposes of the study, we also examined 2I–1R days—days possessing a responsive buying tail instead of an initiative buying tail (Figure 4–114). The results, compiled from Treasury bond data over the June 24, 1986, to May 29, 1987, period are shown below.

The results suggest that, over the period studied, 3–I and 2I–1R structure identified relatively low-risk trading opportunities with astounding reliability. We note, however, that these findings are derived from one market studied over a limited period of time. Other markets behave differently, and all markets change over time. A few of the significant findings are highlighted below.

1. In 94 percent of the days following a 3–I day, the market traded at prices better than the previous day's value area during the first 90 minutes of trading (higher on 3–I buying days and lower on 3–I selling days). This figure was 71 percent following 2I–1R days.

2. In *every* case the market allowed time for a trader to exit trades *without loss*. However, it is important to note that in a few cases the opportunity did not last for long.

3. Some 59 percent of the days following a 3–I day closed at prices better than the previous day's value area, while only 3 percent closed worse. In all, 97 percent of the days following a 3–I day closed within or better than the previous day's value area. For 2I–1R days, this figure measured 82 percent, with 18 percent closing worse.

Figure 4–114   2I-1R day in the June Japanese Yen, May 4-8, 1989.

Price	May 4		May 5	May 8
			.	.
7546	.		.	.
7544	.	Responsive	y	.
7542	.	Selling	y	.
7540	.	Tail	y	.
7538	.		y	.
7536	.		yz	.
7534	.		yz	.
7532	.		yz	.
7530	.		yz	.
7528	y		yz	.
7526	yA		yzA	.
7524	yzABC		yzA	.
7522	yzABC		yzA	.
7520	yzABCHI		yzA	.
7518	zABCDHIJK		yzAB	.
7516	zCDEHIJK	Initiative	yAB	.
7514	DEFGHIJK	Selling	yB	.
7512	DEFGHIJK	TPO's	yB	.
7510	EFIK		yB	.
7508	EK		yB	.
7506	KL		yBC	.
7504	KL		yBC	.
7502	L		OBC	.
7500	L		yC	.
7498	L		CKLM	.
7496	L		CEKL	.
7494	.	Initiative	CDEK	.
7492	.	Selling	CDEFIJK	.
7490	.	Range	CDEFGHIJ	.
7488	.	Extension	CDEFGHIJ	.
7486	.		DEFGH	yzAB
7484	.		DEF	yzAB
7482	.		E	yzAB
7480	.		.	yzB
7478	.		.	OBC
7476	.		.	yBCD
7474	.		2I-1R DAY	yBCD
7472	.		.	CD
7470	.		.	D
7468	.		.	DEF
7466	.		.	DEFGHK
7464	.		.	DEFGHKL
7462	.		.	FGHKLM
7460	.		.	GHIKL
7458	.		.	HIJK
7456	.		.	HIJK
7454	.		.	HJK
7452	.		.	JK
7450	.		.	

A 3–I develops when three specific factors indicating a day's attempted direction—tails, range extension and TPOs—all point the same way. When these three elements are generated in unison, they alert the trader to the potential for a high probability trade, a trade that almost has to be done.

Neutral-Extreme Days

A Neutral day indicates day timeframe balance and is characterized by range extension on both sides of the initial balance. In a sense, both other timeframe participants are active in a day timeframe "vertical tug-of-war." If the market closes near the middle of the range, then control is even. If, however, the close occurs on one of the day's extremes, there is a clear "victor," and the following day is likely to open in the direction of the closing activity.

To test this Special Situation, we studied Treasury bond activity from June 24, 1986, to August 12, 1987. Like the 3–I day, we evaluated Neutral-Extreme days for their continuation into the first 90 minutes of the following session, and also through to the day's close. Over the year-long study, the continuation properties of the Neutral-Extreme days were almost as impressive as those represented by 3–I days.

Neutral Day Closing on an Extreme

Initial 90 Minutes				*Next Day's Close*		
Better	*Within*	*Worse*		*Better*	*Within*	*Worse*
64%	28%	8%		45%	28%	27%

In 92 percent of the cases studied, the market traded within or above the previous day's value area during the initial 90 minutes of trade. Sixty-four percent of the time this activity occurred *above* the value area during a Neutral day closing on the highs, or *below* the value area on a Neutral day closing on the lows. These figures dropped to 73 percent and 45 percent, respectively, when compared to the following day's close.

In terms of trading applications, suppose that Neutral structure develops, and it is apparent that the market will close near the highs. A long placed within the value area will usually offer good trade location into the following day. In the majority of cases, you will have time to monitor early activity for continuation during the next day. If directional conviction reverses, 92 percent of the time you will have an opportunity to exit your long within the previous day's value area.

Again, we note that that these findings are derived from one market studied over a limited period of time. Other markets behave differently and all markets change over time.

The Value-Area Rule

We have mentioned many times the slowing properties of volume. Unless something significant has changed, price movement will often slow upon reentering an area of previously accepted high volume, as the market spends time trading there again.

The value area represents the range where the greatest *volume* of trade took place in the day timeframe. If the market opens outside the value area on the following day, then the previous day's value area has been rejected by other timeframe participants. Due to the presence of the other timeframe participants who caused the initial rejection, the top of the previous day's value area generally provides support against price probes back down into value, and the bottom of the value area will offer resistance against auction attempts to the upside. *However, if price should be accepted (double TPO prints) within the previous day's value area, there is a good possibility that the market will auction completely through that value area.* We have deemed this Special Situation the "Value-Area Rule."

Entering an area of established value represents a test of the market's most recent assessment of value. If the test results in acceptance, it is only logical that market participants will conduct trade throughout that region of value. For example, in Figure 4–115, the soybean market opened below the previous day's value area, reentered value and proceeded to trade completely through it, closing on the high.

Monitoring the market's close after value has been penetrated and price has auctioned all the way through is a subtle nuance of the Value Area Rule. If the market opens lower and trades up through the previous trading session's value area, a close on the highs is an indication of market strength (just as a close on the lows below the previous day's value area after a higher open is a sign of market weakness). On the day following our soybeans example in Figure 4–115, the market had to trade higher to find sellers and cut off buying.

The Value-Area Rule does not suggest that every time the market pierces the bottom of the previous day's value area (from below) you should blindly buy. It is equally important to objectively evaluate overall

Figure 4–115 The value area rule in July Soybeans, May 26-30, 1989.

	May 26	May 30
718.50	.	.
718.00	.	K
717.50	.	K
717.00	.	KL
716.50	.	K
716.00	.	JK
715.50	.	JK
715.00	.	JK
714.50	.	JK
714.00	.	FJK
713.50	.	FHIJK
713.00	H	FHIJK
712.50	HI	FHIJK
712.00	HIJK	FGHI
711.50	HIJK	FGHI
711.00	HIJK	FGHI
710.50	DHIJK	FGHI
710.00	DHIJK	FGHI
709.50	DFGHIJK	FGI
709.00	DEFGHIJK	GI
708.50	DEFGHJK	FGI
708.00	DEFGK	F
707.50	DEFG	F
707.00	DEF	F
706.50	DEF	EF
706.00	DE	DEF
705.50	DE	DEF
705.00	DE	DEF
704.50	E	DEF
704.00	E	DEF
703.50	E	DEF
703.00	.	OEF
702.50	.	DEF
702.00	.	DE
701.50	.	D
701.00	.	D
700.50	.	D
700.00	.	D
699.50	.	D
699.00	.	D
698.50	.	D
698.00	.	.

market conditions and specific circumstances before employing a Special Situation trade. The following considerations should be taken into account before executing a Value-Area Rule trade:

1. Distance from Value   The closer a market opens to the previous day's value area, the greater the chances of it penetrating and traveling through that value area. The logic behind this lies in the concept of market balance. A market that opens within range or value is in relative balance, thus perceptions of value have not changed significantly, and there is a good probability that trade will be conducted within the same value area. Conversely, if a market opens away from accepted value, it is out of balance. Therefore, the market is less likely to return to trade in the previous day's value area, since the forces that caused the imbalance have altered the underlying condition of the market. We caution, however, that if such a break-out of balance should be rejected by responsive participants, the return to value could be sudden and forceful, to the point that price auctions straight through the value area and completely through the previous day's range.

2. Value Area Width   Narrow value is a sign of poor trade facilitation and lower volume. Because volume slows price, narrow value areas are more easily traversed than wider, high-volume value areas. Therefore, the Value-Area Rule carries a higher probability when price enters a narrow value area.

3. Market Direction   The direction of the current longer-term auction has an obvious influence on the momentum, or strength behind the value area penetration. When price auctions up into value during a buying trend, for example, the chances for continuation are much better than if the market were in a downward trend.

Summary   If a trader enters a Value-Area Rule trade without evaluating other market conditions, the probability that price will trade all the way through the value area is little better than a flip of a coin. The power of the Value-Area Rule lies in your interpretation of surrounding market conditions. Through an understanding of the confluence of balance, value area width and market direction, you can identify the situations during which the Value-Area Rule offers a high degree of reliability.

Spikes

A "spike" is generated when price trends swiftly away from established value during the last few time periods of a trading session. Specifically, a spike begins with the time period marking the break-out. For example, in Figure 4–116 the S&P market broke away from value during N period on May 5. Therefore, the spike's range extends from the top of N period (311.00) down to the day's low at 308.00.

Ordinarily, a break-out from value can be monitored for continuation in following time periods. However, when it occurs at or near the end of the trading day, the crucial element of time (Price × Time = Value) is absent. Thus, the trader must wait until the next day to judge the price movement for follow-through and conviction. Where the market opens and subsequently builds value relative to the previous day's spike sends clear signals regarding the underlying directional conviction of the market.

Acceptance versus Rejection   Whenever price moves quickly away from value, it takes *time* to validate the new levels. If price subsequently slows, allowing volume to "catch up" and TPOs to accumulate, then value has been accepted at the new price levels. Thus, a market that opens within a spike created during the previous day indicates confirmation of that area. The price spike is also *accepted* if the following day opens beyond the spike—above a buying spike or below a selling spike. An open in the direction of the spike indicates the probe is not yet over. The market will likely continue to auction in the direction of the spike, seeking new value.

Conversely, a spike is *rejected* if the subsequent trading session opens in the opposite direction from the spike. For example, after a buying spike, an open below the base of the spike would constitute rejection of the upward price probe.

Openings Within the Spike   An opening within the spike indicates that the market is balancing. Thus, two-timeframe, rotational trade will likely develop within or near the spike's range for the duration of the day. In Figure 4–116, for example, the S&P market opened at 308.20 on May 8, 1989—within the 308.00–311.00 selling spike created on the previous trading day. The market then balanced, confirming the previous day's probe to lower value. In a second example in Figure 4–117, the S&P opened at the bottom of the May 2 selling spike. Price auctioned higher and found resistance near the spike's highs (311.00), providing several opportunities for alert traders to place shorts with good day timeframe trade location.

On a side note, during days that open and accept value within a spike generated on the previous day, we use a variation of the Range Estimation rules (introduced in Section I) to estimate the day's range.

Figure 4–116   Open within a spike—definition of range, June S&P 500, May 5-8, 1989.

	May 5	Spike Range	May 8
	.	.	.
312.80	.	.	.
312.60	JK	.	.
312.40	DJK	.	.
312.20	CDGJKL	.	.
312.00	CDEFGHIJL	.	.
311.80	CDEFGHIJLM	.	.
311.60	OCDFLM	.	.
311.40	BCM	.	.
311.20	BCM	.	.
311.00	BCMN	N	.
310.80	BMN	N	.
310.60	MN	N	.
310.40	N	N	.
310.20	N	N	.
310.00	N	N	.
309.80	N	N	.
309.60	N	N	.
309.40	N	N	.
309.20	N	N	.
309.00	NP	NP	.
308.80	NP	NP	.
308.60	NP	NP	C
308.40	P	P	BCDNP
308.20	PQ	PQ	OCDENP
308.00	P	P	BCDEMNP
307.80	.	.	BCEMN
307.60	.	.	BCEKLMN
307.40	.	.	EKLMN
307.20	.	.	EFKLMNQ
307.00	.	.	EFHIKLMN
306.80	.	.	FGHIJKMN
306.60	.	.	FGHIJKMN
306.40	.	.	FGJM
306.20	.	.	F
306.00	.	.	.

Figure 4–117   Open within a spike, June S&P 500, May 2-3, 1989.

	May 2		May 3
312.80	.	.	.
312.70	D	.	.
312.60	CD	.	.
312.50	CD	.	.
312.40	BCD	.	.
312.30	BCD	.	.
312.20	BCD	.	.
312.10	BCD	.	.
312.00	BCDL	.	.
311.90	BCDJLM	.	.
311.80	ODIJLM	.	.
311.70	BDGHIJKLM	The Spike	.
311.60	DGHIJKLM	.	.
311.50	DEFGHIJKLM	.	.
311.40	DEFGHIJKLM	.	.
311.30	DEFGKLMN	N	.
311.20	DEFKMN	N	.
311.10	DEMN	N	.
311.00	DEMN	N	.
310.90	DMN	N	.
310.80	DN	N	.
310.70	N	N	M
310.60	N	N	GM
310.50	N	N	GMN
310.40	N	N	GMN
310.30	N	N	FGMN
310.20	N	N	EFGMN
310.10	N	N	BEFGMNP
310.00	NP	NP	BEFGHMNPQ
309.90	NP	NP	BCEFGHIKMNP
309.80	NP	NP	BCEFGHIKMNP
309.70	NP	NP	BCDEFGHIKLMNP
309.60	NP	NP	BCDEFGHIJKLMN
309.50	P	P	BCDEGIJKLM
309.40	PQ	P	BCDEGIJKLM
309.30	P	P	BCDEGIJK
309.20	.	.	OCEJK
309.10	.	.	BCEJK
309.00	.	.	CJ
308.90	.	.	C
308.80	.	.	C
308.70	.	.	.
308.60	.	.	.
308.50	.	.	.

Normally, the entire previous day's range is used to estimate the current day's range potential. In the case of an open within a spike, however, the spike is treated like a "new day." Thus, when estimating the range on a day that opens within a previous day's spike, we use the length of the spike as our estimate, not the whole day's range. In Figure 4–117, for example, the spike on May 2 extends from 311.30 (the top of the break-out period) to 309.30, a range of 200 points. The following day recorded a range just one tick short of 200 points.

Openings Outside the Spike   Whenever a market opens outside the previous day's range, the market is out of balance. The same general rule applies to openings beyond the spike's range, but the magnitude of the imbalance varies depending on where the market opens relative to the direction of the spike.

Bullish Openings   An open above a buying spike signifies a market that is extremely out of balance—initiative buyers are in obvious control. Ideally, a trader should seek to place longs near the support offered by the top of the spike. In Figure 4–118, crude oil opened above the price spike on the 3rd and established substantially higher value. The opportunity to secure excellent trade location for longs was created when B period met resistance at the 20.15 spike top. Be aware, however, that if the market should auction down into the spike, thus negating its supportive top, price could move very quickly.

When the market opens above a *selling* spike (rejects the spike), sentiment is still bullish for the day timeframe, but for different reasons. This sort of conflicting activity often occurs when price has "gotten ahead of the market," inviting the responsive participant to auction price back into previously perceived value. A case in point is crude oil activity following a selling spike on May 8. On May 9, crude oil opened above the 8th's 19.36–19.60 selling spike (Figure 4–119). After auctioning down three ticks and finding strong support at the top of the spike, the market auctioned higher for the remainder of the day.

Bearish Openings   When a market opens *below* a *selling* spike, day timeframe sentiment is extremely bearish, as is the case with Crude Oil in Figure 4–120. When Crude Oil opened below the spike, traders were alerted that the previous day's selling spike was *leading* value. The eventual development of a selling Trend day exhibited the clear acceptance of lower prices. An open below a *buying* spike represents rejection of the spike and is also bearish for the day timeframe, but not to the extent of the scenario outlined above.

Figure 4–118   Open outside of a spike—bullish (above a buying spike), Crude Oil, May 3-4, 1989.

	May 3	May 4
	.	.
2062	.	
2060	.	KL
2058	.	KLM
2056	.	JKL
2054	.	IJKL
2052	.	IJKL
2050	.	EIJKL
2048	.	DEFIJKL
2046	.	DEFGHIL
2044	.	DEFGHI
2042	.	DEFGH
2040	.	OEFGH
2038	.	BDF
2036	.	BCDF
2034	.	BCDF
2032	.	BCD
2030	.	BC
2028	.	BC
2026	.	B
2024	.	B
2022	.	B
2020	.	B
2018	.	.
2016	.	.
2014	L	.
2012	L	.
2010	LM	.
2008	L	.
2006	L	.
2004	L	.
2002	L	.
2000	L	.
1998	L	.
1996	L	.
1994	L	.
1992	L	.
1990	BIL	.
1988	BHIL	.
1986	BHIJL	.
1984	BHIJL	.
1982	OHIJKL	.
1980	BHIJKL	.
1978	BDHIJKL	.
1976	BCDHIJKL	.
1974	BCDHIJKL	.
1972	BCDEGHJKL	.
1970	BCDEGHJL	.
1968	BCDEGHJL	.
1966	BCDEG	.
1964	BCDEG	.
1962	BCEFG	.
1960	EFG	.
1958	EFG	.
1956	EFG	.
1954	EFG	.
1952	E	.
1950	.	.

Figure 4–119   Open outside of a spike—bullish (above a selling spike), Crude Oil,   May   8-9,   1989.

	May 8	May 9
	.	.
1995	.	.
1994	.	JL
1993	.	JL
1992	.	JL
1991	.	JL
1990	.	JKL
1989	.	JKL
1988	O	IJKL
1987	BC	IJKL
1986	BC	IJKL
1985	BCD	IJKL
1984	BCD	IJKL
1983	BCD	IJKL
1982	BCD	IJKL
1981	BCD	CIJKL
1980	BCD	CDIJKL
1979	BCD	CDIKL
1978	BCD	CDIKL
1977	BCD	CDIL
1976	BDE	CDILM
1975	DE	BCDEFHIL
1974	DE	BCDEFGHIL
1973	DE	BCDEFGHL
1972	DEF	BCDEFGH
1971	DEF	BCEFGH
1970	DEF	BCEFH
1969	EFG	BEFH
1968	EFG	BEH
1967	EFG	BE
1966	EFGHI	BE
1965	EFGHI	BE
1964	EFGHI	BE
1963	EFGHI	O
1962	EFHI	B
1961	EFHI	B
1960	EFHIJ	B
1959	EFIJ	.
1958	FJ	.
1957	J	.
1956	JL	.
1955	JL	.
1954	JL	.
1953	JL	.
1952	JL	.
1951	JL	.
1950	JKL	.
1949	JKL	.
1948	JKL	.
1947	JKL	.
1946	JKL	.
1945	JKL	.
1944	KLM	.
1943	KL	.
1942	KL	.
1941	KL	.
1940	KL	.
1939	KL	.
1938	L	.
1937	L	.
1936	L	.
1935	.	.

Figure 4–120   Open outside of a spike—bearish (below a selling spike), Crude Oil,   May   5-8,   1989.

	MAY 5	MAY 8
	.	.
2044	.	.
2042	B	.
2040	B	.
2038	BC	.
2036	BCDE	.
2034	BCDEFG	.
2032	BCDEFGH	.
2030	CDEFGH	.
2028	DEFGH	.
2026	DEHJK	.
2024	DEHJK	.
2022	HIJK	.
2020	OIJK	.
2018	HIJKL	.
2016	IJKL	.
2014	KL	.
2012	L	.
2010	L	.
2008	L	.
2006	L	.
2004	L	.
2002	LM	.
2000	L	.
1998	L	.
1996	.	.
1994	.	.
1992	.	.
1990	.	.
1988	.	O
1986	.	BC
1984	.	BCD
1982	.	BCD
1980	.	BCD
1978	.	BCD
1976	.	BCDE
1974	.	DE
1972	.	DEF
1970	.	DEF
1968	.	EFG
1966	.	EFGHI
1964	.	EFGHI
1962	.	EFGHI
1960	.	EFHIJ
1958	.	EFIJ
1956	.	JL
1954	.	JL
1952	.	JL
1950	.	JKL
1948	.	JKL
1946	.	JKL
1944	.	JKLM
1942	.	KL
1940	.	KL
1938	.	KL
1936	.	L
1934	.	.
1932	.	.
1930	.	.

Spike Reference Points   During the trading session following a price spike, the spike's extremes often provide useful day timeframe reference points (Figure 4–121). After a higher open, for example, auction rotations are often supported by the spike's top. Similarly, the bottom of a price spike offers resistance on days that open lower. However, it is important to note that the spike extremes are only valid reference points for the first price probe into the spike. If the market returns to test the spike several times in the same half-hour time period, then the chances are good that price will eventually auction through the spike extreme. An additional test into the price spike in a subsequent time period would create double TPOs, in effect establishing value within the spike. In crude oil on the 8th (Figure 4–120), double TPO prints above the 19.98 spike bottom would negate its reliability as a resistance level.

Balance-Area Break-outs

Imagine a large stone precariously balanced on a mountain peak. In a gale force wind, the stone might come loose and tumble down the mountainside. When it falls, it falls quickly in one direction. If the wind is less forceful, the stone may rock to one side and then tumble in the other direction. A balanced market acts in a similar fashion. And, financially speaking, a market that is breaking out of balance can be just as dangerous as a falling rock.

The identification of a balance area depends largely on your timeframe. For example, a ledge (Section I) may constitute a balance area to a day trader. To a swing trader, however, a balance area might be five days of overlapping value. A long-term trader might consider a major bracket to be a balance area. When something upsets the balance, price moves are often sudden and forceful.

Balance area break-out strategy is straightforward—go with the break-out. Thus, if price is accepted outside the balance area, place trades in the direction of the new activity. In Figure 4–122, Treasury bonds had recorded basically eight days of overlapping value within a relatively well-defined balance region spanning from 97–03 to 98–16. On April 9, a narrow initial balance forming near the short-term bracket low alerted traders to a potential Double-Distribution Trend day. When C period broke below the balance-area lows set on April 3 at 97–32, traders should have entered short positions. Buy (exit) stops should have been placed a few ticks above the point of break-out, for a price return into the balance area would indicate rejection by responsive buyers.

Occasionally, the market "rocks" one way, then breaks-out in the opposite direction. This sort of activity often occurs when the locals or

Figure 4–121   Spike reference points.

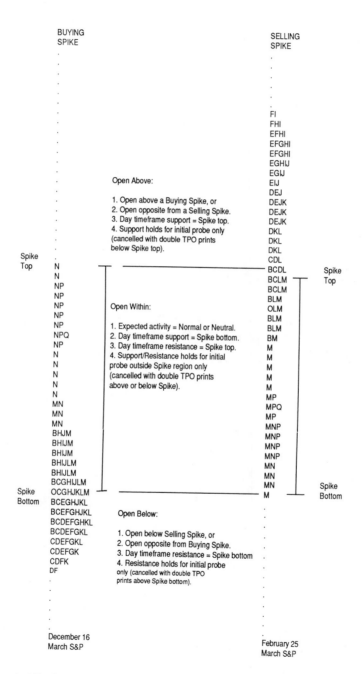

December 16
March S&P

February 25
March S&P

Figure 4–122 Balance area break-out occurring in June Treasury Bonds, March 30-April 9, 1987.

	March 30	March 31	April 1	April 2	April 3	April 6	April 7	April 8	Apr. 9
99 0 /32	.	.	.	.	.	.	.	.	.
98 31 /32	.	.	.	.	.	.	.	.	.
98 30 /32	.	.	.	.	.	.	.	.	.
98 29 /32	.	.	.	.	.	.	.	.	.
98 28 /32	.	.	.	.	.	.	.	.	.
98 27 /32	.	.	.	.	.	.	.	.	.
98 26 /32	.	.	.	.	.	.	.	.	.
98 25 /32	A	.	.	.	.	.	.	.	.
98 24 /32	A	.	.	.	.	.	.	.	.
98 23 /32	A	.	.	.	.	.	.	.	.
98 22 /32	A	.	.	.	.	.	.	.	.
98 21 /32	A	.	.	.	.	.	.	.	.
98 20 /32	A	.	.	.	.	.	.	.	.
98 19 /32	A	.	.	.	.	.	.	.	.
98 18 /32	A	.	.	.	.	.	.	.	.
98 17 /32	A	.	.	.	.	.	.	.	.
98 16 /32	A	L	.	.	.	B	.	.	.
98 15 /32	A	LM	.	.	.	BCH	.	.	.
98 14 /32	A	L	.	AB	.	ABCHI	.	.	.
98 13 /32	AB	AL	.	AB	.	ABCDGHIJ	.	.	.
98 12 /32	AB	AL	.	AB	.	ABCDGHIJ	.	.	.
98 11 /32	ABD	ABIL	.	AB	.	ABCDEGHIJ	.	.	.
98 10 /32	ABDE	ABIJL	.	ABD	.	ABCDEGHIJ	.	.	.
98 9 /32	ABCDEFG	ABIJL	.	ABD	.	ABEGIJ	.	.	.
98 8 /32	ABCDEFG	ABIJKL	.	ABCDE	H	AEFGIJK	.	.	.
98 7 /32	ABCDEFG	ABIJKL	.	ABCDE	H	AEFGJK	.	.	.
98 6 /32	ABCDEFG	ABCIJKL	.	BCDE	H	EFJK	.	.	.
98 5 /32	ABCDEFGI	ABCIJK	.	BCDE	GH	EFKL	.	.	.
98 4 /32	BCEGIJ	ABCIJK	.	CE	GH	EKLM	D	.	.
98 3 /32	BCGHIJ	ACIJK	E	CE	GHIJK	EKL	CD	.	.
98 2 /32	CGHIJ	ACI	E	E	GHIJK	KL	CD	.	.
98 1 /32	CGHIJ	ACI	E	E	FGHIJK	KL	CDE	.	.
98 0 /32	CGHIJK	CI	EF	EF	FGHIJK	L	CDE	.	.
97 31 /32	CGHIJK	CDI	EFL	EFJ	FGHIJK	L	CDE	.	.
97 30 /32	CHIJK	CDI	EFL	EFJ	FGIJK	L	CDE	A	.
97 29 /32	HIJK	CDI	EFGL	EFJ	FIJK	L	CE	A	.
97 28 /32	HIJKL	CDHI	CDEFGJL	FGJK	EFIJKL	L	BCEFG	A	.
97 27 /32	HKL	CDEHI	CDEFGJKL	FGIJK	EFIJKL	.	ABCEFG	AB	.
97 26 /32	HKL	CDEHI	CDEGJKL	FGIJK	DEFIKL	.	ABCEFG	AB	.
97 25 /32	KL	DEHI	BCDEGHIJKL	FGIJK	DEFKL	.	ABCEFG	AB	.
97 24 /32	KLM	DEGHI	ABCDEGHIJKL	FGHIK	DEFKLM	.	ABCEFGH	ABJ	.
97 23 /32	KL	DEGH	ABCDGHIJKLM	GHIKLM	ADEFL	.	ABCEFGHK	ABDJK	.
97 22 /32	KL	DEG	ABCDHIJKL	GHIKL	ADEFL	.	ABCEHIJK	ABDHJK	.
97 21 /32	KL	DEFG	ABCDHIKL	GHIKL	ADEFL	.	CHIJK	BDEHIJKL	.
97 20 /32	KL	DEFG	ABDHK	GHIKL	ADL	.	CHIJK	BCDEHIJKL	.
97 19 /32	KL	DFG	ABDHK	HKL	ADL	.	HIJKL	BCDEHIJKL	.
97 18 /32	KL	DFG	ABD	HKL	AD	.	HIJKL	BCDEGHIJKL	.
97 17 /32	KL	FG	AB	HL	ABD	.	IJKL	CDEGHIJL	A
97 16 /32	.	F	AB	HL	ABD	.	IJL	CDEFGHIJL	A
97 15 /32	.	F	AB	HL	ABCD	.	IL	CEFGHIL	AB
97 14 /32	.	F	A	L	BCD	.	IL	CEFGHIL	AB
97 13 /32	.	.	.	L	BCD	.	IL	CEFGHLM	AB
97 12 /32	.	.	.	L	BCD	.	IL	EFGL	AB
97 11 /32	.	.	.	L	BC	.	L	EFGL	AB
97 10 /32	.	.	.	L	BC	.	L	F	AB
97 9 /32	.	.	.	L	BC	.	L	F	ABC
97 8 /32	.	.	.	L	BC	.	L	F	ABC
97 7 /32	.	.	.	L	BC	.	LM	.	BC
97 6 /32	.	.	.	.	BC	.	L	.	BC
97 5 /32	.	.	.	.	BC	.	.	.	BC
97 4 /32	.	.	.	.	B	.	.	.	C
97 3 /32	.	.	.	.	B	.	.	.	C
97 2 /32	.	.	.	.	.	.	.	.	C
97 1 /32	.	.	.	.	.	.	.	.	C
97 0 /32	.	.	.	.	.	.	.	.	C
96 31 /32	.	.	.	.	.	.	.	.	C
96 30 /32	.	.	.	.	.	.	.	.	CD
96 29 /32	.	.	.	.	.	.	.	.	CD
96 28 /32	.	.	.	.	.	.	.	.	CD
96 27 /32	.	.	.	.	.	.	.	.	CD
96 26 /32	.	.	.	.	.	.	.	.	CD

CD
D
DE
DE
DE
DEF
DEF
DEF
DEFH
EFGH
EFGH
EFGH
FGH
FGH
FGHIJ
FGHIJ
GHIJ
GHIJ
HJ
HJ
J
J
J
J
J
J
J
J
J
J
JL
JKL
JKLM
JKL
JKL
JKL
JKL
JKL
KL
KL
KL
KL
KL
KL
KL
KL
KL
KL
K
K
K
K
K

96 25 /32
96 24 /32
96 23 /32
96 22 /32
96 21 /32
96 20 /32
96 19 /32
96 18 /32
96 17 /32
96 16 /32
96 15 /32
96 14 /32
96 13 /32
96 12 /32
96 11 /32
96 10 /32
96 9 /32
96 8 /32
96 7 /32
96 6 /32
96 5 /32
96 4 /32
96 3 /32
96 2 /32
96 1 /32
96 0 /32
95 31 /32
95 30 /32
95 29 /32
95 28 /32
95 27 /32
95 26 /32
95 25 /32
95 24 /32
95 23 /32
95 22 /32
95 21 /32
95 20 /32
95 19 /32
95 18 /32
95 17 /32
95 16 /32
95 15 /32
95 14 /32
95 13 /32
95 12 /32
95 11 /32
95 10 /32
95 9 /32
95 8 /32
95 7 /32
95 6 /32
95 5 /32
95 4 /32
95 3 /32
95 2 /32
95 1 /32
95 0 /32
94 31 /32
94 30 /32
94 29 /32
94 28 /32
94 27 /32
94 26 /32
94 25 /32
94 24 /32
94 23 /32
94 22 /32
94 21 /32

shorter-term traders auction price beyond a known reference point (in this case a balance-area high or low), to see if there is new activity to sustain the price movement. If there is no response, then the opposite participant can enter the market with confidence, driving price with strong directional conviction. On February 6 in Figure 4–123, price auctions below the three days of overlapping value in the S&P market. Since the rule of this Special Situation is to *go with the break-out*, traders should have been short when D period auctioned below 297.20. When no follow-through developed and price traded back into the balance area, however, shorts should have been exited at minimal loss. With the knowledge that there was no activity below the lows, traders should have been prepared to buy a break-out to the upside, which occurred on the following day at 300.40. A balance area break-out is a trade you "almost have to do." Risk is minimal and profit potential is very high.

In hindsight, a balance-area break-out trade looks like such an easy trade to make. However, when you have spent the last few days watching price move sideways, it is not so easy to enter the market initiatively. It feels as if the trade is late, for technically, better trade location could have been secured on previous days. In reality, a break-out is usually the start of a much bigger move, and trades placed with the initiator are ultimately *early*. Taking advantage of these market-created opportunities is essential to gaining the confidence and experience that is vital to becoming a competent trader.

Gaps

The last Special Situation we will discuss is the *gap*. A gap is an opening outside the previous day's range, signifying a market out of balance. A gap is created when the other timeframe perceives price to be away from value and enters the market aggressively, forming excess in the form of an "invisible tail." The salient feature of a gap (that holds) is that it should offer significant support or resistance to price, and it therefore stands as a valuable guide for day traders and an important reference point for longer-term traders.

Gaps fall into three broad categories: (1) *Break-away* gaps, (2) *Acceleration* gaps, and (3) *Exhaustion* gaps. Briefly, a Break-away gap occurs when the market is in the early stages of a long-term trend. This sort of gap is fueled by new, initiative other timeframe participants possessing strong directional conviction. An Acceleration gap develops within a trend and reaffirms the conviction and strength of the trend's direction. Finally, an Exhaustion gap will sometimes mark the end of a trend. In the final stages of a buying trend, for example, more and more participants are gradually convinced that the market is indeed trending. Eventually, practically everyone is a buyer. The final consensus is so strong that the market gaps higher as the last doubters jump on board. Once everyone is long, however, there is no one left to buy and the trend is effectively over.

Whether or not a gap is a Break-away, Acceleration, or Exhaustion gap will greatly influence the likelihood that it will hold. However, what we are concerned with here is the Special Situation properties of gaps. Thus, the following discussion treats all gaps the same by evaluating each in the present tense.

Day Timeframe Significance of Gaps   Generally speaking, most gaps are eventually filled—some on the same day. In the day timeframe, if a gap is going to be retraced (filled) by responsive participants, the rejection will usually fill the gap within the first hour. The longer a gap holds, the greater the probability of its continuation.

The Special Situation rule for trading gaps is to trade with the initiative activity that caused the gap, placing stops at the point where a price rotation would effectively erase the gap by trading completely through it. Figure 4–124 represents an ideal gap trade in crude oil. Shorts placed in the first half hour of trade with the gap lower and subsequent Open-Drive activity resulted in good trade location during a selling Trend day. Shorts should have been exited if price had filled the gap by trading back above 19.98.

Not all gap days are quite so ideal, however. Like the Value Area Rule, there are outside factors that influence the way a gap should be traded. In Figure 4–125, the Swiss franc opened 26 ticks below the previous trading session's low. Such an extreme gap should have alerted traders to the possible entry of the responsive buyer. The farther away from the previous day's range a market opens, the greater the likelihood that the market has temporarily overextended itself. When this occurs, the responsive participant will often narrow the gap by auctioning price towards the previous day's value. When a market gaps significantly away from the previous day's range, the prudent action is to monitor activity soon after the open before placing trades. In the case of the Swiss franc in Figure 4–125, if the responsive buyer enters, traders should wait until the initiative seller reappears, monitoring the gap for support. When responsive activity waned and two-timeframe trade developed with the downward rotation in A period, shorts should have been entered and buy stops placed at 59.87 (the gap erasure point).

Again, successfully using Special Situations involves a synthesis of market understanding, time and experience. It is difficult to explain the ideal point at which a gap trade should be entered. In many cases,

Figure 4–123 Balance area break-out occurring in the March S&P 500, January 31-February 7, 1989.

	January 31	February 1	February 2	February 3	February 6	February 7
302.70						
302.60						M
302.50						LM
302.40						LM
302.30						LM
302.20						LM
302.10						LM
302.00						LM
301.90						KLM
301.80						KLMN
301.70						KLMN
301.60						JKLMN
301.50						JKLNP
301.40						JKLNP
301.30						JKNP
301.20						HJKP
301.10						HJK
301.00						HJK
300.90						HJK
300.80						HJK
300.70						HJ
300.60						HI
300.50						H
300.40						H
300.30		C				FH
300.20		CD				FGH
300.10		CD				FGH
300.00		CD				FGH
299.90		CD	K			FGH
299.80		CD	K			FG
299.70	N	CD	K			CFG
299.60	N	CDM	JK	C		CDFG
299.50	N	CDM	JK	C		CDFG
299.40	NP	CDM	BJK	BC		CDF
299.30	NP	CELMN	BJK	BC	B	CDEF
299.20	NP	CELMNP	BJKL	BCDN	BC	CDEF
299.10	NP	CELMNP	BJKL	BCDMN	BC	CDEF
299.00	NP	CELMNP	BJKL			CDE

	January 31	February 1	February 2	February 3	February 6	February 7
298.90	NP	CEFIJLMNP	BCJL	BCDMN	BC	CDE
298.80	MNP	CEFIJLMNP	BCJL	BCDEMNP	BC	CDE
298.70	MNP	BCEFHIJLMNP	BCJLM	BDEHLMNP	BC	BCD
298.60	MNP	BCEFHIJLMNP	BCIJLM	BDEGHLMNP	BC	BC
298.50	M	BCEFHIJLMN	IJLMN	BDEFGHIJLMNP	BC	BC
298.40	LM	BCEFGHIJKLM	CHIJMNP	BEFGHIJLN	BCI	BC
298.30	LM	BEFGHIJKLM	CFHIMNP	BEFGHIJKL	BCHI	BC
298.20	LM	BEFGHIJKLM	CFGHIMNP	BEFGHIJKL	BCHI	B
298.10	LM	BEGHIJKL	CFGHIMN	BFGHIJK	BCHIM	B
298.00	LM	BEGIJK	CEFGHIMN	BFGHJK	BCDHIM	B
297.90	KL	BEGK	CDEFGM	BFIK	BCDHIM	B
297.80	KL	BGK	CDEFM	BFIK	BDHIJLMP	B
297.70	KL	BGK	DEFM	BF	BDHIJLMNP	B
297.60	HKL	GK	DEM	B	BDGHIJLMNP	B
297.50	HKJL	G	DEM	B	BDGHIJKLMNP	B
297.40	BHJK	G	DE	B	DGHIJKLMNP	B
297.30	BHJK	.	D	B	DFGIJKLMNP	B
297.20	BCHJK	.	D	.	DEFGIJKLMN	B
297.10	BCHJK	.	.	.	DEFGJKLMN	.
297.00	BCHJK	.	.	.	DEFGKLMN	.
296.90	BCGHIJ	.	.	.	DEFGKMN	.
296.80	BCGHIJ	.	.	.	DEFGMN	.
296.70	BCGHIJ	.	.	.	DEGM	.
296.60	CGHI	.	.	.	DEM	.
296.50	CGI	.	.	.	EM	.
296.40	CFGI	.	.	.	E	.
296.30	CFGI	.	.	.	E	.
296.20	CFGI	.	.	.	.	.
296.10	CEFG	.	.	.	.	.
296.00	CEFG	.	.	.	.	.
295.90	CEFG	.	.	.	.	.
295.80	CEG	.	.	.	.	.
295.70	CDE	.	.	.	.	.
295.60	CDE	.	.	.	.	.
295.50	CDE	.	.	.	.	.
295.40	DE	.	.	.	.	.
295.30	D	.	.	.	.	.
295.20	D	.	.	.	.	.
295.10	.	.	.	.	.	.
295.00	.	.	.	.	.	.

Figure 4–124 A selling gap occurring in Crude Oil, May 5-8, 1989.

	May 5	May 8
2044	.	.
2042	B	.
2040	B	.
2038	OC	.
2036	BCDE	.
2034	BCDEFG	.
2032	BCDEFGH	.
2030	CDEFGH	.
2028	DEFGH	.
2026	DEFJK	.
2024	HIJK	.
2022	HIJK	.
2020	HIJKL	.
2018	IJKL	.
2016	KL	.
2014	L	.
2012	L	.
2010	L	.
2008	L	.
2006	L	.
2004	L	.
2002	LM	.
2000	L	.
1998	L	.
1996	.	.
1994	.	.
1992	.	.
1990	.	.
1988	.	O
1986	.	BC
1984	.	BCD
1982	.	BCD
1980	.	BCD
1978	.	BCD
1976	.	BCDE
1974	.	DE
1972	.	DEF
1970	.	DEF
1968	.	EFG
1966	.	EFGHI
1964	.	EFGHI
1962	.	EFGHI
1960	.	EFHIJ
1958	.	EFIJ
1956	.	JL
1954	.	JL
1952	.	JL
1950	.	JKL
1948	.	JKL
1946	.	JKL
1944	.	JKLM
1942	.	KL
1940	.	KL
1938	.	KL
1936	.	L
1934	.	.
1932	.	.

Figure 4–125 A selling gap occurring in the June Swiss Franc, April 28-May 1, 1989.

	April 28	May 1
6019	.	
6018	C	.
6017	C	.
6016	C	.
6015	C	.
6014	C	.
6013	C	.
6012	yCD	.
6011	yCD	.
6010	yCD	.
6009	OCDE	.
6008	yCDE	.
6007	yCDE	.
6006	yCDE	.
6005	yzACDE	.
6004	yzACDEF	.
6003	yzACDEFGH	.
6002	yzABCDEFGH	.
6001	yzABCDFGHIJ	.
6000	yzABCDFHIJ	.
5999	zABCDIJ	.
5998	zABCIJK	.
5997	zABIJK	.
5996	zBJKL	.
5995	BJKL	.
5994	BL	.
5993	BL	.
5992	L	.
5991	L	.
5990	L	.
5989	LM	.
5988	L	.
5987	L	.
5986	.	.
5985	.	.
5984	.	.
5983	.	.
5982	.	.
5981	.	.
5980	.	.
5979	.	.
5978	.	.
5977	.	.
5976	.	z
5975	.	z
5974	.	z
5973	.	z
5972	.	z
5971	.	z
5970	.	yz
5969	.	yz
5968	.	yzA
5967	.	yzA
5966	.	yzA
5965	.	yzA
5964	.	yzA
5963	.	yA
5962	.	yA
5961	.	OA
5960	.	yA
5959	.	A
5958	.	A
5957	.	AB
5956	.	AB
5955	.	AB
5954	.	ABLM
5953	.	ABL
5952	.	BL
5951	.	BDL
5950	.	BCDL
5949	.	BCDIKL
5948	.	BCDFIJK
5947	.	BCDEFHIJK
5946	.	CDEFHIJK
5945	.	CDEFGHIJK
5944	.	CDEFGHIJK
5943	.	CDEFGHJ
5942	.	CDEFG
5941	.	CE
5940	.	C
5939	.	.

blindly placing a trade in the direction of the gap will eventually result in a successful trade. However, without monitoring early activity, a trade placed too early might suffer undue exposure if price temporarily auctions against the position.

Starting out with poor trade location can be both financially and mentally taxing, often to the point that the trader is forced to exit what would have developed into a good trade. Our Swiss franc example provides a good example of how this can occur. A trader who sold immediately with the selling gap could easily have been forced out of his or her short position, given that the Swiss auctioned against the position for better than the first half hour of trade. Traders who anticipated responsive buying after such a sharp break from value would have probably waited for a return of the selling auctions before entering shorts. With the responsive buying over (at least temporarily), traders placing short positions would have had more confidence, and therefore a better chance at completing a successful trade. In this case, notice that both scenarios would have ended in similar trade location. The difference between the two trades is the level of accompanying anxiety.

Gaps do not hold every time. On some occasions, the buying or selling auction that produced the gap will fail, inviting responsive participants to return price to previous value. When this occurs, however, there are usually clear signs that the gap will be erased. In the case of the gold market in Figure 4–126, gold gapped below the previous day's range. After a quick test to the downside, the responsive buyer entered and drove price up through the gap and into the value area of April 28. All of this activity occurred during the first half hour of trade. Traders who sold with the selling gap should have covered when gold auctioned above 379.60 in Y period.

Gaps are created by aggressive other timeframe activity. They are significant reference points as long as they hold. If, however, responsive participants overcome the initiator and return price through the gap, then conditions have changed and the gap is no longer a significant trading guide.

Summary

Special Situations are not fail-safe answers, but they do offer a trader some degree of comfort and security. Still, your imagination should not stop at these limited examples. By incorporating the different methods for evaluating directional conviction and performance, a trader can identify other circumstances that offer high leverage and low risk. To put it simply, the big picture is made up of many small, more specific com-

Figure 4–126   A "filled" gap occurring in June Gold, April 28-May 1, 1989.

	April 28	May 1
3836	.	.
3834	y	.
3832	y	.
3830	y	.
3828	yz	.
3826	yzA	.
3824	yzA	.
3822	yzAB	.
3820	OzAB	.
3818	yzAB	z
3816	zABJ	z
3814	zABIJ	z
3812	zABCDEIJ	zIJK
3810	zABCDEGHIJK	zIJK
3808	zABCDEFGHIJK	yzAHIJK
3806	zABCDEFGHIJK	yzAHIJKL
3804	zABCDEFGHIJKL	yzABFHIJK
3802	zBCGHIJK	yzABFHJ
3800	zBCGK	yzABCDEFGH
3798	zK	yABCDEFGH
3796	z	yBCDEF
3794	.	yCD
3792	.	yC
3790	.	y
3788	.	y
3786	.	y
3784	.	y
3782	.	y
3780	.	y
3778	.	O
3776	.	y
3774	.	y
3772	.	.
3770	.	.

ponents. By synthesizing these factors into a more all-encompassing market understanding, you will increase your chances of success. Consistently successful trading is the result of a unique combination of opportunity, experience, and market *understanding*.

Markets to Stay Out Of

Special Situations are useful for identifying trading opportunities that possess a relatively high degree of security. On the opposite end of the spectrum, but no less important, are those times when one simply should not trade at all. A trader who forces a trade when there is no real opportunity in the market is like a basketball player who forces a shot when he is off-balance or heavily guarded—the chances of scoring are low. A good basketball player who does not have a clear shot will generally not shoot the ball. Similarly, experienced traders who do not see a clear market opportunity do not "force" the trade. The harder you have to look, the lower the potential for a good trade. In such a situation, it is best to stand aside and wait for an opportunity to develop.

The following discussion covers four market situations which signify the existence of relatively little trading opportunity:

1. Nontrend Days
2. Nonconviction Days
3. Long-Term Nontrend Markets
4. News-Influenced Markets

Nontrend Days

The most obvious market to stay out of is the Nontrend day. On a Nontrend day, the market is not facilitating trade with any participant and opportunity is low, for the day's range is small and activity is scarce. Figure 4–127 shows a typical, low-volume Nontrend day that occurred in bonds on May 8, 1989.

Nonconviction Days

A less obvious type of low opportunity market is a Nonconviction day. Structurally, a Nonconviction day often appears to be no different than a Normal, Normal Variation, or Neutral day. However, the Nonconviction

---

Figure 4–127   A Nontrend day occurring in June Treasury Bonds, May 8, 1989.

89 23 /32	.
89 22 /32	H
89 21 /32	zADEHKL
89 20 /32	zADEFGHIKLM
89 19 /32	yzACDEFGHIJKL
89 18 /32	yzABCDFGIJK
89 17 /32	yzBCIJ
89 16 /32	OB
89 15 /32	yB
89 14 /32	B
89 13 /32	.
89 12 /32	.
89 11 /32	.

---

day exhibits none of the other timeframe directional conviction that these standard day types typically display—there are no recognizable reference points for a day timeframe trader. During a Nonconviction day, the open is often of the Open-Auction variety, occurring within the previous day's value area. Price rotates randomly back and forth with very little confidence throughout the day.

In hindsight, a Nonconviction day's range can be misleading, for it appears as if a number of good opportunities should have been generated as the day progressed. In the thick of such low-confidence activity, however, traders are provided no real reference points by which to base their trading decision. Consequently, traders often end up forcing trades that just aren't there.

Figure 4–128 provides a good example of a Nonconviction day in the gold market. After an Open-Auction, gold spent the remainder of the trading session auctioning back and forth with no apparent directional conviction. The completed Profile looks like a Normal Variation day, but at no point was there a clear indication of other timeframe presence. On

Figure 4–128 A nonconviction day occurring in June Gold, May 24, 1989.

```
3656    .
3654    DFGJ
3652    CDEFGHJ
3650    CDEFGHIJK
3648    yCDEFGHIJK
3646    yCDGHJKM
3644    yACJ
3642    OzABCJ
3640    yzABC
3638    yzABC
3636    zAB
3634    zA
3632    .
```

such a day, it is relatively easy to lose objectivity due to the lack of market sentiment. When a Nonconviction day develops, it is best to stay out of the market altogether, for any trading decision would be based on conjecture and random price rotations.

Long-Term Nontrend Markets

On a larger scale, longer-term activity may at times exhibit a lack of directional conviction. While longer-term traders should not have positions in the market, there may still be plenty of opportunity for day timeframe traders. In Figure 4–129, for example, crude oil exhibited extremely erratic behavior for several weeks, auctioning back and forth with no longer-term conviction. Although this was clearly a market to be avoided by longer-term traders, the resulting price spikes and gaps offered several high-percentage trades for day timeframe traders.

Figure 4–129   A long-term non-conviction market. Crude Oil, May 2-8, 1989.

	May 2	May 3	May 4	May 5	May 8
2062	.	.	.	.	.
2060	.	.	KL	.	.
2058	.	.	KL	.	.
2056	.	.	JKL	.	.
2054	.	.	IJKL	.	.
2052	.	.	IJKL	.	.
2050	.	.	EIJKL	.	.
2048	B	.	DEFIJKL	.	.
2046	B	.	DEFGHIL	.	.
2044	B	.	DEFGHI	.	.
2042	B	.	DEFGH	B	.
2040	B	.	BDFGH	B	.
2038	B	.	BDF	BC	.
2036	B	.	BCDF	BCDE	.
2034	BC	.	BCDF	BCDEFG	.
2032	BC	.	BCD	BCDEFGH	.
2030	BC	.	BC	CDEFGH	.
2028	BCEG	.	BC	DEFGH	.
2026	BCEFG	.	B	DEHJK	.
2024	BCEFG	.	B	DEHJK	.
2022	CDEFGHK	.	B	HIJK	.
2020	CDEFGHK	.	B	HIJK	.
2018	CDEHK	.	.	HIJKL	.
2016	CDHK	.	.	IJKL	.
2014	CDHIKL	L	.	KL	.
2012	HIJKL	L	.	L	.
2010	HIJKL	L	.	L	.
2008	HIJKL	L	.	L	.
2006	HIJKL	L	.	L	.
2004	IJKL	L	.	L	.
2002	IJKL	L	.	L	.
2000	IJL	L	.	L	.
1998	IL	L	.	L	.
1996	IL	L	.	.	.
1994	L	L	.	.	.
1992	L	L	.	.	.
1990	L	BIL	.	.	.
1988	L	BHIL	.	.	B
1986	L	BHIJL	.	.	BC
1984	L	BHIJL	.	.	BCD
1982	L	BHIJKL	.	.	BCD
1980	L	BHIJKL	.	.	BCD
1978	L	BDHIJKL	.	.	BCD
1976	.	BCDHIJKL	.	.	BCDE
1974	.	BCDHIJKL	.	.	DE
1972	.	BCDEGHJKL	.	.	DEF
1970	.	BCDEGHJL	.	.	DEF
1968	.	BCDEGHJL	.	.	EFG
1966	.	BCDEG	.	.	EFGHI
1964	.	BCDEG	.	.	EFGHI
1962	.	BCEFG	.	.	EFGHI
1960	.	EFG	.	.	EFHIJ
1958	.	EFG	.	.	EFIJ
1956	.	EFG	.	.	JL
1954	.	EFG	.	.	JL
1952	.	E	.	.	JL
1950	.	.	.	.	JKL
1948	.	.	.	.	JKL
1946	.	.	.	.	JKL
1944	.	.	.	.	JKL
1942	.	.	.	.	KL
1940	.	.	.	.	KL
1938	.	.	.	.	KL
1936	.	.	.	.	L
1934	.	.	.	.	.
1932	.	.	.	.	.
1930	.	.	.	.	.

News-Influenced Markets

The final "stand-aside" scenario is a day prior to a major news announcement. Generally, many other timeframe participants have balanced their positions prior to a scheduled news announcement. Thus, the day or two just prior to the news is often left in the hands of the locals and other shorter-term traders. The resulting low volume environment can be dangerous, for rumors and predictions can cause price to rotate wildly.

Summary

Staying out of a market is more difficult than it sounds. When there are few clues regarding directional conviction, it is easy to lose objectivity. Sitting in front of a quote monitor all day without placing a trade requires a tremendous amount of patience. Even the most experienced traders begin to hear that little subjective voice: "It has got to break. TPOs favor sellers . . . sell it." When the market has no confidence, *stand aside until new activity develops*. Not only do bad trades lead to losses, but they also keep you from entering a good trade when opportune conditions finally arise.

News

The release of a major news announcement (such as Gross National Product, Merchandise Trade, or Producer Price Index) often creates a violent "knee-jerk" reaction by the market's participants. Trying to anticipate the news item and how it will affect market sentiment is a highly dangerous gamble. Once the news information is out, price moves so violently and with such speed that it is nearly impossible to make a rational trading decision (or locate your trade where you want it). This is due to the manner in which the news is generally announced. The initial number usually causes a sudden price reaction, depending on early estimates that form market opinion. Soon after the actual announcement, however, there is often a revision of previous periods' figures, which can cause further erratic movement. Finally, the components that make up the economic figure come out, often causing yet another reaction to the number. All of this activity takes place in an extremely short period of time. The resulting sporadic price spurts can wipe out a substantial amount of capital in minutes.

Long before a piece of news is ever announced, the market's participants form expectations that begin to influence market activity. The consensus opinion (available in *Barron's* and various news sources) is, in effect, built into the market prior to the news announcement. If a trader is aware of the market's preconceived notions regarding the pending news, then he or she can evaluate the true strength or weakness of the market by observing the reaction to the actual numbers.

Let us look at a real market example. Before the Producer Price Index (PPI) was announced on May 12, 1989, the bond market was expecting a number between +.06% and +.08%. Due to bearish expectations, bonds had been in a short term down auction, as evidenced by point 1 in Figure 4–130. The direction of the major auction, however, was up (point 2). The actual number released was +.04%, which indicated lower inflation than expected, a bullish sign for bonds. The market immediately rallied some 16 ticks (Figure 4–131). Shortly after, it was announced that an increase in oil contributed +.07% of the figure. Thus, had it not been for oil, the PPI would have actually been *negative*. This extremely bullish news caused bonds to rally nearly two full points to 90–26. Many market participants lost money because they had anticipated a bearish number. It is extremely difficult to trade during the volatility created by a news announcement.

Traders could have gained valuable information on the 12th if they had entered the market prepared with the following information:

1. Direction of the major auction.
2. Known reference points.
3. Market expectations for scheduled news announcement.

The direction of the major auction was up, despite the short-term selling rotation due to bearish expectations. The market had broken below several days of overlapping value (not in view) on May 9, establishing two important reference points: the 9th's high (89–16) and the point at which the market broke lower (89–04). As previously mentioned, the consensus opinion was that the PPI should have been between +.06% and +.08%. When the number was announced as bullish for bonds, the market auctioned through the first reference point (point 1 in Figure 4–131) easily, and slowed at the highs for the 9th (point 2). The subsequent announcement of the PPI's components was also bullish, and the market exploded to the upside. Despite the recent down auction, bonds had no trouble auctioning two points higher on May 9. It became apparent that underlying market conditions were strong.

Figure 4–130   A news event's affect on June Treasury Bonds. Data courtesy of Commodity Quote Graphics.

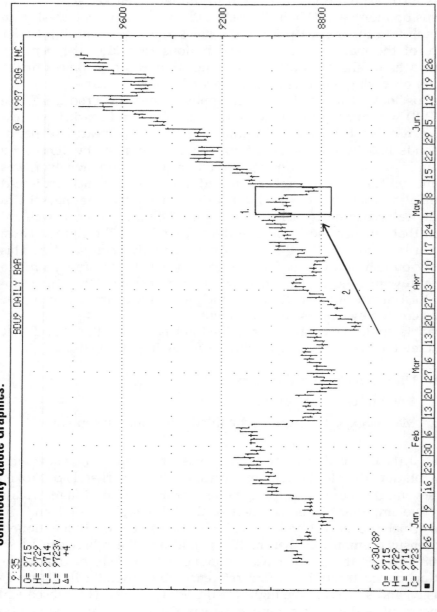

The following list displays the basic news/market sentiment relationships, and our previous bond example is illustrated by the third scenario (denoted by an asterisk). The major auction was up, the news announcement was bullish and the market reacted by auctioning substantially higher in the day timeframe. These circumstances indicate a market that is strong and continuing higher.

Direction of Major Auction	News Announcement	Day Timeframe Direction	Market Sentiment
1. Up	Bearish	Up	Very strong
2. Up	Bearish	Down	Neutral, expected
3. Up*	Bullish	Up	Strong
4. Up	Bullish	Down	Very weak
5. Down	Bearish	Up	Very strong
6. Down	Bearish	Down	Weak
7. Down	Bullish	Up	Neutral, expected
8. Down	Bullish	Down	Very weak

Summary

Instead of getting emotionally and/or financially whipped back and forth along with the market during a major news announcement, traders can use the news to their benefit by following these steps:

1. Balance your inventory so that you hold no position going into the scheduled announcement (except for long-term traders).

2. Make note of market expectations, recent market direction and salient reference points.

3. Monitor activity after the actual number is announced to determine underlying market sentiment (use above reference chart, if necessary).

4. Monitor ensuing activity near recent reference points for confirmation or rejection of apparent conviction.

5. If an opportunity is present, enter trade. Place stops at previous known reference points—exit if conditions arise that contradict market sentiment.

Figure 4–131 A news event's affect on June Treasury Bonds, May 8-15, 1989.

	May 8	May 9	May 10	May 11	May 12	May 15
91 8 /32	.	.	.	.	.	.
91 6 /32	.	.	.	.	.	yA
91 4 /32	.	.	.	.	.	yAFG
91 2 /32	.	.	.	.	B	yzABCDEFG
91 0 /32	.	.	.	.	zBIJ	yzBCDEFGH
90 30 /32					zABDFGIJKL	zBCDGHIJKL
90 28 /32					zABCDEFGHIJKL	zGHIJKL
90 26 /32					yzABCDEFHIJKL	zJK
90 24 /32					yzABCDEHK	z
90 22 /32					yzA	.
90 20 /32					yz	.
90 18 /32					yz	.
90 16 /32					yz	.
90 14 /32					y	.
90 12 /32					y	.
90 10 /32					y	.
90 8 /32					y	.
90 6 /32					y	.
90 4 /32					y	.
90 2 /32	.	.	.	.	y	.
90 0 /32	.	.	.	.	y	.
89 30 /32	.				y	
89 28 /32	.				y	
89 26 /32	.				y	

Figure 4–131
Continued

```
89 24/32                                                                                    . . .   y
89 22/32   H                                                                                        y
89 20/32   zADEFGHIKL                                                                               y
89 18/32   yzABCDEFGHJKL                                                                            y
89 16/32   yzBCIJ                                                                                   y
89 14/32   yB                y                                                                      y
89 12/32                     yzAH                                                                   y    (2)
89 10/32                     yzABCDH                                                                y
89  8/32                     zABCDEFGHI                                                             y
89  6/32                     AEFGHIJ                                                                y    (1)
89  4/32                     GHIJ                                                                   y
89  2/32                     J                                                                      y
89  0/32                     J
88 30/32                     JK                        z
88 28/32                     JK                        yzA
88 26/32                     JK                                           K
88 24/32                     KL                        z            ABJKL
88 22/32                     KL                        yzA          ABCJKL
88 20/32                     L                         yzABCJ       yzABCDJK
88 18/32                                               yABCDIJ      yzACDEFIJ
88 16/32                                               ABCDHIJ      yzDEFGHI
88 14/32                                               DEHJKL       yFGHI
88 12/32                                               DEFGHJKL     yFGHI
88 10/32                                               EFGHKL       yHI
88  8/32                                               EFGHK        y
88  6/32                                               GK           y
88  4/32
88  2/32
88  0/32
```

Beyond the Competent Trader

Let us look back to David, the aspiring pianist, and his path to becoming an expert musician. When he reached competency after years of learning and practice, he had mastered the technical and mechanical aspects of playing the piano. Yet, he had not transcended the physical notes on paper to become an expert. Similarly, a good market understanding is only part of the equation for achieving expert results. Many traders who develop a solid academic background still do not make enough money to justify being in the market.

To progress beyond the average, beyond the middle of the bell curve and into the upper extremes of excellence, you must achieve self-understanding. To become a proficient trader, it is necessary to become so intimate with the mechanical aspects of the market that they form a holistic pattern in your mind. Only then can you begin to understand how your own personal strengths and weaknesses directly influence your trading performance. As Adam Smith said in his book *The Money Game*, "If you don't know who you are, the market is an expensive place to find out."

We have reached the end of the Competent chapter. The study of the basic theories behind evaluating market-generated information through the Market Profile is now complete. We have covered a tremendous amount of information in a relatively short time. So before we move on to the next step in the learning process, take some time to review and solidify the concepts we have discussed. Observe the market. Test and apply your market understanding. Build the experience that will clear the fogged corners of the window to reveal the big picture.

CHAPTER 5
PROFICIENT

Throughout the book, we have followed the five levels of skill acquisition through a college student named David. After hearing a moving rendition of Beethoven's "Moonlight Sonata," David decided he wanted to learn to play the piano. He started the learning process by studying purely derivative sources—taking lessons and reading books on music theory. After becoming familiar with the basics, David began to practice while continuing his derivative learning. In other words, the instruction and mechanical knowledge acted as a catalyst, allowing David to actively apply and develop the theory into actual musical ability. He was building experience.

Finally, after years of practice, lessons, and study, David transcended the realm of derivative knowledge. He simply knew the theory and technique backwards and forwards. When David sat down at the piano, the fingering had been committed to muscle memory and the notes and time signatures were so fully assimilated in his mind that he no longer actively thought of them while playing. David had reached the level of proficiency that allowed him to express his thoughts and feelings through an instrument as though it were an extension of his emotion.

Becoming proficient in any endeavor is a highly personal process. Think about something you excel in, something that has become an instinctive, intuitive ability. Perhaps it is an athletic talent such as golf or tennis. Maybe you have a knack for fly fishing, sailing, or chess. Whatever it is, remember the way you felt when you finally performed the activity perfectly.

Suppose that after years of working on your golf swing through lessons, Arnold Palmer books, and hours at the driving range, you play the perfect round. A proficient golfer intuitively combines course conditions, wind, the ball's lie, stance, club selection, position, and the actual stroke to achieve the perfect shot. Imagine the exhilaration of having the ability to make such a shot 70 times in one round. A perfect round transcends all derivative learning. It is the culmination of knowledge and experience. When all the factors come together, the golfer can "feel" the shot. Developing and learning to recognize that feeling of excellence is the result of a synthesis of derivative and empirical knowledge—of academic learning and hands-on experience.

A futures trader who has progressed beyond competency also begins to intuitively feel when conditions are right for a successful trade. Again, this intuitive ability is fostered by more than just a sound fundamental base. Through market experience, you will begin to recognize certain situations where all the concepts and theories come together and you "feel" the trade. Once you have reached this stage of market understanding, the difficult part becomes learning to trust your intuitions—to trust the feeling of opportunity. In other words, a proficient trader must begin to learn and develop *self-understanding.*

In the final stages of learning, experience becomes the primary teacher, and introspection the vehicle for excellence. In this chapter, we will discuss the importance of self-understanding and its relation to becoming an expert trader.

The Results Equation: Market Understanding ×
(Self-Understanding+Strategy) = Results[1]

The results equation is an oversimplified formula for achieving successful trading returns. It is built upon three concepts: market understanding, self-understanding, and strategy. Up to this point, we have covered the large volume of theory that leads to a sound market understanding. In addition, we have discussed many trading strategies based on specific structural features, such as opening types and Special Situations. We have also examined the strategic application of more general concepts such as other timeframe control and trending versus bracketed markets. These structural strategies arise from an understanding of the

---

[1] J. Peter Steidlmayer and Kevin Koy, *Markets & Market Logic*, The Porcupine Press, Chicago, 1986, p. 5.

marketplace, but they are useless if a trader does not have the confidence to implement them.

A truly effective strategy must incorporate your strengths and weaknesses into a comprehensive "game plan" that uses your abilities to their fullest potential. The pivotal element in turning market understanding into a practical, successful trading strategy is self-understanding. You may have developed a thorough understanding of the marketplace and a reliable *academic* trading strategy, but without an understanding of yourself, you will not be able to effectively employ that strategy. Your trading results will not rise above the bell curve average. And, as we have mentioned before, the "average" market participant does not make money. To become proficient, you must begin the ongoing process of learning to understand yourself.

Self-Understanding: Becoming a Successful Trader

Most of us do a great deal of soul-searching before we choose a profession. Whether we realize it or not, in this process we consider not only the intellectual and academic requirements of the profession, but also how that vocation meets our own psychological and emotional needs. What does it take to become a surgeon, and can I deal with patients that die on the operating table? Do I want to work for someone else, or do I want to call my own shots? Do I want to manage people, or would I prefer to do research on my own? Do I want a profession that is steady and predictable, or would I prefer to have each day be entirely different?

Additionally, we also consider whether or not we possess the innate skills that can spell the difference between success at one profession over another. Do I have the precision hand-eye coordination to become a professional baseball player, the mathematical mind to work as a physicist, the writing style to become a reporter, or the mechanical aptitude to become a mechanic or electrician? These basic skills are usually identifiable early on. When choosing a profession, we need to consider whether we possess the skills required to succeed at that profession. While there are many ways to develop these skills through education, coaching, and experience, the seeds must already be planted if they are to grow.

Most individuals have never given much thought to the underlying skills necessary to become a successful trader. Consequently, when they begin to trade they wander into a very dangerous area totally unprepared. The personal characteristics that generally accompany success in the futures market include maturity and stability, a strong sense of self-competitiveness (as opposed to team-competitiveness), the inner strength to maintain contrary opinions, an orderly mind, and the ability to make a decision and act with confidence.

The ultimate decision to become a professional futures trader involves a melding of your personal skills with your financial and emotional needs. Many view futures trading as a glamorous profession in which it is possible to make a lot of money with very little effort. Few professions are truly glamorous, however, and to the most successful futures traders, the greatest reward is often emotional, while the financial reward is regarded as secondary. If this comes as a shock to you, consider our Olympic athletes. Although a few are compensated well through sponsorships, the majority of these individuals are in the athletic profession first for the emotional value—for the inner feeling of accomplishment that comes with mastering a sport, with winning the game. The financial rewards are secondary and flow naturally as a consequence of their success. And this, it seems, is where most futures traders err. They are drawn to, and in a sense intoxicated by, the lure of the financial reward, while never giving a second thought to the emotional or intellectual requirements of success.

Most traders, like drunk drivers, should be taken off the streets. They are trading under the influence—under the influence of the many advertisements that blanket the pages of trading magazines and newspapers with claims and near promises of quick, easy success. Each month, a new guru is touting a break-through system that turns a computer into a black box gold mine. Enter the orders and scoop out your profits. These glittery ads spark interest and induce sales, but they are misleading.

In contrast, how would you respond to an advertisement that read:

"Wanted: People willing to undergo specialized training in how to succeed. This program will require rigorous intellectual schooling, intensive introspection geared toward identifying invisible blocks to success that are trapped within you, and then a long behavior-modification process necessary to overcome these inner obstacles. At the same time, you will undergo a daily on-the-job training program. Requirements for this training program are as follows: intellectual ability, a meaningful amount of capital, and the willingness to immerse your entire self-esteem into the program. It is anticipated that you will lose most, if not all, of your capital and will be forced to rationalize the whole experience to maintain your self-esteem. Although it takes a minimum of two years to reach a moderate level of success, soon after this initial training program the majority of you will drop out because it is too hard, takes too much time,

requires too much flexibility, is not well defined and there are not enough concrete rules. Of the few that remain, less than 10 percent of you will enjoy the feeling of exhilaration that goes with completing what you set out to accomplish. Like the artist who only gets better, your newly acquired skill and experience will be just the start of a process that can continue for a lifetime. You will be equipped to succeed at your profession. You will be an entrepreneur."

This imaginary advertisement could apply to virtually any serious professional venture. It is not meant to convince you not to trade. Rather, it is meant to dispel the glamorous illusions that surround the field of futures trading. You have already experienced the difficulty of learning the vast amount of theory that makes up market understanding. Developing self-understanding is just as difficult—perhaps more so, for self-understanding cannot be learned from a derivative source.

Self-Observation

The Profile graphic enables a trader to objectively organize and observe the market's behavior, which leads to the development of market understanding. Similarly, self-observation is essential to developing self-understanding. One of the most effective methods to observe and reflect on your actions is to keep a trading journal.

For a trading journal to be useful, you must be honest and consistent, writing down thoughts, feelings, and surrounding circumstances before, during, and after each trade. Observing how your emotions affect the outcome of each trade can reveal your propensity for risk, your intuitive skills, the affects of outside circumstances, and a myriad of other factors that contribute to self-understanding.

Eventually, you will begin to identify behavioral patterns and the types of events that directly affect your trading performance. Perhaps you are overly affected by conflicting news sources and professional opinions. Maybe you find it difficult to trade against the crowd and are easily shaken from your convictions by contrary opinion. For example, you may notice that every time you make a trade based on a fundamental source, you exit too early and have little confidence in the trade. If this is the case, it may be best to simply not expose yourself to outside opinion. Or, perhaps you want to be a longer term trader, but find you have trouble sleeping during nights when you are carrying outstanding positions. By keeping a trading journal, you can begin to understand how you affect your trading results.

The Whole-Brained Trader

Although we still know relatively little about the vast capabilities of the human brain, research has revealed that the brain is divided into two separate hemispheres, each having very different functions. Bennett W. Goodspeed describes these differences in *The Tao Jones Averages*:

> . . . our left hemisphere, which controls the right side of the body, is analytically oriented. It reasons logically and sequentially and is responsible for our speech. It is adept at math, accounting, languages, science and writing. Like a computer, it is programmable and is nurtured by our highly analytic educational process. The properties of the left brain are not unique; man has developed computers that can duplicate those functions.
>
> Our right-brain hemisphere, which controls the movements of the left side of the body, *is* unique. It operates non-sequentially, is intuitive, artistic, has feelings, is gestalt-oriented (sees the forest and not just the trees), and controls our visual perceptions. Since it is nonverbal, it communicates to us through dreams and 'gut reactions.' The right hemisphere provides and stores all of our nonverbal experience—a vast amount of input, certainly much more than we can verbally retrieve.[2]

The difference between right and left brain function explains a great deal about the diversity of interest and talent in the human species. Every individual has a different right/left brain balance, resulting in a vast array of mental and physical abilities. Someone who is very left brain oriented might become an excellent scientist or administrator, whereas a right-brained person would more likely become an artist or playwright.

The division of right- and left-brain thinking is readily apparent in the futures market as well. The technicians who analyze historical data, economic figures, charts and other technical information are primarily left-brain oriented. Conversely, floor traders who rely on instinct are acting according to right-brain intuition, or "gut feelings." Unfortunately, attempting to trade with only the left or right hemisphere will result in an imbalance and poor results. The most successful traders are able to achieve a balance between the analytic left brain and the holistic right brain—they are whole-*brained* traders.

[2] Bennett W. Goodspeed, *The Tao Jones Averages*, Penguin Books, New York, 1983, pp. 22–23.

The Left Hemisphere

The left hemisphere is highly attuned to time, rules, and facts. It has been shown that this half of the brain, while very precise, is capable of processing only small amounts of information at a time. Therefore, attempting to trade with only the left, factual portion of the brain is very limiting—it incorporates only one viewpoint. Yet, there are times, such as in preparation and planning for the day, when it is necessary to be very exact and calculating. To grasp the facts, you must often consider them very rationally and individually. Still, the left hemisphere is seldom able to successfully coordinate the vast amounts of conflicting information disseminated by the market each day.

Imagine yourself sitting in front of your quote monitor, observing a trading day when the markets seem to have gone haywire. You murmur in a barely audible voice, "I cannot believe what is happening in the market today." Your left brain is whispering to you. The analytic decisions you made based on rationally processed facts have not been confirmed by the market. By immersing yourself in technical indicators and scientific study, the real, evolving nature of the marketplace slipped right past you.

The Right Hemisphere

The left brain stores knowledge. However, only through fine-tuned interaction with the intuitive right hemisphere can you successfully synthesize that knowledge and develop understanding. The right hemisphere is generally known as the creative, emotional half of the brain. It is dominated by free association and holistic processing of mass amounts of information.

A trade based on pure emotion may have an even lesser chance of success than a trade based on calmly calculated fact. Nonetheless, once the market opens, it is impossible to analyze the vast numbers of interacting elements that are combined, absorbed, and reflected by the market at any point in time. It takes a careful balance of academic knowledge and intuition based on a larger understanding to trade successfully.

Combining the Two Hemispheres

It is possible to mentally "change gears" in order to use both hemispheres of the brain. Each has its clear advantages and powers. After the market's close, for instance, the analysis of the day's activity and preparation for the following trading session are best accomplished by using predominantly left, analytical talents. On the other hand, when the market is in full gear, the fast-processing, free-associating right brain should have more control. Ideally, we should strive to operate in a more "central" hemisphere, freely calling on both sides of the brain to contribute when needed.

> Neither [hemisphere] should be blindly followed, as to do so would be to act in a half-brained way. Nor should we ignore either, for each effectively represents half of our brain. By understanding both and being able to use the correct hemisphere for the correct task, we can be more whole brained and effective in our decision-making.[3]

Recall our discussion of Bears' linebacker Mike Singletary in Section I of Chapter 4. Between games, Singletary uses his analytical left-brain skills to design a game plan and thoroughly understand the opposing team's offense. When the game starts, however, he does not have time to actively process the overwhelming amount of incoming stimuli. He then operates in a right-brain dominated mode, relying on intuition and holistic pattern recognition to guide his actions.

Experts in any field, like Mike Singletary, make whole-brained balance appear easy. This misconception is apparent to any trader who has had a gut feeling about a trade or an opinion based on careful analysis, only to see the market move in the opposite direction. Like any worthwhile endeavor, whole-brained trading takes time, patience, and experience to master.

You may come to realize that you are a predominantly right-brained or left-brained person. This is the first step in achieving balance. By knowing your left/right brain strengths and weaknesses, you can begin to develop a trading strategy that best uses your individual talents.

Strategy

As we near the end of Proficient, we look at the role and importance of strategy. Throughout the book, we have discussed many trading strategies based on market structure. However, there is a difference between a complete strategy and just managing a trade. Individual trades are guided by a set of rules based on market understanding. A complete

---

[3] Bennett W. Goodspeed, *The Tao Jones Averages*, Penguin Books, New York, 1983, pp. 49–50.

trading strategy, on the other hand, is more of a holistic game plan, built upon an infrastructure of market understanding, self-understanding and structural guidelines.

Every trader has a different timeframe, different goals, and different needs and emotions. Consequently, developing a strategy is a unique, individual process in which we each mold our strategy to best use our strengths and support our weaknesses. In this discussion, then, we focus on the *business* aspects of strategy, purposely avoiding the more personal elements of self-understanding.

A Business Strategy

There are many facets to running a business. You must first consider the *tangibles*, such as capital, risk, cash flow, taxes, and other general expenses. Then, there is the upkeep and use of informational sources, basic record keeping and performance evaluation/measurement. Of equal importance are the *intangibles*, such as knowing your competition and the role of time—both in managing your own time and introducing a new product. Also within this category are qualities like dedication, daily execution, and overall strategic planning that are ultimately the driving force behind any successful business.

Trading is a business. It involves the same tangible and intangible elements of any business strategy. We will examine many of these crucial areas, first from a general business perspective, and then within the context of how together they form a strategic trading plan.

Capital　When running a business, two golden rules apply to capital: (1) make sure that you are adequately capitalized to begin with; and (2) *conserve it.* A business that is undercapitalized is handicapped from the start. A new venture must be able to absorb unexpected start-up costs, as well as fund projects that may be important to longer-term survival.

There are obvious costs to trading, particularly when one is just starting out. It is critical that traders are adequately capitalized for their style of trading. For example, day traders generally do not need to be as highly capitalized as longer-term traders who hold positions overnight. However, even a day trader needs enough capital to take advantage of a market-created opportunity to "take a trade home" with minimal risk, such as that which is often provided by a 3–I day.

Undercapitalization leads to "tick-watching." Traders who must constantly worry about taking a loss are less likely to be objective in their interpretation of the market and, therefore, how they manage their positions.

Location Locating a business is similar to locating a trade. Where would you prefer to build a gas station, on a four-way corner just off the interstate, or somewhere between two traffic lights on a road divided by a median strip? Trades, too, are located based on cost/revenue considerations. Where would you prefer to buy for a longer-term trade, near the longer-term lows with strong apparent excess to lean on or somewhere in the middle of the longer-term range? A poorly located trade suggests that you are assuming greater risk for less than optimal reward.

How do you achieve optimal trade location? *Planning.* Do your homework, identify regions of potential good trade location afforded by excess, balance areas, and brackets, and then put your orders in ahead of time. When you are in the thick of the trading day, the best trade location often looks like the worst at the moment it is reached (Remember, the best trades generally fly in the face of the most recent activity). It becomes extremely difficult to pull the trigger—to make the trade. That little subjective voice begins to cloud your rational decision-making ability to the point that you just sit there frozen, watching a good opportunity slip away.

Many times ideal trade location seems too far away for the market to move in one day. *Put the order in anyway.* The anxiety that often accompanies such dynamic moves can keep you from entering the trade unless the order is already in the pit. In addition, if the trade location is truly ideal, then those prices will not be offered long enough to enter a position unless you have already placed your order. Just as a good chess player always plays several moves ahead of his opponent, playing ahead of the market is what secures good trade location.

Timing Negotiating skills are an important part of business, and *patience* is crucial to successful negotiation. For example, now and then every business has to deal with its suppliers. Would you rather negotiate when the product is plentiful or scarce? The timing of your negotiations often has a direct impact on the price you will pay.

Timing a trade is just as important as timing in a negotiation. Like the business that waits until its supplier has excess, traders should patiently wait for the market to demonstrate excess before they act. Many traders had strong bearish opinions prior to the stock market crash in October 1987. However, those who sold too early were forced out of the market (for financial reasons) long before the global selling began. Traders who are consistently too early need to be more patient in their negotiations with the market.

Information Every business decision and every trading decision are based on facts gleaned from market information. The car dealer only restocks his inventory if his information sources suggest that he will be able to sell the new cars. His information tells him the size of the market, the willingness of the consumer to buy, how many cars he should purchase from the manufacturer and what he should charge for his stock. These same decisions must be made in any market.

Information influences virtually every aspect of a business strategy. In a sense, your information sources are your eyes in the market. That is why it is essential to trade based on reliable, objective information. Many traders surround themselves with so many opinionated and conflicting sources that their decision-making abilities are paralyzed. Think back to Jim Kelvin, the currency trader introduced at the beginning of the book. He knew that the yen was weak, based on purely objective market-generated information. Unfortunately, he also considered several other conflicting technical and fundamental sources that made him doubt his intuitive ability.

If conflicting sources are hindering your trade, eliminate them. Good businesspersons will narrow their information down, select the most reliable sources and get rid of the rest. Streamlining your information helps you arrive at decisions faster and *earlier.*

Historically, the best and most profitable businesses have entered their respective markets *before* all the information was available. They saw an opportunity and acted on it before it became obvious and the whole world jumped in. A successful trader does not wait until structure has provided 100 percent confirmation. Identify the opportunity and then do the trade.

Know Your Competition   Perceptive businesses understand their competition and the kinds of responses to expect from them and devise their strategy accordingly. What will the other players do if price drops too low or rises too high? General Motors has a pretty good idea what the Japanese car makers will do given any number of price-related decisions. Such knowledge of participant behavior is applicable to trading as well. Successful traders have a good inclination of how other market participants will react to a given change in price.

From a trading standpoint, one part of knowing your competition should involve making a continual assessment of whether the other market participants (your competition) are "too long" or "too short." For example, if a market that had been in a sustained up auction suddenly breaks in the day timeframe and stalls, creating a "b" formation, participants were probably too long. Through an understanding of the competition, you know that the activity was most likely a long liquidation break, and the buying auction will continue. *Every successful businessper-*

son and every successful trader understands the behavior of the other participants.

Know Yourself In addition to knowing your competition, you must know yourself. What is it you do best? Under what conditions do you find it difficult to be objective? There are many examples of businesses that have grown very successful by identifying and concentrating on their specific strengths, such as Midas Mufflers and McDonald's hamburgers. Learning to recognize, accept and work with your strengths and weaknesses is perhaps the most difficult aspect of becoming an expert trader.

Earlier in Proficient, we discussed the You portion of trading at length. However, a derivative source can only offer suggestions and provide ideas for growth. Self-understanding must be developed through continual self-observation and introspection. Keep a trading journal. Find patterns of thought and circumstance that lead to successful trades and actively incorporate those patterns into your trading strategy. Eliminate negative influences that cause bad trades and promote irrational thought. Self-understanding is an ongoing process essential to an effective overall strategy.

Consistent, Daily Execution A healthy business turns out revenues day after day. The old adage "successful trading is a lot of small losses and a few big winners" is simply not true. It still may be that the really big profits are made on a few trades, but the first goal is to see that the overhead is covered on a daily basis. A lot of small losses actually contribute to the overhead. A proficient trader will generate revenues virtually every day.

Consistency breeds objectivity. Consistency produces cash flow and takes care of current expenses, such as (in trading) office space, quote equipment, medical insurance, and so on. Consistency also eases tensions, so that the business can operate from a clear state of mind, look ahead, and plan expansion.

Inventory Both in a general business and trading, inventory management often spells the difference between success and failure. The goal, of course, is to buy at the most advantageous price. And, like investing in real estate, that generally means that *you have to buy inventory when no one else wants it*, or else you do not get the ideal price. Similarly, a trader will seek to initiate larger positions when the market appears to be near its longer-term highs or lows. Price generally reaches a longer-term high when the entire market is buying, and therefore when it is least popular to sell. Conversely, price reaches a longer-term low when the entire market is selling and it is least popular to buy.

Keep in mind, however, that many traders lose a lot of money attempting to pick market tops and bottoms. Be alert to conditions that create market extremes and place your positions just after the high or low has been confirmed.

The handling of inventory varies from business to business, just as traders handle their positions differently. For example, locals handle their inventory much like football ticket scalpers outside the stadium or the grocer in your local supermarket—high volume, low mark-up, the less time spent on the shelves the better. Longer-term traders, however, probably handle their positions with greater patience, much like a jeweler and his diamonds.

There are costs associated with not having enough inventory as well as costs of having too much. If you have no inventory (no positions), your opportunity for revenue declines. On the other hand, if you carry too much inventory, you may not have enough capital or space to take advantage of new opportunities. In addition, as one's inventory grows older, it may lose or gain value depending on changing market conditions. The overriding difference between most businesses and trading, however, is that the futures market controls the price of your inventory. You have less control over risk and opportunity and, therefore, must pay much closer attention to your inventory and changing market conditions.

Risk Every good businessperson keeps a watchful eye on risk. This means dedicating the majority of one's time and capital to playing the short odds rather than the long odds, for the main objective is to stay in business. This concept is well illustrated by a theme common among sales organizations. Generally, the salespersons who continually seek the big deals, hoping to hit the grand pay-off, invariably go broke. On the other hand, the individuals who succeed are those who work on five or six big deals, while spending the majority of their time on the 70 or 80 small accounts that provide consistent revenue. If a decision is made to go after a big deal, it is generally only with a portion of the capital or resources of the business.

As an example of how one might incorporate this concept into one's trading strategy, consider the regulation of "maximum" trades (large, longer-term positions). Suppose that part of your strategy is to trade up to three futures at one time. If so, then perhaps you limit yourself to just one maximum trade at a time. This way, you do not risk all of your trading capital on "big deals" (this is just an example, not a specific recommendation). Similarly, if your capitalization is lower, or if you want to reduce the anxiety that often accompanies maximum trades, perhaps you elect to participate in a maximum trade using option spreads.

Trading requires continual risk evaluation. Like a credit policy at a bank where overnight, intermediate and long-term spending limits are calculated precisely through conscious decisions, with each new trade one must evaluate the accompanying risk.

Goals   There are short-term goals as well as long-term goals. Good businesspeople realize that long-term goals are achieved as a result of the constant, cumulative meeting of short-term goals. *Write down your goals.* Make them clear and concise and strive to achieve them through realistic shorter-term check points. From time to time, review them and make sure they still represent your current wants and needs.

Record Keeping and Performance   All businesses keep records for reasons more than satisfying the IRS. Records help a business remain objective and realistic when evaluating performance. How productive is your sales force? How well is the market responding to your advertising and marketing? Is your overall strategy producing the hoped for results? What is the bottom line?

Record keeping is equally important to trading. Records give you an objective way to evaluate how your trading strategy is faring and whether it is in need of change. Proper record management should tell you more than if you are making money. It should reveal where your trading revenues are coming from, what market conditions and trading techniques are most profitable, whether you are meeting daily expenses, and so on. The better your records, the easier it is to isolate the problem areas, find solutions, and hone in on what you do best.

Dedication   Dedication is one of the "intangibles," unique to each individual and therefore not easily measured or valued. Dedication is doing your homework every day. It is keeping up your charts, getting up that extra hour early to get a head-start on the markets, and putting in that extra hour afterward.

Dedication is not just time and work, it is the heartbeat of a business. It is that personal element, the desire for personal achievement possessed by a handful of individuals. It is the driving force behind any successful business. Just wanting to be successful is not enough, you have to make it happen. *True dedication involves paying a price . . . and there is a price.*

Applications   When dealing in the minute-to-minute or day-to-day specifics of trading, it is sometimes difficult to appreciate the importance of strategy. Many traders have spent thousands of dollars learning the market and developing rules and guidelines for their trading. These aids come in multiple forms, from the Market Profile to rigidly disciplined trading models. Unfortunately, much of this knowledge and money is wasted, unless it is also woven together with a comprehensive strategy that takes into account those attributes that are important to staying in business as a trader. In summary, we offer three very general steps to getting started in developing your trading business.

Step 1: Accept and begin to view trading as a business.

Step 2: Develop a comprehensive strategy based on the concepts of successful business management.   To restate, every business—*and trading is no exception*—needs a healthy interaction of the following areas if it is to survive.

- Capital
- Timing
- Location
- Knowing Your Competition
- Knowing Yourself
- Consistency
- Information
- Inventory
- Risk
- Goals
- Record Keeping/Performance
- Dedication

This very "ideal" listing, collectively considered, forms the strategic shell of trading survival.

Step 3: Formulate specific rules and "mini strategies" that will help guide and mold your individual trades in order to meet the longer-term goals of your trading strategy.   Unfortunately, we as humans cannot function purely on a strategical level. We have to deal with facts, disappointments in our own shortcomings, capital requirements, the day-to-day details of physically and mentally entering and exiting trades, and so forth. Thus, once these longer-term goals have been laid out, we can begin to outline a series of shorter-term goals and trading disciplines to help us fulfill our longer-term strategy.

Figure 5–1 illustrates, in a very general sense, how one trader might design the underpinnings of a business trading strategy. This figure represents a basic set of guidelines that begin to tie the strategy together. Once these basic requirements are established, one must then fine tune

Figure 5–1 Trading strategy flow chart.

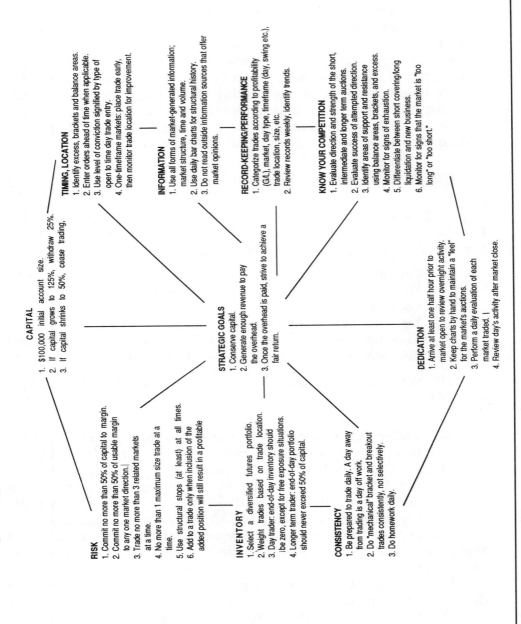

them with yet additional rules, so that eventually a daily, trade-by-trade application can be reached.

Summary

"The poor performance by most professional Wall Street investors is the result of an imbalance . . . a lack of whole-brainedness."

From *The Tao Jones Averages*, by Bennett W. Goodspeed

Most traders eventually become competent, but few transcend the rules and theories to reach proficiency. To progress beyond the average, traders must learn to understand themselves—how their personal strengths, weaknesses, and individual personalities affect their trading results. On the other hand, some traders have a good self-understanding but view their trading as a part-time endeavor or hobby. Trading is a business, and to become proficient a trader must develop a business strategy.

Successful futures trading is the result of a delicate balance between derivative learning and experience, between analytical thinking and intuition. A proficient trader forms a trading strategy built upon an infrastructure of market understanding, self-understanding and structural guidelines. He begins to intuitively feel when conditions are right for a successful trade, balancing left-brain discipline with right-brain creativity. Strive to achieve balance—to become a whole-brained trader.

CHAPTER 6
THE EXPERT TRADER

The knowledge that is gained from books and experience is an integral part of becoming a successful trader, but the path to expert trading begins within yourself. You must believe that you can reach your goals, fulfill your aspirations. Mastering the academics is not enough. An athlete with average ability will be victorious over opponents of greater skill if he believes he can be a champion.

Achieving the level of expert in any pursuit is a challenge that few people attempt, for it requires complete dedication and determination. To reach and maintain excellence, an individual must have a desire to succeed that transcends personal sacrifice. Understandably, most people are not willing to give up the diversity of their lives for a single all-encompassing goal.

Consider anyone that you perceive to be an expert in his or her field. Olympic swimmers spend from four to six hours in the water every day. Great composers and musicians have been known to practice for most of their waking hours. Top salespersons work 12- to 16-hour days. The best creative advertising personnel are always rethinking their accounts, shaping and detailing new ideas. Any highly successful business exceeds the norm by going beyond the rules and calculative rationality to the higher grounds of innovation and excellence.

Do you have what it takes to become an expert trader? We have covered a tremendous wealth of material, from the market's smallest unit to the importance of self-understanding—but the knowledge contained in this book is only the beginning. A derivative source can impart all the learning in the world, but again, much learning does not teach understanding. Benjamin Hoff put it wonderfully simply in *The Tao of Pooh*, "Knowledge and Experience do not necessarily speak the same language . . . there is more to Knowing than just being correct." [1]

In your pursuit of excellence, you may sometimes stumble and feel the frustration of your mistakes. The challenge before you is not without difficulties, but with the inner strength that grows from believing in your potential, you can strive to soar beyond the average—feel the exhileration that goes with completing what you set out to accomplish. As you continue to learn and build experience, remember that your newly acquired skill and understanding is just the start of a process that will continue for a lifetime.

---

[1] Benjamin Hoff, *The Tao of Pooh* (New York: Penguin Books, 1982), p. 29.

APPENDIX 1
Value-Area Calculation

The value area represents the area of greatest trade facilitation and acceptance of value in the day timeframe and is signified by the price region where 70 percent of the day's volume occurred. It can be calculated using either actual price/volume numbers or approximated by substituting TPOs when volume is not available.

Volume Value-Area Calculation

Figure A–1 illustrates how to calculate the volume value area. First, identify the price at which the greatest volume occurred. Then, sum the volumes occurring at the two prices directly above the high-volume price and compare it to the total volume of the two prices below the high-volume price. The dual price total with the highest volume becomes part of the value area. This process continues until 70 percent of the volume is reached.

    In Figure A–1, the greatest volume (22,168) occurred at 96–12. The total volume for the two prices above 96–12 is 34,491 (Sum of Dual Prices) and the two price total below is 43,773. Since the lower total is

---

Figure A–1

Price	Volume	Sum of Dual Prices	Selection Order
96–02	3827		
96–03	5341		
96–04	6107		
96–05	7134		
96–06	8706	21073	7
96–07	12367		
96–08	13971	30871	6
96–09	16900		
96–10	15700	34491	4
96–11	18791		
96–12*	22168		1
96–13	21973	43773	2
96–14	21800		
96–15	19626	37227	3
96–16	17601		
96–17	16496	31417	5
96–18	14921		
96–19	10819	19906	8
96–20	9087		
96–21	6056		
96–22	5071		
96–23	4311		

* High-Volume Price

Total Volume: 327,000   70%: = 228,900

Value Area: 96–06 to 96–20

240,926 = 73.6%

---

greater, it is added to the high-volume price as part of the value area. The same process is repeated, comparing the next two lower prices (96–15 and 96–16), to 96–10 and 96–11 again. The lower total is higher and is, therefore, the next addition to the developing value area. This process is repeated until the volume reaches 70 percent of the day's total volume.

TPO Value-Area Calculation

The calculation of the TPO value area follows the same general steps as the volume value area. First, count the total number of TPOs, including the single prints. Take 70 percent of this number to establish how many TPOs approximate 70 percent of the day's volume. Then, examine the two prices above and below the longest line on the Profile, adding the two with a greater number of TPOs to the longest line. Continue this process until 70 percent of the TPOs are included.

Price	Volume	TPOs	Selection Order
100–04	A		
100–03	A		
100–02	AL		
100–01	AL		
100–00	AL		
99–31	AL		
99–30	AL		
99–29	AL		
99–28	ACGKL	10	4
99–27	ABCGK		
99–26	ABCGHK	16	2
99–25	ABCDEFGHIK		
99–24*	ABCDEFGHIJK	11	1
99–23	BCDEFHIJK	16	3
99–22	BCDEHIJ		
99–21	BCDJ	4	5†
99–20	BCD		
99–19	BC		
99–18	B		
99–17	B		

* High TPO Price

† Only the closest price is used since it fulfilled the 70% or better volume requirement.

Total TPOs = 78   70% = 54.6 or 55
Value area is 99–21 to 99–28 (73%)
For comparison, the volume value area was 99–20 to 99–30

REFERENCE TEXTS AND EDUCATIONAL LITERATURE

Literature

Markets & Market Logic, Trading & Investing with a Sound Understanding and Approach, J. Peter Steidlmayer and Kevin Koy, Porcupine Press, Chicago, 1986. Introduction to theory.

CBOT Market Profile (Manual 1), A Time Distribution Analysis That Explains Market Behavior, J. Peter Steidlmayer and the Chicago Board of Trade, Chicago Board of Trade, Chicago, 1984. Out of press and available only in photo-copy form. Basic theory and reference guide to using the Liquidity Data Bank.

The Profile Report, Results Through Market Understanding, Self Awareness and Strategy, Dalton Capital Management, Inc., Chicago, established in February, 1987. Monthly journal on market-generated education, research and trading.

Applications Of The Market Profile, A Trader's Guide to Auction Markets, Donald L. Jones, CISCO, Chicago, 1988. Concise reference guide to available literature, with direct applications.

Steidlmayer On Markets, A New Approach to Trading, J. Peter Steidlmayer, John Wiley & Sons, New York, 1989. Steidlmayer background, some theory and new concepts.

Courses on Audio Cassette

Operating In The Present Tense, Dalton Capital Management, Inc., Chicago. Introduction to theory and applications. 7½ hours, includes detailed manual.

Beyond The Rules, Dalton Capital Management, Inc., Chicago. Advanced course. 7½ hours, includes detailed manual.

Recommended Reading

The Tao Jones Average, A Guide To Whole-Brained Investing, Bennett W. Goodspeed, Penguin Books, New York, 1983.

A Whack On The Side Of The Head, How To Unlock Your Mind For Innovation, Roger von Oech, Ph.D., Warner Books, New York, 1983.

Mind over Machine, The Power of Human Intuition and Expertise in the Era of the Computer, Hubert L. and Stuart E. Dreyfus, The Free Press (MacMillan), New York, 1986.

ABOUT THE AUTHORS

James F. Dalton

Jim Dalton is a senior vice president of PaineWebber, Inc. within the firm's Managed Accounts Services Division. This is a unique industry position, involving management oversight of the Managed Futures Division as well as serving as Product Manager for the PaineWebber ACCESS Program, a program that provides professional money management and investment consulting services to wealthy individuals and institutions. Mr. Dalton coordinates the selection and implementation of both equity and futures money managers used by the firm's broker consultants. He also serves as a Director of the Investment Management Consultant's Association (IMCA) and has served on the IMCA Advisory Council.

Mr. Dalton's past experience includes more than 25 years in securities, options and commodities. He began his career with IBM prior to entering the securities business in the late 1960s. He served as Executive Vice President to the Chicago Board Options Exchange, as well as President of J. F. Dalton Asssociates, a futures commission merchant. Mr. Dalton also created the Consulting Services Division at a national securities firm.

Eric T. Jones

Eric Jones is a vice president of PaineWebber, Inc. and Director of Product Development for the Managed Futures Division. He is also Editor of *The Consultant's Eagle,* an investment management consulting publication for PaineWebber broker consultants. Mr. Jones is a Certified Investment Management Analyst and a member of the Investment Management Consultant's Association.

Prior to joining PaineWebber, Mr. Jones was Director of Market Research for J. F. Dalton Associates and later assisted Mr. Dalton in the creation of the Consulting Services Division at a national securities firm. He is co-author of *Hedging Foreign Exchange, Converting Risk to Profit.*

Robert B. Dalton

Robert Dalton is Assistant Editor for the *Hendricks County Flyer,* a freelance writer and a student of the markets.

Index